IRELANE UNDER ELIZABETH

ELIZABETH

Matthew J Byrne

BIBLIOLIFE

IRELAND UNDER ELIZABETH.

IRELAND UNDER ELIZABETH.

CHAPTERS TOWARDS

A HISTORY OF IRELAND

IN THE

REIGN OF ELIZABETH.

BEING

A PORTION OF THE HISTORY OF CATHOLIC IRELAND
BY DON PHILIP O'SULLIVAN BEAR.

Translated from the Original Latin

BY

MATTHEW J. BYRNE.

· Carpere et detrahere vel imperiti possunt, Doctorum est, et qui laborantium novere sudorem, vel lassis manum porrigere, vel errantibus iter ostendere.—*St. Jerome.*

Dublin:

SEALY, BRYERS & WALKER,

MIDDLE ABBEY STREET,

1903.

—

PRINTED BY
SEALY, BRYERS AND WALKER,
MIDDLE ABBEY STREET,
DUBLIN.

TRANSLATOR'S PREFACE.

———❖———·

"TRANSLATION in itself is, after all, but a problem, how two languages being given, the nearest approximation may be made in the second to the expression of ideas already conveyed through the medium of the first The problem almost starts with the assumption that something must be sacrificed, and the chief question is, what is the least sacrifice " So wrote Cardinal Newman, in the preface to his " Church of the Fathers," and of course, this problem had to be solved by me, as best I could, before penning a word of the following version of O'Sullivan's history.

I found the brothers Langhorne, the popular translators of Plutarch's lives, commending Amiot, because he " had, indeed, acquitted himself in one respect with great happiness. His book was not found to be French-Greek.   He had carefully followed that rule, which no translator ought ever to lose sight of, the great rule of humouring the genius, and maintaining the structure of his own language " For themselves they said :—" Sensible that the great art of a translator is to prevent the peculiarities of his author's language from stealing into his own, they have been particularly attentive to this point, and have generally endeavoured to keep their English unmixed with Greek. . . Where something seemed to have fallen out of the text, or where the ellipsis was too violent for the forms of our language, we have not scrupled to maintain the tenor of the narrative, or the chain of reason, by such little in-sertions as appeared to be necessary for the purpose "

The plain reading of these propositions would seem to be that the translation should be written as an original work, plagiarised, as it were, from the author, whose writings were being " done into " English, and these rules seem to have the approval of Boileau, Lord Bolingbroke, Beloe—

the translator of Heredotus (1 16)—and to a limited extent
of Newman and others. They have also the attraction
of rendering the translator's work more popular, and
certainly more easy.

On the other hand, Dr. Bloomfield in the preface to his
translation of Thucydides (i xi), emphatically lays it down ·
" It has, indeed, ever been the opinion of our greatest critics,
that what are called free translations of ancient prose
writers, whose matter is of high authority, and, therefore,
whose sense requires to be ascertained with precision,
ought not to be tolerated   Indeed, how instruction or
gratification can be obtained from a translation of an
antient writer which does not faithfully represent the
original, it is not easy to see. But besides fidelity, good
taste requires that the translator should preserve the
manner and characteristics of his author, without which
the utmost verbal accuracy will but inadequately represent
the orginal. As to the style and phraseology of prose
versions of antient writers, few will fail to see that they
should not be neoteric, otherwise the effect thereby produced will be such as cannot but shock a correct taste."

This latter rule has the support of our own O'Donovan
in his introductory remarks to that monumental work—
The Annals of the Four Masters (xl.), and in all his published
translations with which I am familiar. It has been followed
by Dr. Todd (*Wars of the Gael and Gaill, etc*), and Mr.
Hennessy (*Chronicon Scotorum*, lii., liv.), and other translators from the Gaelic, and also by translators for Bohn's
excellent versions of the Classics.

In a letter to Mr Cromwell, Pope says of translation —
" Let the sense be ever so exactly rendered, unless an author
looks like himself, in his habit and manner, it is a disguise
and not a translation " Hence, Montesquieu thanks Dr.
Nugent, " for rendering my work into English so well.
. . . It would seem that you intended to also translate
my style , for there is exactly that resemblance, qualem
decet esse sororum." (*Spirit of Laws* 1 , Introduc.)

Weighing as best I could the arguments pro and con
I finally decided, in the words of the classical Mitford,
to prefer, " occasionally running the risk of some uncouth-
ness of phrase, to those wide deviations from the original
for which French criticism allows large indulgence."

I believe I was mainly influenced by the following
considerations, which may be my apology to those who
dissent from my judgment.

(I.) A profound reverence for O'Donovan.

I imagine it almost impossible that anyone pursuing for eighteen years—as I have done—with ever increasing interest and assiduity, the study of Irish history, could fail to be impressed with an affectionate awe of those Herculean labourers in this field—O'Donovan and O'Curry. It is really not too much to say that nothing written in the English language is of any real authority on the pre-Norman period of our history, which has not passed through either of their hands. None were so satisfied of this as Todd, Petrie and others whose scholarship gilded, indeed, and, perhaps, refined the output of these miners— but to them belongs the credit of the discovery, and of the raising of the ore. Take away their work and only the dross remains, take away the works of all others, and yet the precious metal remains more or less unpolished, according to the time it spent in the masters' hands I believe that after a while one regards the name of O'Donovan or O'Curry as the hall-mark of authenticity in our Gaelic history, and distrusts all material not so marked

The respect I entertained for these patient and persevering labourers, as historians, easily extended to them in other capacities.

II.—The danger of sacrificing accuracy to an attempt at elegance, and so substituting an English composition by myself, for the history of O'Sullivan. I had in mind Dr. Johnson's censure on Pope's version of Homer, and the severe strictures on Dr O'Connor's latin translation of our annals, passed by Drs O'Donovan and Todd. I was also struck by some observations of Dean Butler in his preface to Thady Dowling's annals, published by the Irish Arch. Society (viii.), and of Mr. Leslie Stephen, ridiculing the simplicity of those middle-aged romancers, who transferred to the classical or Hebrew histories the customs of chivalry. (*English Thought in the 18th Century*, ii., 445.)

III.—Being myself rather a student of History, than of histories, I regard O'Sullivan's work more in the light of material for an Irish history of the reigns of Elizabeth and James I., than as itself supplying that want. In this view, accuracy as to dress, arms, currents of thought, and the like, are of equal importance with the chronicling of actual events. Hence I translate " leaden bullets " and use such words as " gunmen " to show the Irish had at such times the use of firearms, etc. Hence, also, the importance of adjectives   A single short sentence will well illustrate my argument. " Elizabetha regina non immerito fuit excommunicationis mucrone percussa a Pio V., Pontifice Maximo." (II., iv. 1)

Now, viewing O'Sullivan merely as an historian, the only fact in this sentence is that Elizabeth was excommunicated by Pius V. Regarding O'Sullivan, however, as an exponent of the sentiments of his countrymen of that age, we have two other important facts, namely, that they approved of this excommunication,—" non immerito " ; and regarded it with awe, as of dreadful effect,—" mucrone percussa" It is canvassed by Moore and others how far religious opinions affected the wars of these times, and on this question side-lights are often of more importance than the direct statements of partisan writers.

Again, an author's credibility is often tested by his style A bombastic and fulsome eulogy is regarded more as evidence of the partisanship of the writer, than as an accurate description Hence, the importance of imitating style.

IV —And finally, I am desirous rather of encouraging the reading of O'Sullivan's own work, than of offering a dissuasive substitute.

I am, indeed, in the words of Cardinal Newman, " very sensible what constant and unflagging attention is requisite in all translation to catch the sense of the original, and what discrimination in the choice of English to do justice to it ; and what certainty there is of shortcomings after all." I can only plead with Horace.—

————Si quid novisti rectius istis,
      Candidus imperti.

I have at this tedious length, discussed the basis of my translation, because, should this volume find favour, I purpose to offer similar versions of Lombard, Rothe, and other contemporary writers of events in Ireland during the reign of Elizabeth, and this preface may serve as an introduction to a series of Tudor historians.

———

The printed materials for an Irish history of our author's times, so far as they have come under my notice, consist mainly of the following :—

I —The State Papers, calendars of which have been officially published, and especially the calendar of Carew Manuscripts.

These calendars are now so numerous, that official guides to their use are periodically published, and the student would do well at the outset to read the late Sir

John Gilbert's *Public Records of Ireland, by an Irish Archivist, London*, 1864.

II —*The Liber Munerum Publicorum Hibcrniæ*, compiled by Mr. Rowley Lascelles, and the reports and indices of the Deputy Keeper of Irish Public Records, and of the Historical Manuscripts Commissioners. Here, too, the search will be for a needle in a bundle of straw without some preliminary training in the method of indexing, etc.

III.—The State Trials, and Sir John Davies' law reports and statutes of the realm. Only the existing statutes are published in the revised editions The student must consult the statutes at large, published by authority of the Irish Parliament in nineteen folio volumes with two index volumes These, from the historian's point of view are like detached pieces of a mosaic—one needs the plan to fit them in their places The student must have a general knowledge of the history of the times before examining these records.

IV.—Beside the official publications there are many excellent collections of State Papers and such like contemporary documents, published by private persons, and arranged in a readily intelligible manner. Such are— Cardinal Moran's *Spicilegium Ossoriense* (vols. I. and III.) ; Mr E. P. Shirley's original letters, etc., illustrating Church of Ireland history ; Dr Maziere Brady's *State Papers concerning the Irish Church, temp Eliz* , Rev Edmond Hogan's *Hibernia Ignatiana*; Mr Hore and late Dr. Graves *The Social State of the Southern and Eastern Counties of Ireland in the* 16th *Century* , Sydney Papers (letters, etc , from Lord Deputy Sydney), Folio, London, 1746 ; Bush's *Desiderata Curiosa Hibernia* (vol 1) ; Mr Gilbert's *Facsimiles.*

V.—The contemporary writers on the Irish side whose chronicles have been printed, are.—

The Four Masters, whose Annals of the kingdom of Ireland as translated and annotated by O'Donovan, are the basis of all Irish History. Vols. v and vi , of O'Donovan's edition comprise our period.

O'Clery's *Life of Hugh Roe O'Donnell*, recently published with a translation, by Rev Denis Murphy, whose last work, *Our Martyrs*, contains excerpts translated from many contemporary accounts of those who suffered for the Roman Catholic Faith, between 1,535 and 1,691 , Our Author, Philip O'Sullivan, whose history is the most readable and complete of the works of the Irish writers of his time , Peter Lombard, Archbishop of Armagh,

1601–25, whose *De Regno Hiberniæ, Sanctorum insula, Commentarius,* has been republished by Cardinal Moran.

David Rothe, Bishop of Ossory, 1618–50, whose *Analecta Sacra*, etc., has also been republished by Cardinal Moran Part III of this work deals with our period.

The second volume of the *Annals of Loch Ce,* as published in the Rolls series

Fr. Meehan's *Rise and Fall of the Franciscan Monasteries,* seems to aim at being a free translation of Donatus Mooney's co-temporary history of the Irish Franciscans. I have never met this latter book, and believe it has not been printed. I understand there is a manuscript copy in the Maynooth library.

Dominic O'Daly, O.P, a translation of whose *Rise and Fall of the Geraldines* has been published by Fr. Meehan

O'Duffy's *Apostacy of Myler Magrath,* a translation of which, by O'Daly, has been published

On the English side we have —

Ware's and Camden's *Annals of the Reign of Elizabeth,* Camden's *Britannica,* which contains Fr. John Good's description of Ireland about the year 1566.

Spencer's *View of the State of Ireland.*

Fynes Morison's *Itynirate,* Part II. I understand this part has been separately published under the title of *Moryson's History of Ireland,* 2 vols., Dublin, 1735.

Carew's *Paccata Hibernia,* which has recently been republished with valuable notes, by Mr. Standish O'Grady.

Stanihurst's description, and Hooker's history, both published in Hollinshed's chronicles.

Bingham's services in Connaught, and Dowcra's in Lough Foyle, both printed in the *Celtic Society's Miscellany,* 1849

John Derrick's *Image of Ireland,* republished in 1883, by Mr Small, Edinburgh

Payne's *Brief Description of Ireland,* published in the *Irish Arch. Society's Miscellany,* 1841

Dymmok's *Treatise of Ireland,* in same Society's *Miscellany* for 1842.

Dowling's Annals, published by same Society, in 1848.

Campion's history has only a brief reference to Shane O'Neill's and Fitzmaurices' insurrection and nothing else belonging to our period.

The History of Sir John Perrot, K.C B, London, 1728.

Barnaby Rich *Description of Ireland,* published in 1610, small 4to.

Fr E. Hogan, S J., has published an anonymous description of Ireland, written in 1598 with copious notes, and the Public Record Commissioners have issued with the volumes of State Papers, Henry VIII., dealing with Ireland, two old maps and a map of Munster. These maps show the territories of the principal Irish clans. See also a list of Descriptions of Ireland in Fr. Hogan's book, p. xii.

Most of the foregoing sources of history are out of print, and to be picked up only at second hand book-stalls, or occasionally at auctions.

I am afraid the time for writing the History of Ireland is still as far off as when O'Curry died, but in the hope of facilitating the future historian, I have collected in the table of contents, under each chapter, all references to its subject matter, contained in contemporary accounts which the kindness of my friends or my own shelves supplied.

Words introduced into the text and not in the original are printed in italics. The names of persons and places are given in present-day form when I was able to identify them, otherwise they are given as in the original text merely dropping the Latin termination.

In conclusion, I have to thank my subscribers, and many friends for kind encouragement and generous assistance in my work, and especially are my thanks due and tendered to The Most Rev. Dr. O'Doherty, Bishop of Derry, himself a master in the science of which I am a devoted student ; Mr. T. D Sullivan our National Bard ; and to my life-long, sincere and valued friend, the Very Rev. Father James F. Murphy, Provincial of the Jesuits in Ireland.

MATTHEW J. BYRNE, Listowel.

MEMOIR OF THE AUTHOR.

———❖———

"THE family of O'Sullivan," says Sir Bernard Burke, "de-
duces its descent from Oholl Ollum, king of Munster, who
reigned A.D. 125." Mr. O'Hart in his *Irish Pedigrees*,
traces their genealogy still further back (4th ed. 1, 245)

Until 1,192 the O'Sullivans were seated in South
Tipperary, on the banks of the Suir, between Clonmel and
Knockgraffan, on which was their principal fort, celebrated
in the third century as the residence of their progenitor,
king Fiacha, who compelled Cormac MacArt, the Ardrigh,
to send hostages thither from Tara (*Annals Four Masters*,
iii., 94-95, n ; *Book of Rights*, 91, n. ; *O'Callaghan's Irish
Brigades*, 374 ; *Lewis's Topographical Dictionary*, 239.)
The Anglo-Norman invaders gradually expelled this family
from its ancient territory, and compelled it to seek a home
in that wildest part of south-west Cork and Kerry, skirting
the Atlantic, and now comprised in the baronies of Beare
and Bantry, County Cork, and baronies of Iveragh,
Dunkerron and Glanlough, in Kerry (*Book of Rights*,
46-91, n , *Annals Four Masters*, iv., 1132 , *O Callaghan's
Irish Brigades*, 374.) The family became divided into
two great sections — O'Sullivan More, in Kerry, and
O'Sullivan Beare, in Cork (*O'Callaghan's Irish Brigades.*)

Mr. Joyce tells us (*Irish Names of Places*, i., 134),
that our author's district acquired its name from Beara,
a daughter of Heber, king of Castile, and whom Oholl
Ollum's father, Owen More, married. On his return
from Spain with his bride, Owen More called the harbour
"Beara" in her honour. This harbour is now Bearhaven,
the island which shelters it is the Great Bear Island, and
the neck of land between Bearhaven and Kenmare Bay
is the barony of Bere or Bear. Prefixed to the second volume
of *State Papers Henry VIII.* (Ireland) are three curious

old maps of Ireland, in the earlier of which (1567 and 1609–11) the names of the Irish septs are set down, showing the districts they occupied, and the territory of " O'Sullivan Biar " is shown as this barony

The O'Sullivans appear to have been settled in their new home early in the fourteenth century, as in 1320 we find them founding a Franciscan monastery at Bantry, in which they and many other nobles chose burial places (*Annals Four Masters*, iii., 523). A century later the line of cleavage between the two families is marked by an entry in the *Annals of the Four Masters*, iii., 566–7, that O'Sullivan More chose a burial place in another Franciscan monastery founded by The MacCarthy More, on a site near the lower lake of Killarney, which an old legend relates to have been miraculously pointed out. At what time our author's family assumed the cognomen " Bear," I have not been able to ascertain. It first occurs in the *Annals of Four Masters* under the year 1485. The name is now always spelled O'Sullivan, but our author wrote O'Sullevan. The Irish word is O'Suilebhain (*O'Hart's Irish Pedigrees*). To count up the various spellings in the patents, etc., of James I., and Elizabeth would be a tedious and profitless task. The deeds of derring-do of the historian's father, and the unhappy dissensions in his family, form part of his history, so need not be anticipated here. Apparently the only materials for a biography of our author are contained in his own works. Harris, the continuator of Sir James Ware, seems to have been unable to discover any others, (*Irish Writers*, 110.)

From the *Catholic History* we learn that his father's name was Dermot (Tom. ii., lib iv , cap. xv., et passim), that his grandfather was also a Dermot, and was The O'Sullivan Bear (Tom. ii., lib. iii., cap. iv., et passim); that his father was a younger son appears from the fact that he was not The O'Sullivan Bear, whose name was Daniel, and to whom our author refers as his " patruelis " (Tom iv., lib. iii., cap. iv.) , that he was born in Dursey Island, off Crow Head (Tom i., lib i , cap. iv.) ; that in the year 1602, while yet a boy, he was sent to Spain with his cousin, son of the O'Sullivan Beare, and who was going as a hostage to Philip III (Tom. iii., lib vii , cap. i.), that he was educated by a Jesuit Father, Synott, "one of his own people," and by Roderic Vendanna, a Spaniard, and other professors (Tom. iii., lib. vii., cap i.) ; that he obtained a commission in the Spanish Navy from Philip III. (*Dedication of History*) ; and that in 1618 he fought a duel oustide Madrid with an Anglo-Irishman, Bath, who had insulted his cousin (Tom. iv., lib. iii., cap. iv.). With his history he published letters to his cousin The O'Sullivan Bear, and Father Synott and Patrick Trant, giving an account of the actions of the fleet in which he took part.

The first-mentioned letter is reprinted at page 391 of *The Celtic Society's Miscellany* (Dub. 1849.)

From a poem prefixed to another of his works, *Decas Patritiana*, we learn that he was one of seventeen children ; that thirteen of his brothers having reached man's estate perished in the dark days of Ireland, meaning the wars of the closing years of Elizabeth's reign ; that after what he calls the sad fall of Ireland, the remaining four emigrated to Spain, whither also came his parents ; that he was educated at Compostella ; that Synott taught him Latin ; Vendanna enlightened him on physics, Marcilla instructed him in divine wisdom , then he engaged in the wars of His Catholic Majesty, serving in the army and navy ; that his brother Daniel also served in the navy, and after many vicissitudes perished in the war with the Turks, and was buried at sea ; that his sister Helena, was drowned returning to Ireland ; that his father, the son of Sheela FitzGerald, lived to the great age of nearly one hundred years, and was buried in Corunna ; and that his mother soon followed her husband to the grave , that her maiden name was Johanna McSwiney , that her mother (Margaret), was of the MacCarthy More family ; and that when he wrote this poem, only his sister Leonora and himself remained of all his family, the former being a nun in the convent of Stelliferi.

From the *Decas Patritiana* (164b) we learn that Philip learned the rudiments of his religion in Ireland from Donagh O'Cronin, who was martyred in Cork in 1601. (See *Our Martyrs*, p. 212.)

Mr Webb says (*Compendium of Irish Biography*), O'Sullivan died in 1660, relying on a letter from Peter Talbot to the Marquis of Ormonde, saying : "The Earl of Birhaven is dead , and left one only daughter of twelve years to inherit his titles in Ireland and his goods here, which amount to 100,000 crowns" Mr. Webb does not show how he identifies the Earl of Birhaven, nor what our author's Irish titles were ; and I should imagine the letter refers to the cousin, the son of The O'Sullivan Bear. (See *Catholic History, III.*, viii., 5) The historian must have been about ten years of age when, in 1602, he emigrated to Spain, as he was able to translate Irish into Latin, and as all his brothers (except Daniel) reached manhood before the war was finished, *i.e.*, 1603.

The only works of which I have any knowledge were .—

1 *The Compendium of the History of Catholic Ireland*, written in Latin, and published at Lisbon in 1621.

2. Letters to The O'Sullivan Bear, Fr. Synott, and Patrick Trant, also in Latin, describing his doings whilst in the navy, and printed with the history.

3 *Decas Patritiana :* or *A Life of St Patrick*, divided into ten books of ten chapters each, published in Madrid, 1629. There is a neatly bound copy of this rare work in Marsh's Library, Dublin. The first book gives a summary description of Ireland, the birth, education, and early life of St Patrick, whom he states to have been born in Armoric Gaul. The second book opens with an account of the learning and arts in Ireland before St. Patrick's arrival, and asserts the knowledge of letters   Here also is a relation that a description of the person and passion of Our Saviour was given by a pilgrim eye-witness to King Connor MacNessa. O'Sullivan asserts that the Apostle James preached the faith here, and that his father, Zebedee, was our first Archbishop. In this second book he relates the mission and first successes of St. Patrick. Then follow five books dealing more particularly with the mission in the several districts, a separate book being devoted to Meath Connaught, Ulster, Munster, and Leinster respectively. The eighth book deals with miscellaneous acts, such as the expelling of serpents, etc., and also relates his preaching in England and the Isle of Man, his miracles and death. The ninth book is devoted to Patrick's Purgatory, to which also he gives up the second book of his *Catholic History*. The tenth book is a glorification of the Irish for their steadfastness in the creed preached by St. Patrick.

4. In the same volume as the *Decas Patritiana* are Latin elegies in the author's praise by Don Geo. Mendoza and Don Antonio Sousa, with O'Sullivan's verses in reply and the long poem on his family which I have already cited. Mendoza's poem, after congratulating O'Sullivan on the publication of his history, refers to the other works still lying in darkness, and hence we know of the following works .—

5. A confutation of the histories of Giraldus Cambrensis, and Stanihurst as calumnies on the Irish. This work was called *Zoilomastix*. I do not know if it be now extant.

6. A work on astronomy.

7 Various lives of Irish saints. O'Sullivan himself tells

us in the *Decas Patritiana* (lib ii., cap. i. ; lib. vi., cap. viii.) that he had written lives of SS. Kyran of Saiger, Abban, Albe, and Declan, none of which have been published. His life of St. Mochudda is published in the *Acta Sanctorum*, (i. 47) of Colgan.

8. With the *Decas Patritiana* he published a reply to the famous Archbishop Ussher's censure on his history. which reply he called *Archicornigeromastix*. As Ussher's work would not be allowed into Spain, being heretical, O'Sullivan was obliged to answer what he had not seen. The entire tract is simply an abuse of Ussher, to whom he applies every coarse epithet he could command. This work reflects little credit on its author, and it is a pity it did not give place to some worthier effort.

9 To the Dempsterian controversy as to Ireland's title to the ancient name of Scotia, O'Sullivan contributed his *Tenebriomastix* vindicating Ireland's title.

O'Flaherty, of *Ogygia* fame, tells us (*Ogygia Vindicated*, 69) he had a copy of this work, and that it was not published. He describes it as " a large volume in Latin, not yet printed, where he also inveighs against all the Scotch impostures whereof I have a copy." Lynch, the celebrated Gratianus Lucius, quotes (*Cambrensis Eversus*, cap. xxv., ii. 662) from this work, and gives this description of it, " Philip O'Sullivan   . has already crushed and utterly demolished Camerarius in a work consisting of six books, which is as much superior to his adversary's in nervous eloquence as it is in the justice of its cause. His ardour was indeed too vehement for my tastes ; but a son of Mars must get some indulgence for virulent invectives, as those who live in the camp generally resent injuries more indignantly and punish them more severely than others."

10 Bound with the *Patritiana Decas* is a long letter to an Irish Jesuit, Cantwell, urging him to publish a history of Ireland he had undertaken   This letter is in reality an essay on the writing of history. Colgan speaks very highly of O'Sullivan (*Acta*, 791).

11. Harris never saw the *Zoilomastix*, but says O'Sullivan was supposed to have drawn up the account of Irish affairs presented to the king of Spain by Florence Conroy, Archbishop of Tuam.

12. There are occasional references in the history to some other work from which our Author takes extracts. See Chapters 11 and 19 of Book IV., Tome II. If these excerpts are typical of the lost work, we might conjecture it was a martyrology of the reign of Elizabeth. These

b

quotations are in a much more florid style than the history, and may have been juvenile essays   They are, at all events, no fair specimens of his historical exactness, and it is a pity that in transferring them to the pages of solemn and solid work the author's ripened criticism was not applied to modify the poetry which overlies and tends to discredit the facts which are in the essentials strictly accurate.

INDEX TO REFERENCES.

———❖———

To facilitate reference to different editions I have given the Books and Chapters where the works are so divided, as well as the page in edition used by me.

ANN.—Annals of the Kingdom of Ireland, by the Four Masters, from the earliest period to the year 1616 Edited by John O'Donovan, LL D , M.R.I.A 2nd Edition. Hodges, Smith and Co, Dublin : 1856

BRADY— State Papers concerning the Irish Church in the time of Queen Elizabeth, edited by W. Maziere Brady, D.D. Longmans, London, 1868.

CAMPION—Ancient Irish Histories The Works of Spencer, Campion, Hanmer and Marleburrough In 2 Vols Vol I containing Spencer's View of the State of Ireland, and Campion's Historie ⸗ of Ireland Hibernia Press, Dublin : 1809.

DES. JR —The Description of Ireland and the state thereof, as it is at this present, in anno 1598. Edited by Rev. Edmund Hogan, S.J. Dub.: 1878

DOWLING—The Annals of Ireland, by Friar John Clyn and Thady Dowling, Chancellor of Leighlin, edited by the Very Rev Richard Butler, A B , M.R.I A. Irish Arch. Soc., 1849.

(References are to years.)

DOW. NAR.—A Narration of the Services done by the army ymployed to Lough Foyle, under the leadinge of mee Sr Henry Dowcra, Knight, etc., etc Printed in Miscellany of the Celtic Society, Edited by John O'Donovan. Dublin : 1849.

(References are to pages of Miscel.)

DOW. REL.—Dowcra's relation of service done in Irelande. Printed in Miscellany of the Celtic Society Edited by John O'Donovan Dublin . 1849.

(References to pages of Miscel.)

FITZSIMONS—Words of Comfort to Persecuted Catholics. Written in exile anno 1607. Letters from a Cell in Dublin Castle, etc., by Father Henry Fitzsimons, S.J Edited by Rev. E. Hogan, S J Gill Dublin. 1881

HIB. IG —Ibernia Ignatiana seu Ibernorum Societatis Jesu Patrum Monumenta Collecta etc, à. P. Edmundo Hogan. Tomus Primus. Dub : 1880.

COMPENDIUM

OF

THE HISTORY OF CATHOLIC IRELAND

DEDICATED TO

DON PHILIP OF AUSTRIA

Most potent Catholic king and monarch of the Spains, the Indies,
of other kingdoms, and divers dominions.

BY

Don Philip O'Sullivan Bear of Ireland

WITH THE SANCTION OF

The Holy Inquisition, the Ordinary, and the King.

———

PRINTED AT LISBON BY PETER CRASBEECK;
Printer to the King,
In the year of our Lord 1621

———

Translated and Edited by Matthew J. Byrne.

INDEX TO CHAPTERS

---∴---

ON THE CUSTOMS AND RELIGION OF THE IRISH;

TOME I   BOOK IV

TOME II. BOOK I

HOW IRELAND WAS ACQUIRED BY THE ENGLISH.

TOME III.   BOOK I.

ON THE FIFTEEN YEARS' WAR.

Spencer 153-4.

TOME III. BOOK II

ON THE FIFTEEN YEARS' WAR.

TOME III   BOOK III.

ON THE FIFTEEN YEARS' WAR.

TOME III.   BOOK V.

ON THE FIFTEEN YEARS' WAR

TOME III BOOK VI

ON THE FIFTEEN YEARS' WAR

TOME III   BOOK VII:

ON THE FIFTEEN YEARS' WAR

TOME III.   BOOK VIII

ON THE FIFTEEN YEARS' WAR.

CONTENTS OF VOL. IV.

———❖———

BOOK I

ON THE FOUR FIRST PRINCIPAL STAGES OF THE PERSECUTION.

———

BOOK II

ON THE PARLIAMENT ; THE FIFTH STAGE OF THE PERSECUTION.

BOOK III

ON SOME EXAMPLES OF TYRANNY.

DEDICATION.

——❖——

PHILIP O'SULLEVAN
TO
DON PHILIP OF AUSTRIA

Most potent Catholic King and Monarch of the
Spains, the Indies, of other kingdoms, and
divers dominions

Most potent Monarch ! I venture to commit this,
my Compendium of Irish Affairs, to the patronage of
your Catholic Majesty, for many reasons. I pass over
its being due to you in earnest token of a grateful spirit,
by me who, in an honorable commission all too generously
bestowed by your royal father, bear arms in your fleet ·
I refrain from dwelling on yourself or pleading the course
becoming your officer I omit enumerating the generous
and noble succours to the Irish people afforded by yourself
and the mighty monarchs, your father, and grandfather.

But there is one reason I cannot refrain from mentioning.
You are the strongest bulwark and protector of the
christian family . Ireland for christian piety and devotion
to the holy faith is overwhelmed with the most tremendous
load of calamities. You are striving to spread amongst
all peoples, and far and wide to propagate, the worship
and splendour of the holy and apostolic religion, and to
enlarge the confines of the Roman Church · Ireland has
never swerved from that law which Christ our Redeemer
instituted, the blessed Apostles preached, and the Roman
Pontiffs instructed us to cherish   You are ever a barrier
to the pestilence of hellish heresy : Ireland is overwhelmed
with the most violent fury of heresy   You are the refuge
of Catholics Ireland turns to you as to an asylum.   You
above other kings are most justly styled " Catholic "
Ireland stands forth Catholic, amidst the monstrous confusion of the errors of the north

Add to these the singular piety of your disposition and the eminently admirable spirit wherewith in the very beginning of your reign you commenced so excellently to establish your sway, forbidding all apostates from the Catholic faith access to your kingdoms, and determining that the Batavians and other assertors of nefarious doctrines and persons ill-disposed to the christian law should be reduced by force to proper obedience to the church, so that the holy faith of our Saviour should appear practised and honored, not only in those realms which were handed down to you by your ancestors, but, also, it is hoped that your labours and zeal will in a short time under happiest auspices restore and re-establish it in its former splendour, authority and dignity in other realms in which, dishonored by the crimes of impious men, it has fallen to the lowest depths   For these reasons I have thought that this History of Catholic Ireland, which 'till now hath lain in the dark, should go forth into the light under the patronage of your royal majesty.   Long live your invincible majesty

PHILIP O'SULLEVAN.

DON PHILIP O'SULLEVAN OF BEAR IN IRELAND

To the Catholic Reader

ALTHOUGH, Catholic reader, in ancient times and even at this present day, there have been many and various affairs of the kingdom of Ireland well worth knowing and commemorating, yet its records, either wholly unpublished, lurk in darkness shrouded in the thickest mist, or are so much written in the Irish language that they are confined to the home circle and have not been sufficiently published by anyone in Latin.

And so those who have compiled the church histories of our times have either altogether passed over that island in silence, or recorded the fewest and most meagre particulars of it, notwithstanding that it endured for the preservation of christian piety the severest trials—aye, greater than is generally known.

Hence, some foreign writers justly complain that there is no Irish historian bringing to light the knowledge of his country's affairs, and placing them before the eyes of foreign people, and this is all the more strange because at this very time there are many religious and secular Irishmen distinguished for their talents in theology, philosophy, canon and civil law, and the study of other sciences.

Verily, unless I am deceived in my judgment, the current of present events, and the accumulation of many calamities deter our people from the attempt. For we are so distracted and tossed about on the most turbulent waves and by the confusion of all our affairs that there is no leisure for writing. Whence might be said of us that verse which Ovid sings of himself :—

> Though were my soul with fortitude sustained,
> As great as his whom Anytus arraigned :
> Yet, since the wrath of Gods so far transcends,
> The utmost rigours to which men's extends ,
> Wisdom itself, falls shattered by its weight
> And even he whom ' wise man ' Delphi hight,
> Unnerved—would fail to write in my sore plight

Moreover, it is necessary either to basely lie, which is contrary to the laws of history, or to offend those with whom in Ireland lies the government and the power of life and death How few would care to run so great a risk ? Whence it is that our invincible martyrs, who, suffering the greatest tortures resolutely, gave up their lives for the law of Christ the Redeemer. our most pious confessors, who worn out with the filthiness and squalor of fetid prisons, winged their way to the glory of empyrean realms ; our most eloquent Orators, who have encountered the fury of infernal doctrines , our most valiant and renowed generals, and magnanimous soldiers, who preferred to fall in arms fighting strenuously and devotedly, than to submit to heretics—an accursed race of men , our women, who, endowed with masculine resolution, have never yielded to fear of the heretics , our children and infants, whose lives the sword of the heretic so little spared— are deprived of their just credit and to what graves their bodies are consigned, therein also are their fame and memory interred Such considerations impel me to undertake the writing of this history—a task to accomplish which demands both greater ability and leisure than is mine, tossed about as I am, in the general wreck of my fatherland

However, I resolved to save from oblivion and destruction the fame of the greatest and most distinguished Irishmen, who displayed great virtues, both in fighting for the Catholic faith and in peace , for men celebrated in history, after the body is turned into dust, live as if endowed with a kind of immortality, as the same poet happily testifies

> In song is valour made immortal,
> And rescued from death's gloomy portal,
> It's fame lives on through generations
> Stone nor iron, time's depredations
> May resist , and all must yield to age
> Yet long will live the written page
> The record tells of Agamemnon
> And tells us also about each one,
> Who fought against him, and who for him.
> Were Thebes not sung in ancient rhythm,
> Who now would know the chieftains seven ?
> And so e'en older things are proven,
> And later tales preserved till now
> E'en Gods (if reverence will allow),
> With all their might, need poet's song,
> To sing what meeds to them belong.

In a less lofty strain, however, I will commence describing the nature of the Island , the origin of its people , their customs, religion, and fortunes, especially since the rise of the present heresies   Nor will I omit those feats which the enemies of the Catholic religion and ourselves valiantly and bravely achieved, and how our countrymen were conquered by them, but will set down their triumphs more carefully than they are recorded by their own writers to this present day.   Nor will I anywhere wrong them or pass upon them unmerited censure or defraud them of their just credit whenever they acted equitably, lest passing over such, I should bury the truth.   And so farewell, my Catholic reader.

TOME II., BOOK IV.

OF

DON PHILIP O'SULLEVAN OF BEAR IN IRELAND

ON THE VARIOUS VICISSITUDES OF IRELAND UNDER
ELIZABETH.

THE more notable events in Ireland during the reigns of
Henry, Edward, and Mary, I have related in the foregoing
book. There now remains to be told what befell during
the forty-three years of Elizabeth's rule. All of these,
however, are not detailed in this present book, but only
so much of them as happened during the twenty-nine
years from the year 1558 to the year 1588. As this was
a considerable period of time, so it supplies us with many
instances of unconquerable ecclesiastical martyrs; of the
fickle and shifting faith of the silly and the base, of the
atrocious tyranny of the heretics; of conspiracies of the
nobles, of wars, battles, and various celebrated events well
worth knowing.

CHAPTER I.

GENERAL SKETCH OF THE TYRANNY OF ELIZABETH AND
DISTRACTIONS OF IRELAND.

IMMEDIATELY on the death of the Catholic Queen Mary, she
was succeeded by her sister Elizabeth, the daughter of
Henry VIII and Anne Boleyn, and who became queen
in the year of our Redeemer 1559. As soon as she wielded
the sceptre, imitating her father, she excited the most
violent and fierce storms against the professors of Christian
truth. In England she nearly extinguished the Catholic
faith and religion, then she set herself to detach the Irish
from the faith. The system of her persecutions has been

A

given above, and is here also repeated. The most blessed
sacrament of the Eucharist, in which Christ our Lord
is really and truly present is removed from the churches
and the eyes of the people ; sacred images are burnt ; priests
banished ; and the entire Catholic people groan under injustice , churches are contaminated either by profane uses
or execrable heretical superstitions. Ecclesiastical revenues
are bestowed on most abandoned heretics ; all things
established for the honour of God are defiled   Catholic
bishops, friars, priests, either in hiding or disguised in
secular apparel, scarcely dare to walk abroad.   In their
places Lutherans, Calvinists, and other sects of heretics
are supplied   The messenger of faith, religion, piety, virtue,
is banished , licentiousness, lust, crime, heresy, is hospitably
received   The queen is declared head of the church in
her own kingdoms, and all must admit her to be head
and attest same by an oath   These ordinances began to be
enforced by the royal ministers and magistrates first in the
queen's towns despite the greatest opposition and firmness
of the townsmen , then they were carried into the territories
of the Irish chiefs, and here because the chieftains were
nowise willing to conform, various artifices were devised,
by means of which they were despoiled of their property,
gradually overthrown and punished with death.   Hence
the sword was drawn   The kingdom blazed, burned, and
perished with war, slaughter, and famine. As long as
some of the Irish were in arms for the liberty of the Catholic
religion and of themselves, so long a cessation from persecution
was allowed to other chiefs and to the queen's towns, until
the defenders of liberty were destroyed. Queen Elizabeth,
the instigator of all these crimes, was not undeservedly
smitten with the sword of excommunication by Pope Pius V.
We shall relate, although not all, yet in great part, the
events most deserving of mention which occurred during
those twenty-nine years of Elizabeth's reign.

CHAPTER II.

THE MEMORABLE MARTYRDOM OF JOHN TRAVERS, D.D.

WHAT Alanus Copus (*Nicholas Harpsfield*) and Father
Henry (*Fitzsimons*), of Dublin, have related about John
Travers, an Irish doctor of sacred theology, who fell in
Henry's or Elizabeth's time (I have not definitely ascertained
which) is worth repeating   This man wrote something

against the English heresy, in which he maintained the jurisdiction and authority of the Pope. Being arraigned for this before the king's court, and questioned by the judge on the matter, he fearlessly replied—"With these fingers," said he, holding out the thumb, index, and middle fingers, of his right hand, "those were written by me, and for this deed in so good and holy a cause I neither am nor will be sorry." Thereupon being condemned to death, amongst other atrocious punishments inflicted, that glorious hand was cut off by the executioner and thrown into the fire and burnt, except the three sacred fingers by which he had effected those writings, and which the flames, however piled on and stirred up, could not consume.

CHAPTER III.

THE MOST MEMORABLE OF THE REMARKABLE VICISSITUDES OF SHANE O'NEILL, CHIEF OF TYRONE.

GREATER butchery of ecclesiastics was prevented by various risings of the nobles, some of which are now to be related, and in the first place those excited by Shane O'Neill, chief of Tyrone,[1] which are as follows:—Con O'Neill, chief of Tyrone, having paid the debt of nature, left two sons, Shane and Fardorch, born of different mothers. Shane succeeding on his father's death as chief of Tyrone, was held in great esteem amongst the Irish, old as well as new, of which latter race was his paternal grandmother, the daughter of the Earl of Kildare : nor was his jurisdiction narrow, for he annexed to Tyrone a great part of Tyrconnell as a ransom for Calvagh O'Donnell, chief of Tyrconnell, when he was taken prisoner, as I related above. The English, therefore, greatly feared him as they were not ignorant that the power of this Catholic hero would resist the persecution of Catholics which they were plotting and had already begun to carry out Wherefore desirous of diminishing his power, they eagerly seized an opportunity which offered. Between him and his brother Fardorch there arose a dispute about their father's property. The

---

[1] The famous Shane an Diomuis, or John the Proud, son of Con Bacagh O'Neill, whom O'Sullivan calls Quintus. Fardorch or Frederick is generally known as Matthew, and was an illegitimate son of Con Bacagh Shane O'Neill said he was son of a blacksmith's daughter

latter honoured with the title of baron (*of Dungannon*)
the English incite to war, and inflame him with the hope
of obtaining the chieftaincy, and with no want of alacrity
help him with royal forces   A troop of Englishmen is also
sent to O'Donnell, who freed from his captivity went to
England to ask aid of the queen.   With this assistance,
though chiefly by the suffrages of the clansmen who readily
deserted   O'Neill,   O'Donnell   recovered   the   whole   of
Tyrconnell.   And now O'Neill was fiercely attacked on
the one side by O'Donnell, and on the other by his brother,
Fardorch, and on both by the forces of the queen.   Moreover,
the regiment of Scots which he drew from Scotland
for the war, mutinied and pillaged his country, on account
of their hire not being punctually paid.   Nevertheless
O'Neill, in the very beginning of the war, wiped out
Fardorch.   Leading the rest of his army against the Scotch
regiment he slew three thousand Scots.   Besides this,
seven hundred English whom the queen sent to O'Donnell's
assistance,   under command of Randal an Englishman,
were destroyed by divine vengeance   There is in the
chieftaincy of Tyrconnell a town overhanging Lough
Foyle, which is an episcopal seat of great fame, under the
patronage of St Columba, hence it is called Dire
Colum Kell (*Derry*), that is, " the Grove of Columba's cell."
English heretics having landed in this town, they,
against the wish and command of O'Donnell, expel the
priests and monks, invade the holy churches, and in one
church place for safe keeping gunpowder, leaden bullets,
tow-match, guns, pikes, and other munition of war.   In
other churches they performed the heretical rites of Luther,
Calvin, and others of that class of impious men   They
left nothing undefiled by their wickedness   St. Columba
(it is supposed) did not long delay the punishment of this
sin   The natives confidently assert that a wolf of huge
size and with bristling hair coming boldly out of the nearest
wood to the town and entering the iron barriers, emitting
from his mouth a great number of sparks, such as fly from
a red hot iron when it is struck, proceeded to the place
in which the powder was stored and spitting out sparks
set fire to powder and church.   I will not take upon myself
to vouch for the truth of this story· upon fame and long-
standing tradition let it rest.   This which is admitted by
all, I may assert, viz., that the gunpowder suddenly took
fire, the English who were in the church were burnt up,
and those who were patrolling round the church were
struck with burning tiles and killed ; those who fled to

neighbouring houses or into the adjoining lake were killed
by pursuing tiles, some of which were thrown five hundred
paces from the town.   And thus without a single Irishman
being wounded, miserably perished Randal with seven
hundred English except a few witnesses of the slaughter,
who, returning to their English fellows, gave an account
of the catastrophy in their native and peculiar manner
in these words :—" The Irish god, Columba, killed us all."
Mark the words of the barbarous heretics ! as if the Irish
worshipped St Columba as a god, and not as a faithful
servant of God, who, because he observed the command-
ments of his Creator, and because of his holy and innocent
life, is noted in the calendar of the saints for many miracles
In his lifetime, being filled with divine inspiration, he
foresaw that this holy city would be violated by heretics
When he was oppressed with great grief on this account,
being asked the cause of his sorrow by his companion
Baethan, " Anguish," said he, " Baethan, that Randal should
be in this grove."   Which prophecy committed to writing,
but after long ages unintelligible, was clearly spoken of
this Randal of the English.

O'Donnell who, though a Catholic, introduced heretics
into the holy town to defile holy things, also quickly suffered
meet punishment   When, after the destruction of these
English, he was leading against O'Neill a large army of
his own clansmen, he suddenly fell dead from his horse,
overtaken by some sudden disease in the heyday of his
health and vigour.   His brother Hugh O'Donnell succeeded,
and O'Neill carrying on hostilities against him as against the
deceased, surprised and having raised some troops, surrounded
him, ill-protected by a few attendants   O'Donnell having
lost a few of his men sought safety in flight, but, on the
same day having rallied his forces, he returned again to
fight the victor with a determination to be avenged   Many
fell on both sides fighting stoutly   At length O'Neill,
his line having been broken and his forces destroyed, with
difficulty escaped with a few followers, no whit however
disspirited, for on the eighth day after, having quickly
collected forces, he encountered the queen's troops and
obtained that famous victory which is called " of the red
coats," because among others who fell in battle were four
hundred soldiers lately brought from England and clad
in the red livery of the viceroy   Although made famous
by this victory, he unluckily fell not long after.   That he
might have greater forces against the queen and O'Donnell,
he had brought a regiment of Scots from Scotland, and,

when he was off his guard amongst them and fearing
nothing, he was surrounded by Scottish soldiers, mindful
of the cutting off of the Scotch regiment a short time before,
and falling under almost innumerable stabs of poinards,
he was slain despite the efforts of the officers to restrain
the fury of the men.   Thus the Scotch regiment avenging
the death of their fellow-country-men put an end to this war.

The chieftaincy of Tyrone was thereupon added to the
queen's dominions, but to little purpose as Turlough O'Neill
forthwith took possession of it, worn with war and for the
most part wasted   Against Turlough the queen afterwards
excited Hugh O'Neill, son of Fardorch, aided the latter
and honoured him first with the title of baron and then
of earl.   This will later on be shown by us in its proper
place.

* * *

CHAPTER IV.

ON THE EARL OF CLANRICKARD

AFTER the pitiable murder of John O'Neill, Richard Burke,
Earl of Clanrickard, whose estates in Connaught stretched
far and wide, was cast into prison by command of the queen,
for it had been determined and resolved by the English
that the Irish nobles whom they well knew would be
assertors of the Catholic faith should be rooted out completely.   The earl's sons, Ulick and John, provoked by the
queen's injustice, declared war and did not desist from
their proceedings until their father was restored to his former
liberty   He afterwards dying left them surviving, the
one as Earl of Clanrickard and the other as Baron of
Leitrim.

* * *

CHAPTER V.

ON THE O'MORES AND O'CONNORS OF OFFALY.

NOT long afterwards Leinster was convulsed with tyranny
and confusion   The chieftaincy of Leix was (as we
have seen above) taken from O'More and added to the
royal crown.   Rotheric (*Rory*), son of O'More, ill brooking
this, endeavoured to recover his patrimony by arms in a

fierce struggle of six years' duration.   At one time making truces, and, on the expiration of these, again renewing the war   Amongst others the following was a memorable event —He had taken as prisoners of war Harrington, a privy councillor, and Alexander Cosby, governor of Leix, both Englishmen.   The English opened negociations for ransoming these, but about the same time a huntsman of Rotheric's enraged on account of a fine inflicted on him by his master, fled to the English and arranged with them to betray Rotheric, and set Harrington and Cosby at liberty   Harpole, an Englishman, under the guidance of the huntsman, set out with two hundred soldiers against Rotheric. Rotheric had built a house in the midst of a dense and impassable wood and fortified it by a ditch, access being had by two avenues.   When the huntsman had arrived here on a stormy night, " here," said he, " sleeps Rotheric with his wife, John O'More, a kinsman, and one old man, and he has Harrington and Cosby in chains, but such is his daring and valour, as you so often found, that lest he escape by that luck by which he has so often surmounted other perils, spread for him this net which I usually lay for deer " Ridiculing the advice of this man the English block the two avenues, surround the door, and fire into the house. Rotheric, being aroused, struck with great presence of mind at Harrington and Cosby four or five times with his drawn sword.   Rushing from his house he, with his sword, intrepidly knocked down Harpole who was nearest to the door, and although the latter was not wounded, being protected by a coat of mail, yet all were struck with fear, so that the former brandishing his sword escaped unhurt through the midst of his enemies, his kinsman following. His wife and the old man were slain by the heretics when they entered the house   Harrington, severely wounded, especially in the left arm, but Cosby unhurt, because he hid himself behind Harrington when Rotheric was striking, were set at liberty.   Some days after, five hundred English and Irish mercenaries under command of Fitzpatrick, chief of Ossory, invaded Leix.   Rotheric led four hundred Irish against them, but before he came in sight, leaving his own men to reconnoitre the strength and position of the enemy, he fell by chance into their midst with only two companions, with whom he perished under many wounds.   On hearing this news, Rotheric's soldiers filled with rage rushed thirsting for vengeance against the enemy and routed them, and after many were slain the commander with difficulty escaped on horseback.

CHAPTER VI.

TYRANNY OF COSBY, AN ENGLISHMAN.

WHEN disturbances were allayed tyranny used ever increase. Francis Cosby, governor of Leix, and his son Alexander raged savagely against the entire Catholic body. He summoned the men of his province to Mullagh Mast for a convention to discuss matters of administration. He suddenly surrounded the assembly with armed bands, and of the family of O'More killed on the spot one hundred and eighty unarmed and unsuspecting men He lived mostly at Stradbally, where before his doors grew a tree of great height and abounding in spreading branches. From this he was accustomed to hang not only men but also women and children for no crime. When women were hanging from the tree by a halter he took an incredible pleasure in at the same time hanging by the mother's long hair their infant children It is said that when the tree was without the corpses of Catholics hanging from it, he was wont to say—" You seem to me, my tree, shrouded with great sadness, and no wonder, for you have now long been childless. I will speedily relieve your mourning. I will shortly adorn your boughs with corpses."

CHAPTER VII.

ON CATHAL O'CONNOR, MACFORT, AN ENGLISHMAN, AND AN INSTANCE OF ENGLISH TREACHERY

ENRAGED by this cruelty Cathal O'Connor renewed the rising, inflicting great devastation on the English, and often vainly attacked by them. At last MacFort, an Englishman, opened a treaty of peace with him He said he would not trust his safety to the promises of MacFort unless the latter produced the order and warrant of the queen. A day was arranged between them on which MacFort should produce the warrant When the day arrived, MacFort on horseback and Cathal and Conal MacGeoghegan on foot (as arranged) came to a parley, no safe pass having been given. Nor did this seem necessary since the horseman could easily escape from the foot, and it was not likely one man would venture to attack two. Besides Cathal and Conal were speaking from a high and steep bank, and MacFort did not ascend thither. After MacFort had frequently shown them a parchment document which he would not give to be read, he was going away without anything being settled, when Cathal became desirous of ascertaining what the parchment contained, so springing from the high ground at horse and rider he so balanced his body as to get his arms round the neck of MacFort and dragged him from the saddle to the ground Conal followed his comrade. Both tried to snatch the parchment from MacFort. He endeavoured to put the parchment into his mouth, crunch it with his teeth and swallow it. They compelled him to disgorge the parchment by strongly pressing his jaws with their hands In it was written (as I learn) an order from the queen by which MacFort was directed to capture Cathal whenever he could, either by craft or force, and when caught to put him immediately to death. Having learned this perfidy, Cathal and Conal with their swords slew MacFort, whom otherwise they would have let go unhurt. After this Cathal went to Spain, whence returning again to Ireland he perished in the shipwreck of the Spanish fleet at a port of Gallicia, which is commonly called Corcubion (*Corruna*). Conal escaping with impunity ended his days in Ireland.

CHAPTER VIII

THE FITZGERALDS OF MUNSTER.

BUT not even the Munsters enjoyed immunity from English injustice. The FitzGeralds of Munster were provoked to take up arms there. In order to understand how this came about we shall say something of their origin We have elsewhere shown that there were in Ireland two families of FitzGeralds, one in Leinster of which we have spoken above, the other in Munster, and of which we are now to treat. The chief of this family on its first introduction into Ireland was called MacThomas, which name was changed by the English to the title of Earl of Decies or Desmond (which is the same) Now John FitzGerald, Earl of Desmond, had three sons—James the eldest, Maurice the second, and John the youngest. The two

younger died leaving issue :—Maurice left Thomas (who
soon died) and James , John left Thomas, James, and
Maurice   James, son of Earl John, who became earl on
his father's death, begat four children.   Thomas surnamed the Red, by the daughter of Viscount Roche, whom
he divorced, and   married a daughter of the chieftain
O'Carroll, by whom he had Gerald and John   After her
death, a daughter of the chieftain MacCarthy bore him
James   Now when dying he is said to have provided by
a written will that Gerald, the second in point of age, should
be his heir and successor in the earldom.   To Thomas,
the eldest, he also left no inconsiderable property   With
these, however, the latter was not content, aspiring to the
earldom and chieftainship of the illustrious family, but in
vain, for it is said he was set aside for Gerald by the clansmen, and that he failed also in his case before the privy
council, whether justly or no is not here to be canvassed
The dominion of this family through the influence and favor
of the English kings, and constant aggression on their
neighbours, had in a short time grown to that extent that
the earl of Desmond was regarded by the English themselves
as a powerful subject   For although some of the old
Irish chiefs had greater resources, they were counted by
the English not in the number of subjects but of enemies,
although they paid tribute   But as power generally excites
the hatred of many, so with this family, great enmity and
hostility entered its territories, and principally on the part
of the chiefs of Clancarthy, Thomond, and Muskerry, who
treasured recollections of wrongs inflicted by the Geraldines
fighting for the English crown and for the increasing and
pushing of their own dominions.   On this account there
was a standing feud in which, amidst the frequent clash
of arms, blood was with great bitterness freely shed on
both sides.   Nor were the FitzGeralds less odious to many
also of the new Irish lords of English extraction.   By Earl
Ormond and almost the whole family of Butler they were
held in inextinguishable hatred.   Indeed both frequently
fought fiercely for the honor of governing districts and
exacting tribute, and all the while the kings of England,
who held the reins of government in Ireland and ought to
have prevented this incendiarism, connived at the ruin of
both families, which were Catholic.   Nor were the
FitzGeralds, barons of Lixnaw, often less odious, but as they
sprung from the same Geraldine stock were often warred
upon   Wherefore, when an opportunity offered, during
the reign of Elizabeth, John FitzGerald (brother of Earl

Gerald), whilst yet a youth defeated John Butler in battle and slew him with his own hands.   This, and a recollection of his ancestors' wrongs, haunted Thomas Butler, brother of the deceased, and surnamed the Black Earl of Ormond, a Protestant in religion owing to his being educated in the English court, but who before his death was converted to the faith, as I shall show later on   He having learned that Earl Gerald with a few companions was in that part of Decies which adjoins Ormond, got together a larger band of soldiers and surrounded him   Gerald although far inferior in numbers, nevertheless prepared to trust his safety to battle rather than to flight.   The few being surrounded were overcome by the numbers of their adversaries.   Gerald himself received a bullet wound in his foot and fell fighting bravely.   Thence he was taken by Ormond to Affane and cured by the great care of the doctors, who, however, were not able to prevent his ever after limping slightly   Having been cured he was sent into England to the queen, who had him committed to the tower of London, partly to gratify herself by removing this stout impediment to persecution, and partly anxious because there was at large John FitzGerald, brother of the earl, a high-souled hero, generous, distinguished in warlike arts, and a favourite with the Irish.   She laboured therefore to capture him also, and this was effected without any difficulty, because John neither fled from her nor dared to do the least injury, thinking more of his brother's than of his own safety.   Him also she cast into the same prison as his brother   Ill brooking this, James FitzGerald, son of Maurice, the uncle of Earl Gerald, refused to recognise the queen's authority until she restored his kinsmen to their former liberty   Hence a war broke out   There followed James's party, other kinsmen of his, almost all the followers of the earl, and nearly the whole family of the FitzGeralds of Munster ; some from lower Munster, principally gentlemen of the MacSweeny family, named Edmund, Eugene, and Murrough, uncles of mine , some from the principality of Bear, under command of Dermot O'Sullivan, my father , and other spirited youths.   By their aid and valour James got and endeavoured to hold possession of the country of his kinsman the earl   The queen ordered her lieutenants in Ireland to march against the rebels, and easily aroused the Earl of Ormond's hatred of the Geraldines. She incited Thomas FitzGerald, surnamed Roe, a foolish man, eldest brother of Earl Gerald, with the hope of obtaining the earldom, and named him governor of the earldom, which, no doubt, seemed to him the next step to the title of earl.   She played on the tempers of the Irish chiefs ; relaxed her persecutions ; intimated that she fought not against religion but to assert her right to govern.   Thus the war swelled, and it was wonderful what luck attended the campaigns of James and of his lieutenants the MacSweenys and others.   He routed the royal forces at Kilmallock town   He was victorious at Mount Sannid, and successfully encountered them at Kuillchugi wood (Kuill-chugi).   At the church of Cloyne he slew General Morgan and destroyed his forces, and in other places came off victorious.   Nor did he cease from his undertaking until his kinsmen, the earl and John, were released from prison and restored to their former position, and himself promised pardon.

CHAPTER IX

WAR OF MACCARTHY AND EARL DESMOND—JAMES FITZGERALD SAILS FOR SPAIN.

SOON after James' rising was calmed down a war broke out between Earl Gerald and Donald MacCarthy, Chief of Clancarthy and earl of Valencia, and at the river Maine a battle was fought which was rather a slaughter than a fight , for while some illustrious gentlemen of MacCarthy's fell, and amongst others Murrough and Eugene MacSweeny, whose assistance James had formerly employed against the heretics , of Fitzgerald's forces only Colus, brother of Maurice, succumbed   Shortly after, James, , thinking (as it seems to me would have been the case), that on account of the English he would be very unsafe in Ireland, crossed over to Spain with his wife and two young children.

CHAPTER X.

RICHARD, PRIMATE OF IRELAND, A FAMOUS HERO.

IRELAND was long miserably convulsed by these misfortunes   When the turmoil of war was becalmed the English had, after the old fashion, nothing but fury against holy bishops, friars and priests   About this time was arrested the

Primate of Ireland, of whose life and death in prison a few memorable incidents are here recorded.

Richard O'Melchrebus, commonly called Creagh, and by some writers Cravaeus, was the son of a merchant of the town of Limerick in Ireland, of well-known integrity and respectability, and after the manner of his people receiving a Christian education and instruction in letters in his childhood, he became inflamed with piety and zeal for divine knowledge As a young man engaged in his father's business, he, in company with other merchants, sailed for Spain in a trading vessel laden with a cargo. Having sold his goods there and bought others to traffic with, and these being shipped, and all prepared for the return journey, a favourable wind blowing, the hour was appointed at which all merchants should embark. On this day when at early morning they came to the ship, Richard said to his companions that he must hear the holy Mass before he embarked, and that having heard it he would join without delay Intent on seeing the celebration of the holy Mass he was left behind by his companions, who shortly weighed anchor and set sail Seeing them from the land and calling them, he saw them together with the ship and cargo suddenly sink within the very harbour. Greatly struck by this incident he gave thanks to God that he himself had been preserved, and resolved to lead another life less perilous to his body and far safer for his soul. He applied himself therefore entirely to study Excelling in piety, and by no means unskilled in learning, he was in a short time ordained priest and consecrated Archbishop of Armagh and Primate of Ireland. He returned immediately to his native land, bringing the fruits of divine wisdom and sanctity instead of worldly and paltry merchandise, that with these helps he might afford a salutary aid to the souls of his people stricken by a most vehement persecution under Elizabeth. The holy bishop entering upon his sacred office was arrested by the English priest-hunters and sent into England. Cast into the Tower of London, and whilst in chains long and frequently pressed by bribes and threats and assailed with menaces he never would desert the Catholic religion. Amongst others let us make known this remarkable incident. The archbishop was brought before the tribunal of the Privy Council, a plan having been previously arranged and concerted by the heretics that the keeper's daughter should charge the bishop with having made an assault upon her to violate her chastity. The holy bishop standing before the tribunal

was falsely accused of this crime (as arranged). The girl
of beautiful appearance, and decked out, entered the court
amidst great expectation of the councillors and all bystanders   When she turned her eyes upon the innocent
man she was dumb, and could not answer a word to the
commands of the councillors to speak, not did her voice
return until within herself she silently changed her wicked
resolution, and then instead of what she had previously
arranged and the councillors expected and ordered, she
suddenly broke out to the contrary, saying that she had
never seen a holier man than the archbishop, that she had
never been tempted to sin by him, much less assaulted
nor had even her clothes been touched, and that this she
could not deny even if she had to die for it.   The holy
bishop however was recast into the same prison, and after
some days gave up his soul to his Creator.

CHAPTER XI.

PATRICK O'HEALY, BISHOP OF MAYO, AND HIS COMRADE,
CONNATIUS O'ROURKE, FRANCISCANS AND FAMOUS MARTYRS.

No milder course was taken with Patrick O'Healy, Bishop
of Mayo, and his companion, Connatius O'Rourke, of whom
I have already written as follows :—In that most doleful
time during which Elizabeth, Queen of Britain, after
destroying the church in England, was assailing the Catholic
religion in Ireland also with the utmost violence, there
flourished Patrick O'Healy, an Irishman of by no means
humble origin, who having embraced the order of the
Seraphic Francis, in Spain, stayed some years diligently
studying in that most famous academy of Complutus (*Alcala.*)
Then after he had elsewhere and finally at Rome, in the
convent of Ara Cœli, proved to all the innocence of his
life and his sincerity by many evidences of holiness and
penance, he was consecrated bishop by Pope Gregory XIII.
in the year of our Redeemer 1579, and laden with gifts
was sent into Ireland, that country requiring him to assist
it struggling against the deadly contagion of English heresy.
When he reached Paris on his journey he earned in public
debates in the university then widely famous a reputation
for great ability and very uncommon learning   With

him went his companion (*Chaplain*) Connatius O'Rourke, son of the chieftain O'Rourke, a man of a noble ancestry, reckoned amongst the first in Ireland, a light of the Seraphic (*Franciscan*) Order, and of irreproachable character. Both having embarked in a ship weighed anchor for Ireland. When they arrived there they landed on the open shore, whence going towards Askeaton, which was a town of Earl Desmond's, they were captured by the Queen's emissaries and soldiers—Earl Gerald FitzGerald and his brother John and other kinsmen being absent They were sent in chains to Limerick city, where they were shut up for fifteen days in a dark and fetid prison. When Drury, an Englishman and Viceroy of Ireland, thought them sufficiently tried by this punishment and likely to give in, they answered him that on the contrary that place appeared to them sweeter and more enjoyable than the most delightful garden replete with many scented flowers and cheered by the glowing sun and a pleasant puff of air cooling the heat of autumnal midday. The furious viceroy determined to punish them more severely, and ordered them to be brought before him. Then turning an angry eye and truculent countenance upon the bishop, " Why is it," said he, " you mad and wicked man, that you spurn the commands of the Queen and contemn her authority, and make a mockery of her laws ? Be converted, if you be wise ; be converted to the Queen and to her creed. In this way whatever crimes you have committed heretofore shall be forgiven on the simple condition that abandoning the Pope's faction and guidance you attest by an oath that the Queen is head and prince of the church in her own dominions. So not only may you have the bishopric of Mayo, but richer rewards from the Queen, such is her royal munificence " The bishop answering nothing to all this, gently smiled Whereupon the viceroy asked, " What are you laughing at ? " " Give me," said the bishop, " this leave I pray. How could I restrain a smile when you bid me be converted who have never turned from the true religion of God. Wherefore if I should follow the Queen's schism from it, that would not be a conversion but a perversion, since it is always called a conversion to the true religion from the false, but a perversion from the true to the false." " We will pass from these jokes," said Drury, " but I know very well that the design of the Pope and king of Spain to make war on the Queen, especially in this kingdom of Ireland, is well known to you, and that you are in their councils, which you cannot conceal." The bishop made no rejoinder to this, and when he was plied with questions, whilst his hands and feet were broken with a mallet, and splinters driven between the nails and flesh of his hands, he betrayed nothing   His companion Connatius intrepidly followed in the footsteps of his holy superior   The viceroy transferred both from Limerick to the town of Kilmallock, and there sentenced them to death.   When they were brought to the scaffold, which was erected on a hill not far from the gates of the town, the bishop addressed the crowd with wonderful cheerfulness and rare eloquence and sacred learning, confirming the people in the Catholic faith, warning them against the errors of the English ; and then he named a day of reckoning for the viceroy to render an account of his unjust sentence against him, an anointed bishop, and his priestly companion, and for his extensive cruelties against friars, bidding him in the name of the Lord to stand before the divine tribunal before the fifteenth day.   Thereupon our martyrs were hanged with a halter fashioned from the holy girdles with which friars of the Seraphic Order bind their habit.   The bishop was hung between his comrade Connatius and one who was accused of robbery, and whilst he hung was pierced in the forehead by a bullet from an English soldier.   Thus the two martyrs rendered their souls to their Creator.   There are witnesses to attest that those who were present and saw conspicuous and obvious signs were filled with an incredible consolation on account of this miracle ; it is well-known that their bodies hanging from the gibbet were never touched by any beasts, or in the least molested, when the other corpse was torn by wild dogs and birds.   The viceroy quickly fell into a horrible disease, and suffering great pain rotted daily from an incurable corruption, accompanied by a most repulsive stench, and on the fourteenth day from the martyrs' deaths he died at Waterford perpetually tormented by wicked devils   The bodies of the martyrs were in a short time buried by the Catholics.

[CHAPTER XII.

ON MILER, PSEUDO-ARCHBISHOP OF CASHEL.

As it is right that these holy and glorious men who attained by their merits the highest praise on earth and eternal happiness in heaven should be celebrated in books and records, so on the other hand the wicked and abandoned men should not be passed over in silence, in order that not only might the living justly condemn them, but also that posterity might execrate their name   And so Miler, a man not as exalted in birth as famous for wickedness, entered into religion in which he conducted himself in a very irregular way and with very little of the manner of a religious. Consecrated a priest and endowed by the Pope with no little power and authority, he set out from Rome to Ireland as if he were going to denounce the new dogmatic errors of the English, but, perhaps, thinking otherwise in his mind ; for from the time he reached England, I am informed, he used to carry the apostolic letters in a large and beautiful pyx or locket which hung openly from his neck and was obvious to every one, for no other purpose but that he might betray himself and his calling.   Being arrested by the ministers of justice, he was brought, together with the apostolic letters, before Queen Elizabeth or her council, and deserted with little unwillingness the Catholic religion, readily embracing the Queen's sect and bribes before he performed the least duty.   Then made pseudo-bishop of Cashel, he right away in unholy union wedded Anna Ni-Meara. She upon a Friday would not eat meat. "Why is it wife," said Miler, " that you will not eat meat with me ? " " It is," said she, " because I do not wish to commit sin with you." " Surely," said he, " you   committed a far greater sin in coming to the bed of me a friar."   The same woman asked by Miler why she wept : " Because ," said she " Eugene who was with me to-day assured me by strong proof and many holy testimonies that I would be condemned to hell if I should die in this state of being your wife, and I am frightened and cannot help crying lest this be true." " Indeed," said Miler, " if you hope otherwise your hope will lead you much astray, and not for the possibility but for the reality should you fret."   Not long after Anna died consumed with grief. This Eugene who then, as at many other times, had endeavoured to bring her back to a good life was (*O'Duffy*), a Franciscan friar, some of whose rather incisive poems, written in Irish against Miler and other heretics, are extant   Well, the wicked Miler married a second wife, and now lives sinning, not in ignorance but wilfully. He does not hunt priests nor endeavour to detach Catholics from the true religion.   He is now nearly worn out with age.

B

CHAPTER XIII.

THOMAS O'HERLIHY, BISHOP OF ROSS, AN ILLUSTRIOUS HERO.

OF far different moulds were Miler and Thomas O'Herlihy, bishop of Ross, who was present at the famous Council of Trent. Returning to Ireland his lot was also cast in the reign of Elizabeth. It is almost incredible with what zeal he laboured there against heresy, by preaching, administering the sacraments, and ordaining priests Long and diligently sought by the English, he was at last arrested, sent to England in chains and cast into the Tower of London Thence brought before the Privy Council, he with marvellous learning and skill pleaded his cause and refuted charges However, he was not on that account the less maltreated, but was sent back to the same prison. Thence again brought before the council and accused he spoke not a word When asked by the councillors the cause of his silence, "If," said he "justice and right had been done there would now be no need of my pleading, since I have already sufficiently cleared myself of the crimes alleged, and proved my innocence, but since not by law but by your will I am to be dealt with, it seems to me useless to endeavour to legally exculpate myself where justice and law avail nothing to the accused." Thrown into his former bonds he was long tortured with hunger, thirst, and fetid darkness, and his body from filth covered with vermin, and the soles of his feet gnawed by rats. At last he was released, some of the Queen's councillors thinking he was a fool and an idiot. I do not know if it be true, as I heard, that some of the Queen's councillors were corrupted by a bribe from Cormac McCarthy, son of Thady, Irish chief of Muskerry, to free the bishop. Freed from his chains, for some years he discharged his holy duty, and at length fulfilled his holy mission.

CHAPTER XIV.

INSURRECTIONS IN LEINSTER.

ABOUT this time Leinster was convulsed with no inconsiderable disturbances, the origin of which may be gathered from what we now relate. The Leinstermen ill-brooked that the celebration of the holy mass and sacraments of the church should be forbidden to them , that priests should be either proscribed or cast into prison, or slain ; that churches should be defiled with heretical ceremonies ; and at last wearied with long continued persecution, and fearing greater would come upon them, some nobles took counsel how to meet these evils. Gerald Fitzgerald, Earl of Kildare, whom we have shown was restored by Queen Mary, planned to capture Dublin Castle James Eustace, Viscount Kilcullen and Fiach O'Byrne, son of Hugh, a gentleman of birth, both engaged to form a conspiracy amongst the nobility. When correspondence on this subject had passed backwards and forwards between the gentlemen, the wife of one gentleman, a woman full of jealousy, fearing lest perhaps letters were coming from another woman to her husband, seized one of the letters when he was asleep and gave it to a heretic kinsman to read. He, clearly understanding the matter, disclosed it to the viceroy By order of the viceroy thirty-six gentlemen of Leinster and Meath were suddenly and unexpectedly seized and suffered the extreme penalty of the law

The Earl of Kildare, who could have taken up arms, took the matter easily, submitted himself to the judgment of the English, by whom he was thrown into chains, and after a short time he died in prison. The viscount and Fiach with some associates endeavoured to save their lives and liberty with their swords They fought a memorable battle at Glenmalure, where they defeated Grey, an Englishman, the viceroy of Ireland. They killed eight hundred soldiers, and amongst them the cruel butcher of Catholics, Francis Cosby, governor of Leix, of whom we made mention above Carrying on war as opportunity offered during two years, they laid waste the neighbourhood, but after numerous raids and receiving not a few wounds, they were deserted by their men and reduced to straits. The viscount and his brother flying to Spain were received by Philip II., that most pious king, and whilst they lived they were supported and honored by the generosity of the munificent king Thus fell the sons of Rowland, Viscount Eustace and his family, as that ghostly verse, which I cited above, foretold to himself —

> What greedy lust the church's rights usurped,
> That will with blasting blight thy fields oppress,
> And quickly cause that all thy sproutings warped,
> Shall leave an airy space for leaves to dress

Fiach did not lay down his arms until promised safety, and was left in possession of his property.

CHAPTER XV.

THE SECOND WAR OF THE FITZGERALDS OF MUNSTER.

WHILST these events were taking place in Ireland, James FitzGerald, of whom we have written rather a full account, upon his arrival in Spain explained the position of affairs in Ireland to his Catholic Majesty Philip II , and sought aid from him for the Catholics.   Thence he went for Rome through France, where at that time was Conor O'Ryan, a Franciscan bishop of Killaloe, and an Irishman, and Thomas Stukely, who by some is said to have been an illegitimate son of King Henry VIII. of England, by others to have been born of an English gentleman and an Irish mother, by others he is called an Irishman altogether This man professedly in aid of the Irish was harassing the English, either incensed against them or moved by piety, or desirous of revolution and war, in hope thereby to gain something, or perhaps aspiring to rule as a man born of royal blood   At the same place was Sanders, an honor to the English race, flying from their tyranny after he had written a book on the English schism

At that time some bands of brigands grievously pestered Italy ; sallying from the woods and mountains in which they hid, they destroyed villages in midnight robberies and raids, and blocking the roads despoiled travellers

James besought Pope Gregory XIII. to assist the Catholic Church in Ireland, then almost overwhelmed, and at length obtained from him pardon for these robbers on condition of their accompanying him to Ireland, and from these and others he got together about one thousand soldiers.   The Pope appointed them generals ; Hercules Pisano, a brave man and famed for his skill in military matters, and other Roman soldiers who embarked with Cornelius, the bishop, and Doctor Sanders.   James ordered Stukely to make for Lisbon and await him there until his wife whom he left in France, should arrive   Stukely steering his ships from Italian shores for Lisbon, with favourable winds, arrived during those days in which Sebastian, the famous king of Lusitania, was fitting out an expedition against Mauritiana

The king asked Stukely to accompany him into Mau-ritiana, promising on his return that either he himself would cross with Stukely into Ireland or at least would give him additional forces to assert the liberty of that island Stukely freely accepting this promise fell by the forces of the bar-barians in that well-known slaughter of Lusitanians—a famous race—together with the illustrious king Sebastian. The Italians who survived the massacre returned to Spain, where James also had now arrived, and he having enrolled the Italians who survived the massacre of Mauritiana, had, with a few Cantabrians given by his Catholic Majesty, eight hundred soldiers According to Michael of Isseltus, one Sebastian San Joseph was appointed commander of the soldiers by order of the Pope.

These embarking in six ships with a large commissariat, batteries, arms for four thousand Irish, James, Cornelius, the bishop, and Doctor Sanders, sailed from Spain for Ireland and after a prosperous voyage arrived in the harbour of Ardnacantus, which is called Smerwick by the English, and is opposite the town of Dingle. There is in that port a rock, which the natives call the " Oilen-an-oir," well fortified by nature, partly washed by the tide, partly fenced by high rocks, and joined to the mainland by a wooden bridge. This was in the charge of Peter Rusius, a citizen of Dingle, who had there a guard of three or four youths. James finds out where Peter is, and having seized him and bound him, cocked him atop the roof of a sow, † and by his soldiers pushes it towards the rock. Peter shouting out orders his men to surrender the rock. James quickly threw into it six hundred soldiers under command of Lieutenant Sebastian San Joseph. He fortified it during six days of continuous work. Moreover, on the mainland in front of the rock he constructed a trench and mound, and stationed there cannons taken from the ships. It was a very strong fortress, almost impreg-nable. He gathered from the neighbourhood wine, oil, beer, sea-biscuits, and meat. He sent back the ships with the remaining two hundred men In the meantime his cousin, John Fitzgerald, brother of Earl Gerald, and other noble youths joined him To these he explained that he had been sent by the Supreme Pontiff to aid the Irish in asserting the rights and liberty of the Catholic Church against the heretics. On this account he carried the keys inscribed on his banners, because they were fighting

---

† See Appendix " Irish Arms, etc."

for him who had the keys of the kingdom of heaven He
said, however, he would not be satisfied with John's
fidelity until he had done some noble deed whereby he
would provoke the anger and indignation of the heretics
and show that he would be faithful to himself. Thereupon
John entering the town of Tralee killed Davers, a magistrate , Arthur Carter, provost-marshal of Munster, both
English heretics ; Miach, a judge ; Raymond the Black,
and others   The rest of the Englishmen he drove out of
the town   San Joseph was animated by James and
encouraged to strenuously defend the fort, and he gave
as interpreter an Irish gentleman of the Plunkett family
Cornelius the bishop, and Doctor Sanders were left with
John to stir up and excite the good will of the men. James
himself set out with eight Irish horse and eighteen foot
which Thady McCarthy had supplied in order to enlist in
the war others with whom before leaving Ireland he had
communicated the object of his journey. He met on the
way Theobald Burke, Lord of Castleconnell, with Richard
and Ulick his brothers, and a number of cavalry and infantry
greater than his own   These, although Irishmen, Catholics,
and kinsmen of James, nevertheless swayed by an insane
stupidity in order to prove their fidelity to the Queen, fired
on James from a distance   James now crossed the ford of
the narrow pass (Bealantha an Bhorin,) and the Burkes
got to the same place.   James was there struck by a bullet,
and thereby roused to fury he turned round his band
Both sides fought rather more bitterly than successfully.
James putting spurs to his horse rushed into the tide at
the ford, intrepidly followed by his horse and foot.   He
rushed on Theobald with drawn sword, and struck him
a great blow, splitting his skull in two, through the helmet,
and scattering his blood and brains over his breast and
shoulders   When Theobald fell dead from his horse the
Burkes yielded the ford, then James pushing forward they
took to flight, James following close on their heels.   There
perished of the Burkes with their leader Theobald, his
brother Richard, and William Burke, gentlemen ; Ulick, also,
the third brother, was mortally wounded Edmund O'Ryan,
gentleman, lost an eye, and several either fled wounded or
were completely destroyed   On the other side, only James
died within six hours of receiving his wound, having his
sins first forgiven by a priest whom he had with him.
Eighteen soldiers were wounded, of whom Gibbon Fitz-
Gerald, surnamed the Black, stricken with eighteen
wounds, was left hid in a hedge, where he was secretly

nursed by a friend, a doctor. When the latter had left, a wolf coming out of the adjoining woods gnawed the old cast-off bandages tinged with pus and blood, but never attacked the abandoned sick man. The others after they had buried at Cadmeus their leader, lost in the engagement, returned to John FitzGerald. The successor of the deceased lord of Castleconnell was created baron by the Queen for this action.

The news of James' death having spread, the majority of the Irish participators in his plans lost hope and failed to take up arms. Sebastian San Joseph was privately alarmed. The English, on the other hand, plucked up spirit, and applied for aid from England. The Queen ordered an abatement of persecution. She sought to stir up the Irish. The earldom of Desmond is said to have been promised to Thomas Butler, Earl of Ormonde, if he would speedily bring the war to an end. She was afraid that Eugene O'Sullivan, chief of Bear, my kinsman, would join in the war, and so ordered him to be seized unexpectedly and put into prison, nor was he released until the war was over. A garrison under command of Fenton, an Englishman, was placed in Dunboy, the castle of his chieftaincy. With the Earl of Ormonde and other Irish troops, although they were Catholics, especially Anglo-Irish of Meath and their English followers, Grey, an Englishman, the Viceroy of Ireland, got together about one thousand five hundred soldiers, forces very inadequate to storm such a fortification as the Golden Fort. Nevertheless with these and two or three transport ships he blockaded Sebastian by land and sea with a double line, and, having placed his cannon, made an attack. The assailed made small account of the attack, being not only well furnished with artillery and arms, but also thoroughly protected by the nature of the place. Already the heretic had for about forty days in vain plied his cannon on the fort, wasting his strength to no purpose. He was tried by the inclemency of winter at sea and in the open camp, where he was without houses, under shelter of a few camp tents , he was being deserted by the Irish, who were brought thither against their will ; and he was losing some English troops, killed by the fire of the artillery, and amongst others John Shickius (*Shinkwin qy.*), a man of great standing amongst them. However, not to abandon the enterprise which he could not achieve by force, he tried strategy He sent a flag to demand a parley. Plunkett endeavoured to prevent a conference with the English, a callous and treacherous race of men, by whom Sebastian, a credulous and incautious man, might perhaps be deceived.

Sebastian, with whom the command rested, thought a conference should not be refused, and so, having got a safe pass, he approached the viceroy in his camp, with Plunkett as interpreter, and, speaking with his head uncovered, showed himself a man of cringing disposition. The interpreter, however, kept himself covered   The viceroy and commandant proposed peace to each other   Plunkett interpreted their speeches opposite ways, making the commandant say to the viceroy that he would lose his life rather than surrender, and making the viceroy say to the commandant that he was determined to give no quarter to the besieged.   The commandant perceiving the false translations of the interpreter by the inconsistency of the viceroy's face, ordered Plunkett to be carried back to the fort and cast into prison, and negotiated with the viceroy through another interpreter.   Then returning to his men he informed them that he had obtained from the viceroy very fair terms of capitulation.   Plunkett shouted from his chains that the Pope's fort was perfidiously betrayed , that the viceroy would soon be forced by the winter's rigour to raise the siege ; that John FitzGerald was coming to the rescue ; that all the Irish would desert from the English if the commandant held the fort ; that there was enough victuals for the besieged for many months , and finally that there was no trusting the heretics   To the same effect spoke the captains of the Cantabrians and Hercules Pisano, saying that they would not only defend the fort, but even engage the enemy in the open if necessary.   The commandant persuaded the soldiers to side with him, and so through the cowardice of this timid general the valour of the others was overcome, and he who was more anxious to save his life than win glory lost both   He surrendered the fort in the month of December on the one condition, which was secured to the besieged by the oath of the viceroy, that he might march out safe with soldiers, arms, bag and baggage.   However the heretical faithlessness held itself bound neither by honour nor the sanctity of an oath nor by the laws held inviolate amongst all people civilized and barbarous   The fort being surrendered, the defenders were ordered to lay down their arms, deprived of which they were slain by the English except the commandant, who being let off is said to have gone to Italy.   Plunkett was for a short time reserved for a more cruel death   Shortly afterwards he was put to death, having had his bones broken by a mallet. Hence " Grey's faith " became a proverb for monstrous and inhuman perfidy.[1]

Grey returning thence to Dublin placed garrisons in the Munster towns, and applied to the Irish and to England for aid against John FitzGerald He ordered his lieutenants to do their utmost to bring the war to a speedy termination, and not to rest until they either took or killed John. The Earl of Ormonde and other Irish nobles hating the pride and power of the FitzGeralds were easily drawn to serve against them. John with his brother James, his kinsmen and followers, the spirited young men of the MacSweenys (those who were cut off in McCarthy's war being sorely missed by the FitzGeralds), Dermot O'Sullivan, my father, who led the infantry of Bear, and others, endeavoured to protect himself, and at the same time harass the enemy.

From the very beginning of the war Earl Gerald did not dare to approach the royal camp or trust his person to the heretics, being mindful of the long imprisonment in which he had formerly been kept by them ; but, on the other hand, he did not openly break with them or assist his brothers and kinsmen. Moreover, his too accomodating wife had surrendered their only son, James, as a hostage to the Queen that his father would continue friendly. Nevertheless, the Earl was considered the latter's enemy and his towns laid waste with fire and sword. To defend them he took up arms. He had not long taken up arms, and been rather successful at the start, when the Queen offered him pardon and his former privileges and other honourable terms of peace on the one condition that he would surrender to her authority Dr. Sanders, who was an Englishman. Gerald replied that he would never be the betrayer of the holy priest, who not being protected by any of his own people had fled to the supreme Pontiff, and thence had come into Ireland, attracted by its renown for the Catholic faith and the piety of the Irish. When they could not agree about this condition a bloody war commenced, which was fought out during three years with various and varying fortune. We shall relate some of the more important events At Springfield, Tarbert (*Herbert qy.*), an Englishman, with four companies, and

---

[1] The famous Sir Walter Raleigh was present at this siege and massacre. The poet Spencer who came over to Ireland as secretary for Lord Grey justifies this massacre on the ground that the Italians were private adventurers who had presumed to assist rebels and traitors (*Leland*, ii. 283). Great indignation was caused on the continent by this butchery (*Camden*, 243).

John Fitzgerald at the head of five hundred foot and some cavalry, had an engagement. Dr. Sanders bid John be of good cheer, and promised that while he fought, the doctor on bended knees, would pour forth prayers to the Lord for him, nor leave the place unless he conquered. While Sanders on a high mound prayed to God, John engaged in battle, and, though inferior in point of numbers, overthrew the enemy; put them to flight with slaughter; and took their standards and military stores, suffering himself no serious loss.

After a few days Malby, an Englishman, president of the province of Connaught, passing through Limerick city, arrived at the place called Eanach-beg (the little market-place). He was at the head of five hundred English soldiers and more numerous Irish auxiliaries, amongst whom were Ulick and John Burke, sons of the Earl of Clanricarde, and Peter and John Lacy. John hastened to meet them and when he had halted in the distance a few of his men charged the enemy in a disorderly manner and drove them into the nearest fort. Thence the royal troops again sallying forth, despising the smallness of the Catholic forces, boldly attacked and put them to flight, until John came to their rescue. There were slain on that day, of the Catholics, Thomas FitzGerald, son of John, cousin of the earl, and Thomas Brunnus (*Browne*), gentleman, with twenty-three foot.

The royal cavalry from the town of Kilmallock followed John as he went from Clonish to Aherlow, and he successfully skirmished with them. At Pea Field (Goart-na-pisi), Earl Gerald, after he had taken up arms, destroyed ten companies of the Queen's troops. A short time afterward he invaded and ravaged the Butler's country. The Butlers, following, came up with him at Knockgraffan with a numerous army, under command of Edward and Peter Butler, brothers of the Earl of Ormond, MacPiers, Baron of Dunboyne, and Purcell, Baron of Lochmogh, but were defeated by Gerald, and the flower of the Butler army cut off

Daniel O'Sullivan, a young man who was afterwards made chief of Bear, carried on war against the English for the protection of the Spaniards. At the monastery of Bantry he destroyed a company of English, overwhelming them with stones; and at Lathach-na-ndaibh (the slough of the oxen), slew Dermot O'Donovan, who, by order of the English, was wasting Bear. Gerald ravaged the country of Cashel and in endeavouring to restrain him, Roberts, an Englishman, with the townsmen and garrison of Cashel, coming to Scurlochstown (the town of the Surlogs), was routed, and some of the Cashel citizens captured Gerald stormed and dismantled Youghal, a noble and very wealthy town, in the storming of which Dermot O'Sullivan, my father, captain of the foot of Bear, with signal valour and against immense difficulties, scaled the walls by ladders, the besieged in vain resisting When pillaging the town a soldier of his, having forced a strong box, took out a sack full of gold and silver, saying, " Here, most valiant captain, is a lucky find unless it be a dream." Dermot replied, " Do not, my brave fellow, be so greatly charmed with your dream, lest, waking up, you find it be not a true image, but a delusion of the senses " Afterwards Dermot fought Fenton, an Englishman, governor of Dunboy, by various stratagems A company of English soldiers, remarkable for their dress and arms, and who were called the " red coats," sent a short time before by the Queen for the war, were destroyed near Lismore by John Fitzgerald, called the Seneschal, a gentleman of birth, at the head of an inferior number of foot. From Fitzmaurice, Baron of Lixnaw, the heretic had extorted six noble youths as hostages, and these were hung on suspicion of his entering into rebellion Fitzmaurice, transported with rage at this act, slew four English companies with their commander, Achamus (*Hatsim*) having surrounded them at the town called Ardfert, that is the hill of miracles After these victories the die of fickle fortune quickly turned another side, ruining the hopes of the Geraldines

James Fitzgerald, brother of the earl, having gone to ravage Muskerry on account of an old grudge, was taken by Cormac MacCarthy, son of Thady, chief of Muskerry, and, being sent to the English at Cork, was put to death. Another James Fitzgerald, son of John, uncle of the earl, was slain in an encounter by Brian O'Brien, an Irish gentleman. Earl Gerald, ravaging MacCarthy More's country had, with a few men, halted at Aghadoe, while his brother John was making an incursion, when Zouch, an Englishman, coming out of the town of Dingle with sixty horse and a troop of foot following, surrounded the Earl unawares, and encompassing the houses of the unfortified town, slew Maelmurray MacSweeny, a captain, Thady MacCarthy, lord of Coshmang, and David Fitzgerald, gentleman. The Earl himself, half asleep, fled to his castle, whence, sallying forth, having got together some troops, and following Zouch he rescued the captive women and spoils

from him. The loss of Maelmurray was, however, a great
and sore blow to the earl. Not long after this John left
the army with only eight horse, for the purpose of settling
a dispute and quarrel that had arisen between some of his
party who were absent. He was crossing Drumfinen on
a pleasant evening, and, having ridden during the midday
heat, now dismounted to refresh himself by walking with
his comrades, who fearing no danger, thinking the enemy
were a long way off, were on foot leading their horses ·
when, however, the light changed they saw not far off
Zouch approaching with sixty horse Immediately all
remounted on their horses except John, who at other times
was the most dexterous of all, and a man of great courage
and stoutness, intrepid in sudden emergencies, and who
usually mounted his horse with the greatest ease But
now, not even with the aid of others could he mount, for
a torpor came over him and completely non-plussed him,
and his horse, at other times gentle and tame, was now
restive, plunging now on his fore legs and now rearing on
his hind legs. Then John, addressing his comrades, said,
" Fly, my more fortunate brave comrades I cannot mount
my horse I have lost all power This is my fated day "
So leaving him, his seven comrades fled, of whom James
Fitzgerald, lord of Strangkelly (Tiarna Scrona Calli), when
he had gone a little way, exclaimed, " I will not desert John,
a most valiant hero, by whose aid and valour we have often
conquered the heretics, by whose single hand many of the
enemy perished. Best son of the Earl whom I have ever
known ! I will not allow him to perish alone. As he,
when victorious, often rescued me from the hands of the
heretics, I will now share death with him " With these
words he dismounted and took his stand beside John.
Meantime the enemy came up, and both being surrounded,
preferred to be slain rather than give up their arms

By the deaths of John, Maelmurray, and others whom
we have mentioned, Earl Gerald was deprived of a great
part of his resources, and broken down, and nearly
altogether worn out and exhausted of his power. However, he protracted the war nearly a year longer, and then,
reduced to extremities and the greatest poverty, he was
gradually deserted by all, and, maintained by his lieutenant
Geoffrey MacSweeny, hidden in caves or woods. Geoffrey,
submitting to the English, and arrested by Earl Ormond,
was questioned about Gerald but replied he knew nothing
A witness who had seen him with Gerald was produced
When the fact had been proved by an eye-witness, Geoffrey,

thinking he could no longer deny with safety to himself, —death awaiting him if he prevaricated—confessed that he was with Gerald, and promised to deliver him to Ormond provided a sufficient reward were given to him. Being promised the reward, Geoffrey, highly lauded, was sent to bring in Gerald in chains Nor did it seem likely to anyone that for Gerald's sake he would risk reward and fortune, and bring himself in great peril of his life. But Geoffrey had greater piety and more estimable honour, and he transferred Gerald to other lonely places, and there he maintained him by hunting and plundering, until, whilst looking for food, he was intercepted and killed.

Then Gerald, with four or five companions, sought a very dense wood in his own country, which is called Glena-genty (The wood of the Wedge), and lurking here he was surprised and beheaded In memory of this, the place which was then stained by his blood is to-day said to be of bloody hue. The guides of those who tracked him were two brothers, servants of his, and upon whom he is said to have conferred many favours, Eugene and Daniel, who, perhaps, looking for someone else, fell upon him in company with the Queen's minions ; but they perished miserably, being hung, the one in England, for I know not what crime, the other in Ireland during the great war, (of which I am to write later on) by Fitzmaurice, baron of Lixnaw, for this foul crime.

CHAPTER XVI

ON BISHOP CORNELIUS AND DR. SANDERS.

WE must not here omit to mention the death of Dr. Sanders. He was seized before the end of this war with dysentery of the bowels. Up to that time he had been healthy, and though in everyone's opinion he was in no danger, yet at the beginning of the night, he thus addressed Cornelius, bishop of Killaloe —" Anoint me, my good lord, with the last Unction of the dying, for to-night I am to depart this life, being summoned by my Creator." " Surely," said Cornelius, " you are strong in the robustness of your constitution, and do not seem to me to require anointing, or look as if you were dying." However, being more severely distressed by his illness, he was anointed in the middle of the night, and before cock-crow gave up his soul to the Lord, and on the following night was secretly buried by the priests, being carried to the grave by four Irish gentlemen, amongst whom was my father, Dermot. Many were not allowed to be at the funeral lest there should be anyone who might discover the body to the English, who were wont to display their cruelty even against the dead. Cornelius, the bishop, went to Spain, and ended his days at Lisbon, A.D. 1617. Some years after he is said to have written in the margin of Stanishurst's book on the manners and customs of Ireland, opposite each falsehood, this note, " He lies "

CHAPTER XVII

THE LETTER OF THE SUPREME PONTIFF, GREGORY XIII
TO THE IRISH, REPRODUCED.

THESE are the most memorable events of this war, as to which I must not omit the letter Pope Gregory XIII. sent to the Irish .—

" Gregory XIII to all and every the Archbishops' Bishops, Prelates, and Princes, Earls, Barons, Clergy, Nobles, and People of the kingdom of Ireland, Health and Apostolic Benediction.

" A few years ago we exhorted you by our letters to recover your liberty and against the heretics to hold and defend the same under James FitzGerald, of happy memory, who with great zeal was planning to raise the heavy yoke of servitude put upon you by the English deserters from the holy Roman Church ; and in order to encourage you all, and nerve him to meet the enemies of God and of yourselves, and incite you to the more readily and zealously aid him, we granted to all who were sorry for, and confessed their sins, and joined the army of the said James in defence and maintenance of the Catholic Faith, or aided him by advice, countenance, supplies, arms and other warlike things, or in any other way encouraged him in the expedition, a plenary indulgence and remission of all their sins, like as was usually granted by the Roman Pontiffs to those who went to war against the Turks, and for the recovery of the Holy Land. But we have lately, with great grief, learned from you that the said James has fallen (so it pleased the Lord) fighting bravely with the enemy, but that our beloved son, John FitzGerald, his cousin, has succeeded him in this undertaking with singular piety and greatness of soul (may God prosper his cause), and has already achieved many noble and commendable feats for the Catholic faith. Wherefore, with the greatest earnestness we can command, we, in the name of the Lord, exhort, require, and urge all and every of you to aid the said John and his army against the heretics in every way, as you did the said James whilst he lived, and by the omnipotent mercy of God, and the authority of his Blessed Apostles, Peter and Paul, to us confided, we grant and extend by these presents the same plenary indulgence and remission of all sins, as was granted to those who fought against the Turks and for the recovery of the Holy Land, and was contained in said letters, to all you who confess and communicate and aid the said John and his army ; and after his death, if this should chance (which God avert), to those who adhere to and support his brother James, and this indulgence shall continue as long as the said brothers, John and James, live and maintain the war against the said heretics. And because it is difficult to bring these, our letters, before all whom they concern, we will that copies under the hand of a Notary public, and attested by the seal of an established ecclesiastical authority, be accepted everywhere as fully authenticated, and as if these presents were produced and shown.

" Given at Rome, at St. Peter's, under the fisherman's ring, the 13th day of May, 1580, in the eighth year of our Pontificate. *Caes Glorierius.*

" Entered by the Lord General of the Holy Council of the Cross, John de la Rumbide."

THE FOREGOING LETTERS WERE TAKEN FROM THE ORIGINALS, CORRECTED AND COMPARED BY ME, ALPHONSUS DE SERNA ; BY THE APOSTOLIC AND ORDINARY'S AUTHORITY, A NOTARY PUBLIC OF THE ARCHIVES OF THE ROMAN COURT, IN THIS TOWN OF MADRID, DIOCESE OF TOLEDO, THE 14TH DAY OF OCTOBER, 1580.

To accomodate this letter to our history one must know that the Pope's " Jacobus " and my " Jaimus " following the Irish pronunciation, denote the same person.

CHAPTER XVIII.

ON ULICK AND JOHN BURKE, SONS OF THE EARL OF CLANRICKARD.

FROM what we have seen above, it may be clearly gathered
with what great zeal and diligence the English endeavoured
the destruction of the Irish, and how largely the Irish
themselves aided their own destruction by assisting the
English in order to injure one another.   This will appear
more strikingly clear in the example which I shall subjoin.
Ulick and John Burke, sons of the Earl of Clanrickard,
by different mothers, disputed the inheritance of their
deceased father.   The English regarded this occasion as
affording an opportunity for the destruction of both, and
by a secret warrant in writing authorised one to slay the
other with impunity.   It is agreed by all that Ulick had
very little affection for his brother.   John, fearful on this
account, when he was entertained by a kinsman of both
in his castle, kept a wary man of his own followers on guard
at his bedchamber whilst he slept, and caused the keys of
the castle to be given to him.   But there is no security
where perfidy exists.   His host, a perfidious and inhuman
man, having provided a feast and produced his cups, made
the guards drunk, and whilst they slept, soaked with wine,
the keys were abstracted and the doors thrown open, as
arranged, admitting to the castle during the night an
armed band of Ulick's, by whom two noble gentlemen,
retainers of John's, were surprised asleep and put to the
sword.   John, who was sleeping in the next room, roused
by the clamour and uproar, quickly threw on his cuirass
over his shirt, and with drawn sword hastened to defend
the entrance to his room.   He kept all at bay until it was
agreed that he should be delivered safe to his brother Ulick,
who was at the gates ; but there is no trusting the perfidious.   Scarcely had he given up his sword, and taken
off his cuirass, when he was slain by the assassins in the
very chamber, and with cruel wounds in the same year
in which the Earl of Desmond was beheaded.   He left
two sons of whom we treat more fully hereafter, Raymond,
Baron of Leitrim, and William.

CHAPTER XIX.

DERMOT O'HURLEY, ARCHBISHOP OF CASHEL, THE MOST UNCONQUERABLE AND ILLUSTRIOUS MARTYR.

WHEN these wars in which our Island suffered so pitiably were over, a new danger sprang up, far more miserable and monstrous, namely the tyranny exercised against priests and other Catholics. The first who fell under this persecution was Dermot O'Hurley, Archbishop of Cashel, of whom we have already written, as follows :—

Dermot O'Hurley was by birth an Irishman, the son of a gentleman, and in his boyhood was, under the care of his parents, politely brought up, and instructed in the rudiments of letters. As he grew older he made such progress at Louvain and Paris in the higher studies that, if confronted with men of his own age, he was second to scarcely anyone as a grammarian , he was equal to the most eloquent as a rhetorician ; superior to most in jurisprudence ; and in theology inferior to few. Having obtained the degree of Doctor in Theology and Civil and Canon Law, he for four years publicly taught law at Louvain Uniting to these accomplishments a splendid presence, dignity, and gravity of mind, he seemed to the Supreme Pontiff, Gregory XIII., after he had spent some years at Rome and taken Holy Orders, worthy of being consecrated Archbishop of Cashel. As soon as this office was imposed upon him, he returned to Ireland, to perish in that most doleful time for his country when its sceptre was swayed by Elizabeth Tudor, Queen of England, who was not only infected with the stain of most foul heresy, but was also the bitterest enemy of the Catholic Faith and of holy bishops and priests.

The cruelty of their Princess in persecuting the Catholics was carried out by the Royalist governors and ministers, not only in England, where they had now destroyed the splendour of the Faith, but also in Ireland, where the natives, even to this day, patiently endure all extremities for Christ's sake. However, our Archbishop, with the greatest pains and zeal, administered the Sacraments to the flock of his jurisdiction, and expounded the Gospel of the Lord, confirming all in the Faith, and for nearly two years vainly sought after by the English, being protected by the care and devotion of the Irish, and disguising his identity and calling by wearing secular apparel. In this guise other priests also, in Ireland, Scotland, and England, are going

C

about to the present day, since the fury of the English
Kings rages against the Church of Jesus Christ   Eventually
it chanced that one day while the Archbishop was staying
with Thomas Fleming, an Anglo-Irish Baron, at his castle
of Slane, in his own dominion, a grave question was started
at dinner, in the presence of the squint-eyed Robert Dillon,
one of the Queen's judges.   The heretics, giving each his
own opinion, freely proceeded to such extreme folly, that
Dermot, who was present, and long kept silent lest he
should betray himself, could not any longer stand their
rashness, and so, to the great astonishment of all, he easily
refuted the silly doctrines of the heretics, with an air of
authority, and great eloquence and learning   Hereupon
Dillon was led to surmise that this was some distinguished
person who might greatly obstruct heresy   He related
the matter to Adam Loftus, Chancellor of Ireland, and to
Henry Wallop, Lord Treasurer, both Englishmen, and
with whom the government of Ireland then rested, as
the Viceroy was absent.   These ordered Baron Thomas
under heavy penalties, to send them the Archbishop in
chains.   The Archbishop, having meantime left Slane,
was arrested by the Baron and Royalists emissaries in the
castle at Carrick-on Suir in the month of September, 1583,
whilst staying with Thomas Butler, surnamed the Black,
Earl of Ormond, who was much offended and distressed
at the arrest, and afterwards did his best to rescue the
Bishop from the executioners, except that he did not take
up arms as he ought to have done in such a case, and
perhaps would have done, but that he was a Protestant
His other efforts were unavailing
    The Bishop being brought to Dublin, the chief city
of the kingdom, was kept many days in chains in a dark,
dismal, and fetid prison, until that day in the following
year, which is kept under the name of the Lord's Supper,
on which day he was attacked by the heretics in this manner :
First he was brought before Adam, the Chancellor, and
Henry, the Treasurer, and civilly and kindly invited to
follow the tenets of the heretics, and promised large rewards
on condition of abjuring his sacred character , relinquishing
the office received fom the Pope, and (O villainy !) entering
upon the Archbishopric under the Queen's authority.
He told them that he was bound and resolved never to
desert the Church, Faith, or Vicar of Christ Jesus for any
consideration   Then the Chancellor and Treasurer endeavoured to deceive him by cunning arguments, straining
every nerve to establish the truth of their falsehoods Dermot

not relishing this, especially as he was not allowed to reply to their nonsense, bade them, stupid and ignorant men (such was his high spirit), not to offer ridiculous and false doctrines to him, an Archbishop, and Doctor of celebrated academies Then the heretics, filled with anger, exclaimed : If we cannot convince you by argument, we will make you quit this your false law and embrace our religion, or feel our power. The Bishop was bound hand and foot, was thrown on the ground, and tied to a large stake His feet and legs were encased in top-boots (a kind of boot at that time common, made of leather, and reaching above the knee), filled with a mixture of salt, bitumen, oil, tallow, pitch, and boiling water. The legs so booted were placed on iron bars, and horribly and cruelly roasted over a fire. When this torture had lasted a whole hour, the pitch, oil, and other mixtures boiling up, burned off not only the skin, but consumed also the flesh, and slowly destroyed the muscles, veins, and arteries ; and when the boots were taken off, carrying with them pieces of the roasted flesh, they left no small part of the bones bare and raw, a horrible spectacle for the bystanders, and scarcely credible. But the martyr, having his mind filled with thoughts of God and holy things, never uttered a word, but held out to the end of the torture with the same cheerfulness and serenity of countenance he had exhibited at the commencement of his sufferings, as if, flying the heat of the summer sun, he were lying in a dainty bed upon a soft pillow, beneath an overshadowing tree, with spreading leafy branches, and beside a rivulet humming with gentle murmur through fragrant lilies, quietly refreshing himself after hard work and the weariness of long vigils

. When, however, in this savage way, the tyrants had failed to break the unconquerable spirit of the martyr by their more than Phalaric cruelty, he was by their order, brought back to his former prison, a foul place, filled with a dense fog, ready to endure worse torments, if such could be devised.

There was at this time in Dublin, Charles MacMoris, a priest of the Society of Jesus, skilled in medicine and chirurgery, who, because he was of the Faith of Christ, had been imprisoned by the English, and again discharged by them on account of curing some difficult cases for certain noblemen This man visited the holy Bishop in prison, and gave him such medical treatment, that on the fourteenth day he was able to get up from his bed for a little while. The Chancellor and Treasurer, learning of this, and that the Earl of Ormond was coming, by whose influence and power they feared Dermot would be saved, determined in their malign wickedness to put him to death as soon as possible Fearing, however, that the people would raise a disturbance, and rescue their pastor from death if it were generally known by the citizens that he was to be executed, they ordered the dregs of their soldiers and executioners to bring out the Bishop on a car early in the morning, before sunrise, and before the people were up, and hang him on a gallows outside the city.

Which being done, out of all the citizens, he was met by only two and a certain friend who had been extremely faithful to him, and had made him his particular care from the time of his capture. These followed him , and before he was strung up the Archbishop, seizing the hand of his friend, and strongly squeezing it, is said to have impressed on the palm, in an indelible red colour, the sign of the cross—a rare and holy pledge of his gratitude to his most faithful friend. Thereupon he was hung by a halter made of plaited osiers, and in a short time strangled, and, so dying, acquired eternal reward in heaven in the year of Our Lord, 1584, on the seventh day of the month of June.

It is said that on the spot where Dermot perished, a noble lady was delivered from a wicked devil, by whom she had been long tormented William Fitzsimon, a citizen of Dublin, removed the body of the martyr from the place where the heretics had buried it, and placing it in a wooden coffin, interred it in a secret grave Richard, a famous musician, has celebrated this suffering and death in a plaintive and pathetic piece called " The Fall of the Baron of Slane."

CHAPTER XX.

THE MARTYRS GELATIUS O'CULENAN AND HUGH O'MULKEERAN.

HAVING told what I know about that unconquerable martyr, the Archbishop of Cashel, I will now more briefly narrate a few incidents concerning Gelatius O'Culenan, an abbot, and Hugh O'Mulkeeian, a priest Gelatius O'Culenan was born of no mean family, and being educated at Louvain, went on to Rome Returning thence to Ireland, he entered the holy Order of Saint Bernard. Increasing daily in virtue, he was deemed worthy of the Abbacy of Boyle by the Pope, and his holy Order. Shortly after this appointment he was captured by the English, who offered him the bishopric of Mayo, and other vacant sees in the province of Connaught, if he would only forsake the Catholic religion and the Pope's party Thereupon he replied to the heretics, " These are great and generous offers which you make me, but how long will you give me to enjoy them ? " " As long as you live," said the heretics. " And how long will you give me to live ? " said he " We cannot," said they, " fix the term of your life or prolong it, nor can we know the hour of your doom." " Therefore," said he, " it is far better for me to obey Him, and follow His law, Who knows my fated hour, and can give a longer life and grant me an eternal and happy existence in heaven, than for the sake of the vain, fleeting, and deceitful prizes you offer to lose my eternal happiness by complying with the wishes of you, who cannot prolong life by a single moment." The English, enraged at this answer, ordered the friar's fingers, legs, and arms to be crushed with a mallet When even this torture could not shake his constancy they ordered him and Hugh O'Mulkeeran, the priest, and who professed the same sentiments, to be hanged. Hugh was dismayed and wept, whereupon the Abbot asked the executioners to put Hugh first to death, so that he (the Abbot) might give courage in his dying hour to the timid priest, and this was conceded. Hugh being hanged, the Abbot followed, not only intrepidly but cheerfully. And so both being hung on a gibbet in Dublin, speedily ascended to heaven in the year of our Redeemer, 1584, on the 21st day of November, at which date the Abbot had completed 26 years His body was hung on the battlements of Dublin Castle, a sad spectacle to Catholics, and a target at which the English used to discharge leaden bullets

---

CHAPTER XXI.

FIERCE ATROCITIES OF THE ENGLISH IN CONNAUGHT.

NOR was this persecution confined to priests, but was also exercised against other Catholics Richard Bingham, Knight, an Englishman, and the Queen's President of the Province of Connaught, began his administration with such mildness and moderation that he was most acceptable to all, and the Connaught men gave him the honourable title of the Kind President. However, this was not a real but a feigned benignity ; not the simplicity of the dove, but of the fox.   After he had established a great reputation for kindness and goodness, the heretic broke out into more than Phalaric cruelty, greedily spilling the blood of the Catholics.   He hanged O'Connor Roe, aged about 80 years, and slaughtered many of the O'Connors and Burkes.

Flying from this cruelty, two gentlemen of the Burke family betook themselves and their families to a castle in a lake belonging to them.   Thither in boats and pontoons came Bingham, accompanied by a guard of soldiers.   When he disembarked on the island, the Burkes, sallying from the castle, charged him.   The heretics turned tail and rushed to get on board their pontoons   The Burkes pressing on, Bingham threw himself into the water and narrowly escaped by swimming.   Driven by the same barbarous cruelty, Fergus O'Kelly concealed himself and a few companions in a thick wood.   Frequently sallying forth, he attacked the English and was in turn often attacked by them.   At last Bingham pardoned him and received his allegiance, but shortly afterwards, when Fergus was on Christmas night happily taking his supper at home, he was unexpectedly surrounded by a magistrate and band of soldiers sent by Bingham.   While the heretical barbarians were detained breaking open the doors, Fergus sent away his family through an underground passage, which, fearing such an event, he had long previously dug up from his house   He, himself, having loaded a gun, addressed the magistrate by name, as if he were going to beg for mercy from the barbarian, and as the latter was replying Fergus shot him with two bullets.   Having loaded a second gun, he killed another soldier, and the house being set on fire by the heretics, he followed his family through the underground passage   and safely escaped.   Whether he be still living or not, I do not know.

CHAPTER XXII.

SOME SAMPLES OF CRUELTY IN THE MUNSTERS ARE GIVEN.

IN the Munsters, also, the English did not fail to utterly destroy generous men, with barbarous brutality, thirsting for human and Catholic blood   Beginning with my uncles, Gelatius and Brian MacSweeny, they put them to death. My father, Dermot, was also eagerly sought for and his servant Gerald, being captured, was tortured with fire applied to his hands and feet, until the nails and tops of his fingers were burnt off and destroyed, but being a man endowed with great fidelity and resolution, he would not betray his master

Shortly after this, Dermot accompanied by five retainers fell in with one of the Queen's magistrates accompanied by fourteen soldiers, and a sharp fight took place. Finally, Dermot was struck down covered with many wounds, two retainers were killed and three wounded. Nor was the fight a bloodless one for the enemy of whom no fewer fell with their leader, before it was terminated by some men coming up from the nearest hamlets. Dermot and the other wounded men were cured by most attentive nursing. Daniel MacCarthy, son of The MacCarthy, flying from the barbarous fury of the English, haunted wild and inaccessible places, and at times saved himself only by a strong band of armed men. He had a wonder, fully intelligent dog called Kiegan (Keegan geir), which, whilst his master slept, always kept watch, and whenever he scented anyone coming or passing by he used to awake MacCarthy, and going before him, point out a way of escape. When Daniel had thus for some time secured his safety, Thady, a woodsman, who was ill-disposed towards him, slew the dog with a sword although the animal was not doing any harm. For this iniquitous deed Thady quickly suffered meet punishment, for he was hanged from a tree by Daniel.*

The following also, Posterity, which will judge of the old man's actions generously and dispassionately, may, perhaps, regard as an instance of cruelty and ingratitude.

Donough MacCarthy, surnamed the White, an Irishman well known amongst his own people for his hospitality and generosity, entertained the English President of the Munsters not only in a sumptuous and splendid banquet, but also had his servants perform dances and sports. A few days afterwards the President ordered his host, when he came to Cork, to be put to death, alleging that an honest and frugal man could not support so large a retinue and would have no need of so many servants unless for robbery, rapine, and other illegal practices (of which there was no proof.)

---

* See Mr Standish O'Grady's excellent tales " The Bog of Stars and other stories of Elizabethan Ireland " New Irish Library Tale III.

CHAPTER XXIII.

THE ENGLISH FAN DISSENSIONS AMONGST THE IRISH CHIEFS.

IT was not the least of the misfortunes which afflicted that unhappy island, that the Irish chiefs levied war against each other, and the English, with whom the government of the country rested, not only permitted these feuds, but fanned and encouraged them, as we have already seen on several occasions   Here again some other instances should properly be mentioned in the order of time

Between Turlough O'Neill, chief of Tyrone, and Hugh O'Neill, who was afterwards surnamed the Great, Baron of Dungannon, and son of Fardorch, there was a bitter dispute as to the chieftaincy of Tyrone, which the Queen was so far from preventing breaking out into war that actually royalist forces were supplied to each to enable them to carry on the war.   The Baron pitched his camp at a place called Carricklea (the Grey Rock) having with him 2,000 men, a great portion of whom were royalists Thither hastened the O'Neill with 800 men, of whom two companies were royalists under William Mostyn and Surdan (*Parker?*), the majority of the rest were led by the MacSweenys of Munster :—Murrough, surnamed Na-mart, the son of Melmurry, and Murrough, the son of Owen, kinsmen of mine, who, having a taste for war or adventure or flying from the tyranny of the English in Munster, had a few days before led some bands of foot from Munster to Ulster The armies being confronted, the royalist troops on each side seemed to attack each other perfunctorily and without spirit, neither suffering nor inflicting any injury.   The Munstermen routed the other forces of the Baron, put them to flight, and killed many, contrary to all expectations, seeing the former were so very much inferior in point of numbers   A mutual arrange-ment as to the principality was subsequently entered into, and the Baron was created Earl, for the English thought it expedient that one should be a check on the other, so that neither should be able to do anything against the Crown.   And not only in war but also in legal proceedings the English governors endeavoured rather to thwart than to advantage the Irish provincials. Of this I will give an instance ·—When Rossa MacMahon (Rosa bui), surnamed the Sallow, chief of Oriel died, his brother Hugh, surnamed the Red (Aodha Rua), Patrick (Gillaphadrig Mac Art Moil), Ever, chief of Farney (Ebhir Mac Iul) and Brian, Lord of Dartry (Brien Mac Aodha), all of the MacMahon family, went to law about the chief-taincy, before William Fitzwilliam, an English heretic, and the viceroy of Ireland, whom The Red bribed by a promise of 700 cows to give judgment in his favour   The Viceroy decided that Ever should be satisfied with Farney and Brian with Dartry ; he placed a garrison in the town of Monaghan, the capital of the chieftaincy ; and divided the remaining villages and lands between the Red and Patrick, awarding the better lot to him who had promised the bribe and leaving him the title of The MacMahon This was in sooth, a charming judgment, by which a great part of the property over which they were squabbling was taken from each claimant, indifferently, and bestowed upon others who had no title at all   Cicero severely censures a like decision of a Roman judge, Offices, Book I.   The Red, however, would not give the cows, being aggrieved at Monaghan being taken away from him, and alleging that the Viceroy had not adhered to the bargain, where-upon the Viceroy, pretending some crime against him, put him to death at Monaghan, and added his territory to the Queen's possessions.   These, however, Brian, Lord of Dartry, shortly afterwards recovered and was inaugurated The MacMahon in spite of the English, as we shall show later on   Meantime I must not pass over a famous judg-ment of John Perrot, Viceroy of Ireland, in a suit instituted before him between Thady and Cathal O'Connor of Offaly about some booty.   He decreed that the matter be settled by the sword rather than by law, and they, being ashamed of appearing cowardly if they declined this single combat, took seven days to prepare for the duel, during which time Thady incessantly poured forth prayers to God, beseeching the Divine assistance.   Cathal, however, devoted all his care to mastering the art of combat.

On the appointed day, they entered the lists in the presence of Perrot and others, and fought vigourously and skilfully on both sides, inflicting many deadly wounds of which Cathal died within a few days

CHAPTER XXIV.

THE ENGLISH EXTORT HOSTAGES FROM THE IRISH

IN this most lamentable state of things, the English, fearing that the Irish roused by their wrongs and for the sake of their persecuted religion might rebel, extorted hostages from many of them, and dreaded Hugh O'Donnell, Chief of Tirconnell and other Ulster chiefs, from whom they had not hostages. They dare not, however, ask hostages from these, lest they irritate men ready for rebellion, and whom they knew well would no more give hostages than pay a tribute to the English crown What they could not accomplish openly they endeavoured to effect under-hand and by treachery. John Birmingham, an Anglo-Irish merchant of Dublin, was induced by the Viceroy, partly by bribes and promises, and partly by threats, to load a ship with merchandise and embark therein fifty soldiers supplied by the Viceroy, and sailing from Dublin he was carried by favourable winds between Ireland and Scotland into Lough Swilly in O'Donnell's country.

On the news of the strange merchant some young chiefs came down, of whom the principal was Hugh O'Donnell, surnamed "Roe," eldest son of the O'Donnell, then aged fourteen years. Accompanying him were Owen MacSweeny, surnamed "Oge," chief of Tuath, and Owen O'Gallagher a gentleman. These the merchant invited on board to inspect his wares, but when they came on board they were seized by the fifty soldiers and clapped under the hatches. MacSweeny Fanad was released upon his giving them as a hostage his son, Donnell MacSweeny surnamed Gorm. MacSweeny, Tuath was also released upon giving as a hostage a youth of humble birth dressed in his son's clothes. Owen O'Gallagher likewise gave as a hostage Hugh O'Gallagher, his nephew, the son of his brother Cormack Birmingham returning to Dublin handed over to the Viceroy the four hostages, Roe, Gorm, Hugh, and the peasant youth whom the Viceroy dismissed when he ascertained he was not Tuath's son The three noble youths were committed to the castle of Dublin with the other hostages

CHAPTER XXV.

AN ACCOUNT OF THE FIERCE PERSECUTION STARTED BY THE ENGLISH AGAINST THE FAITH.

WHILST Ireland was thus pitifully ruined by the quarrels of the chiefs both between themselves and with the royal crown, and the blood of ecclesiastics was spilled by the English, the chiefs, either worn out by their factions and now exhausted of their resources, or hostages, for many of them being in the hands of the English, seemed little likely to take up arms in defence of the Catholic religion. Hereupon a persecution broke out against the faith of Christ, and the tyrant, Queen Elizabeth, ordered that all should entirely abandon the Catholic faith, forsake the priests, accept the teachings and doctrines of heretical ministers, embrace the Queen's sect, and on holydays attend the services in the churches. And to this were they compelled by fear, terror, punishment and violence. This terrible attack on the Catholic faith was now the more severe and dangerous because just at this time more than ever since the reception of the faith, were Irishmen ignorant of theology, philosophy, and jurisprudence, so that they were unprepared for controversy and for preserving the people in the true religion of Christ Jesus, because through their factions, the confusion of affairs, and the barbarous fury of the heretics, their schools were gone to ruin and scarcely was there any one able to teach publicly the higher studies. The holy communities of friars were for the most part scattered and banished, and in many places priests could not easily be found to baptise infants ; in many places the younger folk knew only so much of the faith as they had learned from their mothers and nurses, and some, indeed, were so ignorant of the evidences of the faith that they knew not how to prove or explain anything beyond that they themselves firmly believed whatever the Roman Catholic Church believed ; that with it was the true doctrine of the Catholic faith , and that they had very little trust in the doctrines of the English whom they believed to be ill-disposed to the faith The royalist towns suffered more through this want of instruction and ignorance

than the countries of the chiefs, because the English used
to congregate in the royalist towns   And this is the reason
why the herds and country people, not to mention the
ancient and modern Irish chiefs, are more pure and
enlightened in devotion to the Catholic faith than the
Anglo-Irish who dwell in the royalist towns   In the
depth of this darkness and ignorance there is no doubt
but that the Irish providentially shunned, ridiculed, and
despised the English preachers and were saved from their
errors by an unseen and secret light of faith which, alone
in a wonderful manner, guided many to follow the true
faith of the supreme Pontiff, from which the English had
recently fallen away.

CHAPTER XXVI.

THADY O'SULLIVAN, A FAMOUS PREACHER, CONFIRMS THE
IRISH IN THE CATHOLIC FAITH

IN these straits the great and good God, who never deserts
his own in the last pinch, sent to the aid of the Irish Thady
O'SULLIVAN, a doctor in Theology, and a light of the
Seraphic Order   This man, having studied Divinity in
Spain, returned to Ireland amidst the blaze of this persecution   He visited Dublin, Waterford, Cork, Limerick,
and other royalist towns.   He travelled the countries
of the chiefs, and all Ireland , expounding the evangelical
law, preserving the people in it, and keeping them away
from the new errors   So elegant was his Irish, so great
his learning, so innocent his life, and such his success, that
the Irish called him the second Patrick, because through
him, God preserved them in the Catholic faith which He
gave them through St Patrick   When the fame of this
great preacher had spread over all Ireland and reached
the English, and when he was eagerly sought for by them,
my kinsman Owen O'Sullivan, chief of Bear, concealed him
until the search was somewhat abated, and saved his life
by seizing two abandoned wretches who had made up
their minds to betray him to the heretics.   Finally, Thady
died a holy death a few days before the beginning of the
great war about which I am to write later on

CHAPTER XXVII.

SOME INTERESTING INSTANCES OF PERSECUTION

I WILL relate here some events of this persecution in which will be shown both the constancy of the Irish and how empty and unstable their own sects appeared to the heretics themselves. To begin with · the noble Irish youths who were held by the English as hostages in Dublin being brought to church on a day which was observed by the heretics as a festival and holyday, set up a great shouting and bawling when the ministers commenced their hymns and music, preventing them from being heard, and obstructing the heretical ceremonies, nor did they desist until they were carried out of the church and sent back to their former prison, whence they were never again summoned to wicked rites

On the day on which the Feast of the Lord's Supper is commemorated, the heretical ministers arranged in a ring or circle, and on bended knees, a large crowd of Irish farmers and rustics whom they forced into church, and one minister bearing a large mass of wheaten bread vainly offered a piece to each ! Another tendered drink out of a large bowl of wine. The first of the rustics who accepted the bread helped himself with the left hand, and immediately taking the cup of wine poured the whole liquor over his long and unkempt beard, pretending that he had drunk it all. But when the second boor found the glass empty, " Why, comrade," said he, addressing the first, " have you not left me any wine ? " whereupon the former, striking the latter in the face with his piece of bread, cried out " If I have drunk all the wine do you eat all the bread " Hereupon mocking laughter, shouting and uproar, broke out and put an end to the whole plan of heretical Communion despite all the ministers could do.

In a certain village near the town of Drogheda, dwelt an English minister, who greatly annoyed the Catholic priest of the village, and other Catholics : now endeavouring to seize the priest, anon complaining of his neighbours, and wanting to be present at marriages, baptisms, funerals, and other sacred rites. Once it happened that a certain neighbour died whose body the rest wished to bury, with

the priest in attendance, and unknown to the minister.
The body was with utmost privacy brought to the church,
surrounded by women—the men were not present for fear
of the English , the grave was just dug and the priest
had begun to say the holy Mass, with one boy answering.
When the heretical minister, who had watched all night,
discovered this, he secretly and stealthily entered the
church, and stood silently at the door, until the Conse-
cration was over.   Then, however, seizing the priest by
the collar, and also laying hold on the chalice and Sacrament,
" Give me," said he, " this chalice and also come with me
yourself, whom I arrest by the authority and command of
the Queen."   Hereupon the women, rising up and quickly
laying hands on the minister, threw him into the dug-out
and open grave, and began to cover him with earth and
stones.   He cried out to stop, begging pardon and promising he would never again, in the smallest way, molest
a priest or any Catholic.   When he had sworn to this,
he was, at the bidding of the priest, let go by the women,
and afterwards kept his oath, not annoying the villagers,
but becoming respected and beloved by them.   Another
minister, being at last tired of persecuting Catholics, allowed
the subjects of his jurisdiction to marry, baptise infants,
and enjoy the ministrations of Catholic priests, provided
they paid his fees and entered marriages so celebrated and
children so baptised in his register or book, lest he be punished by those to whom was confided the power of visiting
and punishing too neglectful ministers.   Similarly another
minister, when a new-born infant was brought to him
before the Catholic priest, and the fee extorted, said, as he
returned the child baptised to the parents, " The fee is small,
but rightly so, since if it be less than full, so also is my
baptism.   Take your child to be baptised by a Popish
clergyman, who will please you better, and give him the
balance of the fee.   I am aware how difficult it is for you
to pay the full fee to him and me, but I require this part
because I have no other means of subsistence.   Therefore
I pray you to excuse me."
    The same minister consoled his wife, whom the children
of the district used to hoot as she walked along the streets
and sometimes cover with spits and slavers, calling her the
priest's wife, with this observation :' " That she was not a
clergyman's wife, nor himself a clergyman, although
enjoying the benefice of a Protestant minister, which he
held to support himself, and that Catholics might live more
freely and Catholically under him than under others."

There was a certain pretended English Bishop (Lyons) who being informed by spies where there was a Catholic priest, secretly sent a messenger to warn the priest to quit that place lest he be arrested by the soldiers, and when he was not found there, the Bishop had the infamous spies severely reprimanded, and warned not to bring him any more falsehoods

A certain priest, being enamoured of a woman, committed himself more than once, and being cautioned by the clergy and rebuked for his crime, he would not do penance, but finally, when the priests endeavoured to inflict a salutary remedy for his public wickedness, went to the heretic Bishop and promised that he would follow the Queen's sect, and give the Bishop satisfaction if he were enrolled in the ranks of the ministers and got an ecclesiastical benefice. The heretic Bishop, however, asked him, "What objects induce you, what persecution compels you, to forsake your old religion ? Is it not cherished by others more pious and more holy, and every way more eminent than yourself ? It is great folly to desert a religion without reason. Do you think that we will place confidence in you who so easily change your early and up to now settled convictions ? With the same inconstancy would you abandon us also I am, indeed not ignorant that it is not for love of the Queen nor zeal of her religion nor any other reason than the lust for a woman whom you do not wish to give up that you come to us But we think less of you than if you remained true and steadfast amongst your own."

CHAPTER XXVIII.

A WONDERFUL MIRACLE IS RELATED

AMONGST the miracles occuring during this tyranny, some of which I have in part related, and others of which I will partly detail, although passing over many of them, yet I cannot pass over the following on account of the importance of the affair.

In Leinster an English Bishop of the Diocese of Ferns, at the head of his heretics, invaded a church dedicated to St. John the Baptist, near the village called Castle Ellis, which is in O'Murphy's country, and destroyed statues

of the Virgin Mother and of the titular Saint, always held
in great esteem by the natives, and also offerings brought
thither by the Catholics and the ornaments of the church,
and caused his English comrades to overturn the altars.
Next he set about plotting cruelties against the Catholic
Irish because they would not assist in this crime   But
before he could carry out his intention, he suffered the
penalty of his crime   For immediately a pain spread all
over him by which he was violently racked and reduced
to madness and dashing his huge body on the ground and
against the stones, he put an end to his impious life.   His
body, buried in the holy church by his brother and comrades, was found the next day outside the church, thrown
up on the walk   The English, thinking the Irish had
done this, again buried the body and put guards, but again
the second night the grave was opened, and the body was
nowhere to be found.   By the greatness of this miracle,
not only did the brother of the pretended bishop and his
comrades embrace the Catholic faith, but it also came about
that even to this day no Englishman dares to violate that
church.   Daniel O'Murphy celebrated this novel and rare
miracle by large gatherings of the neighbours and by
sports

CHAPTER XXIX

BRIEF ACCOUNT OF THE GENERAL STATE OF THE KINGDOM.

To bring to light every instance of this tyranny would be
tedious   Throughout the whole   island this   violent
tyranny   produced   immense   confusion   The Catholics
struggling against the sway and orders of the ministers,
shunning their doctrines, and avoiding their deadly rites ;
sometimes beating the ministers with cudgels, and terrifying
them by night and day.   On the other hand, the
ministers bringing the matter before the magistrates, the
Catholics were thrown into prison and fined by the magistrates.   The Queen and her councillors and magistrates
directed all their zeal and plots to despoil the Irish of their
goods, to gradually overthrow them and take away their
lives   This they had often before tried, being of opinion
that the Catholic religion could not be stamped out in any

other way than by annihilating those in whose breasts it was deeply rooted, nor could the new errors be established as long as those flourished who ever hated them. Therefore many mulcted in heavy fines were reduced to poverty, many men of noble birth were put to death. All were required to produce the patents under which they held their properties, so that means might be found of despoiling them of their goods This might be easily done, as most of the Irish had no patents and did not require them since they were owners of their countries before the time of the English rule

And so the destruction and annihilation of the whole island and Catholic faith were imminent. This was the state of things when that great war began, which it is now time for us to relate.

COMPENDIUM OF THE HISTORY OF CATHOLIC IRELAND

BY

DON PHILIP O'SULLEVAN OF BEAR IN IRELAND.

I am about to write of the memorable war carried on for nearly fifteen years by many of the Irish against Elizabeth, Queen of England, for the liberty of the Catholic religion, from the beginning of the year 1588 to 1603, in which not only was the whole of Ireland utterly wasted and destroyed, but also the flower of the English nobility was cut off, in which great forces, but greater animosities encountered ; and in which the conquerors were often conquered .—Which events are digested in several books

———

TOME III.—BOOK I.

ON THE FIFTEEN YEARS' WAR

I will give in this book the resources and equipment of both parties for the campaign and a summary of the whole war.

———

CHAPTER I.

ENUMERATES THOSE WHO SIDED WITH THE QUEEN.

THE combatants were very unequal in their resources In the first place, the entire power of the heretical kingdom of England backed the Queen and the propagation of her doctrines, and she was also supported by all the resources of that part of Ireland which is called Finegald, or the English province, the majority of the inhabitants of which although they are Catholics, yet are not only of English descent, but also preserve the English laws and institutions and the English language, albeit in a crude and archaic form.

Befriending the same side were the municipalities and towns of Ireland, because merchants and men, addicted to trade and commerce and arts of peace, are not easily induced to take up arms to which they are unused, even for liberty and Catholicity, which they, nevertheless, faithfully profess. The chiefs and nobles of Ireland, who are not only very warlike, but place the chief glory of this life and rest all things in arms, were divided into two great and powerful factions, the one siding with the English and royalists, the other with the Irish and Catholics.

The race of mixed English and Spanish blood, that is the new Irish, influenced by the favour and gifts of the Kings of England, for the most part took sides with the heretics, although themselves Catholics, preferring the cause of kith and kin to the Catholic religion, which they embrace and revere.

Some of the most illustrious of these shall be named :

THE NEW IRISH CHIEFS WHO ADHERED TO THE QUEEN'S PARTY :

MUNSTERMEN—Thomas Butler, surnamed Duff, Earl of Ormond ; Barry More Viscount Buttevant , MacPierce, Baron of Dunboyne ; MacPadrig, Baron Courcy ; Burke, Baron of Castleconnell.

CONNAUGHTMEN—Ulick, and his son, Richard Burke, Earls of Clanricard ; Theobald Burke, son of Richard, surnamed Na-long, claimant for the chieftaincy of the MacWilliam's country ; MacPhoris or Bermingham, Baron of Dunmore.

LEINSTERMEN—Henry, William, and Gerald Fitzgerald, Earls of Kildare , St Lawrence, Baron of Howth

MEATHMEN—Preston Viscount Gormanstown ; Nugent, Baron of Delvin ; Fleming, Baron of Slane.

THE OLD IRISH CHIEFS WHO ADHERED TO THE QUEEN'S PARTY :

(Some chiefs of the old Irish race, imitating the new-comers, also offered their services to the Queen.)

MUNSTERMEN—Donough O'Brien, Chief of Limerick, Earl of Thomond ; MacCarthy Reagh, Chief of Carbery ; Charles MacCarthy, son of Dermot, Chief of Muskerry ; Murrough O'Brien, Baron of Inchiquin.

CONNAUGHTMEN—O'Conor Don, Chief of the Plain of Connaught.

MEATHMEN—O'Melaghlin. The following Meathmen, as to whom there is some question whether they be old or new Irish, also aided the Queen —Barnewall, Baron of Trimblestown, Plunkett, Baron of Louth, Plunkett, Baron of Dunsany ; Plunkett, Baron of Killeen.

Those above named we shall call the Irish of the English or royalist party, to whom should be added the Ulster Anglo-Irish who inhabit Uriel (*Louth*) and others

---

CHAPTER II.

LIST OF THOSE WHO TOOK UP ARMS FOR THE CATHOLIC FAITH.

IN defence of the Catholic Faith, the old Irish deriving their descent from Spain, not only held the first place, but were the mainstay and bulwark of the war. Of these the most illustrious were the following —

ANCIENT IRISH WHO FOUGHT FOR THE CATHOLIC FAITH

ULSTERMEN—Earl Hugh O'Neill, Chief of Tyrone, with his followers, namely :—Magennis, Chief of Iveagh ; MacMahon, Chief of Oriel, Maguire, Chief of Fermanagh ; O'Kane, Chief of Oireacht-Aibhne, James and Randal MacDonnell,Chiefs of The Glynns; O'Hanlon, Chief of Orior.

O'Donnell, Chief of Tyrconnell with his followers :— MacSweeny, Chief of Fanad ; MacSweeny, Chief of Banagh O'Doherty, Chief of Inishowen ; O'Boyle.

MUNSTERMEN—O'Sullivan, Chief of Beare and Bantry ; Daniel O'Sullivan More, whose father, the Chief of Dunkerron, was prevented by old age from taking up arms ; O'Conor Kerry of Iraghti (*Connor*) ; Donough MacCarthy, son of Cormac MacDonough, claimant to the Chieftaincy of Duhallow; Dermot MacCarthy,son of Owen MacDonough, another claimant to the Chieftaincy of Duhallow; O'Driscoll, Chief of Corca-Laighe ; O'Mahony of Carbery ; O'Donovan ; O'Donohoe of Eoghanaght (or *Onaght*) ; O'Donohoe of the Glen

CONNAUGHTMEN — O'Rourke, Chief of Breifny, MacDermot, Chief of Moylurg ; O'Kelly, Chief of Hy-Many.

LEINSTERMEN—Although none of the Leinster Chiefs deserted the Queen, nevertheless, many noblemen took up arms for the Faith, especially of the four families of whom the chief were the Kavanagh's, the O'Conors of Offaly, the O'Mores of Leix, the O'Byrnes.

MEATHMEN—MacGeoghagan, the Chief.

Some of the new Irish nobles followed these.

MUNSTERMEN—Roche, Viscount Fermoy; Richard Butler Viscount Mountgarret; MacMaurice, Baron of Lixnaw; Thomas Butler, Baron of Cahir, Patrick Condon, Chief of Condons; Richard Purcell, Baron of Loughmoe; William Fitzgerald, Knight of Kerry and Lord of Rathannan, Edmund Fitzgerald, Knight of Glin; Edmund Fitzgerald, the White Knight.

I have here recounted only those who were in possession of their properties and estates when they took up arms for the faith. Others also, I will mention in the course of my history, who either deserted the English after they had lost their properties or who acquired during the war estates they had not previously been in possession of. Such were Florence and Daniel MacCarthy, who for a while held the chieftaincy of Clancarthy; O'Conor, Chief of Sligo; James Fitzgerald, Earl of Desmond; MacWilliam Burke, Raymund Burke, Baron of Leitrim; Owny O'More.

These were the most eminent of those who declared war for the Catholic religion, and whom we call the Irish and Catholic party. All, however, did not confederate at the same time, but when some had laid down their arms, others took them up. When some were annihilated, others renewed the war. If all had joined together at one time, they would either have conquered, or at least given the heretics a much greater task   .

There were other noblemen, many of them little inferior in rank to many of those we have mentioned and more renowned in actions, although not chiefs of septs or of the countries where they lived. Such were Niall O'Donnell, Garve, Cornelius O'Driscoll, son of O'Driscoll More, Dermot O'Sullivan, my father, Fiagh O'Byrne, Cormac O'Neill, Cornelius O'Reilly, Dermot MacCarthy Reagh; William Burke; Brian O'Kelly, Richard Tyrrell, Brian O'More; Walter Fitzgerald, Dermot O'Conor; Peter Lacy, Edmund O'More; James Butler; Murrough MacSweeny; Ulick Burke; Daniel MacSweeny; Richard MacGeoghagan; Manus MacSweeny; Maurice O'Sullivan; Thady O'Mahony, Carbery, and very many others on both sides, whom I pass over here, as it would be too tedious to name them.

I also pass over many of the Irish Chiefs who stood idly by and in observing a neutrality, effectively aided the victors.

CHAPTER III

WHY ALL THE IRISH DID NOT SECEDE FROM THE HERETICS, DISCUSSED

OF these magnates who aided the heretics, three or four were heretics, but conscious of their heresy and time servers. The rest were Catholics, who resolutely professed all articles of Catholic belief , who harboured Catholic priests, educated in faith and morals, in Spain, Italy, Germany and Belgium , who were wont to receive the most Blessed Body of Christ Jesus, with the greatest veneration ; and who revered all the rites of the Catholic Church.   This being so, one would naturally ask, how such illustrious and Catholic Princes ? how so many Catholic and pious citizens, municipalities and cities ? how such Christian soldiers ? should not only help heretics, but even assail Catholics fighting for the rights and liberties of the Catholic Church.

In truth, I think, this must have been a punishment of God on Ireland for the crimes of Irishmen.   The municipalities and towns lay the blame on the old and new Irish chiefs of the English faction who did not secede from the heretics, and on their Catholic priests, who were far from exhorting them to war.   Moreover, they say that they felt aggrieved at being so despised and looked down on by the chiefs and nobility of the Catholic faction, that the latter would not seek their friendship or company   The Irish chiefs of the English faction do not all give the same reason for not deserting the Queen : some say they were cowed by the disasters of those who had in former times withdrawn their obedience from the kings of England; that they despaired of the Catholics succeeding, as they were not assisted by the Pope or the Kings of Spain or France , that they hoped the Queen, a woman of many years, would soon die, and that it would be wiser for them to await her soon expected death, than risk themselves and their fortunes, they had no doubt but that when the war was finished those, by whose aid and valour the Queen would have conquered, would obtain from her as a reward for their services, liberty to live as Christians and Catholics; that they feared the power of the Irish chiefs lest if these conquered, themselves would be deprived of their properties , that they had persuaded themselves right and justice were on the side of the English in this and other wars which, with the permission of the Pope, former Catholic Kings of England had waged on many Irish chiefs, not about religion, but about titles to land and government, that at this time, there was no persecution of priests; that the Catholics who aided the heretics were not excommunicated by the Pope, or stricken with the censure of the church; yet they would not have been deterred from the league by all these circumstances had it not been that many priests and friars gave an opinion that it was not only lawful to assist the Queen, but even to resist the Irish party and draw the sword upon it. Indeed, the priests were also divided amongst the two parties. All of the old Irish race threw themselves heart and hand into the defence of the Catholic Faith. Thus also thought and acted most of the priests of the new Irish, but not all, for some stood out against the Irish and Catholic party, who had great influence with the Irish chiefs and cities of the English party.

The Pope, on being informed of these Irish factions, by his decree ordered all Irish, not only to abstain from oppressing the Catholic chiefs, but to assist them. By the supporters of the other faction it was objected that the Pope's letter had been obtained on a false representation. This question was at too late a stage, referred to the famous Universities of Salamanca and Valladolid, where all the doctors agreed that the letter had not been obtained surreptitiously, and the opinion of the Irish priests of the English party was condemned in the year 1603, after the war had been nearly finished, as we shall show at greater length in its proper place. If this judgment of the Universities had been obtained at the beginning of the war, doubtless it would have turned against the heretics the arms which were taken up for them.

CHAPTER IV.

THE IRISH OVERCOME, NOT BY ARMS, BUT BY VARIOUS ARTIFICES.

HOWEVER, the Irish and Catholic party was defeated, not by the valour of the enemy nor by the arms of the heretics, but by various crafts and stratagems. Not the least of the English stratagems was, that as soon as the war broke out they at once ceased persecution and tyranny and did not harass or annoy either the Irish priests of the English faction nor the Irish laymen of their province, although they never tolerated the open profession of the Catholic religion.

By this indulgence they retained the friendship of the Irish chiefs of the English faction, and of some of the priests and cities. For it is the custom of the English, and the policy of the Irish government in war and critical times and difficulties not to provoke the Irish with the least injustice, to make much of them, and load them with presents . in peace and prosperous times, they kill, destroy and ruin   They endeavoured with great assiduity to persuade the Finigald or English province, and the Irish chiefs of the new race that they would be expelled from their possessions and properties by the old Irish who were fighting for the Catholic Faith, if these conquered, and by this misrepresentation they rendered credulous men not only obedient to themselves but made many of them active against the Catholics

The English Governors and clergy by themselves and their followers declaimed against the unheard of cruelty of the Spaniards, and unjustness of their laws, in order to deter the Irish from friendship with them, but there is at this day no Irishman who does not know perfectly well that the truth is otherwise.

The Irish, if they deserted the English a thousand times during the war, were nevertheless as often received back into friendship and all their former offences forgiven and themselves oftentime richly rewarded.   But those who deserted once in times of peace were put to death, and the English, that they might not seem to break faith, falsely charge them with some new offence, and however trivial might be the charge it is sufficient to have them adjudged to death   Indeed, I am not surprised that an equal punishment should await those who never deserted from them, although they were Catholics   For although the English may not hate them more, assuredly they do not love more those Irish who are heretics, however friendly, graciously and plausably they may behave towards them, when they require their assistance and help to destroy Catholics   When the Catholics are destroyed they then mete out the same punishment to heretics whom they know esteem the Catholics and are heretics not from conviction, but in appearance only and through fear. Actuated by a like spirit against the Scots, they spare no Scotchman

Nor should another Protestant device be omitted— namely, the plan of laying waste the Catholic's lands, towns crops and cattle with fire and sword, so that those whom they could not overcome by valour, they conquered by

famine and want, and sometimes they did not spare even
the lands of their own subjects or of the Irish of the English
party, destroying their corn and cattle and forbidding
cultivation, lest these being captured might furnish supplies
to enable the catholics to carry on the war.

Brass coin was, by order of the Queen, sent to Ireland
in the year 1601, by which on the one hand the Queen
replenished the exhausted resources of her army, and on
the other withdrew Irish gold and silver   As soon as the
war was finished this brass money became valueless, to
the great injury of the Irish and of the Queen's tax-payers,
especially merchants   Indeed the Protestants held that
the Irish war would never have been finished while the
Irish had victuals or gold or silver to procure them, and
that their own army should be supplied from England.
These were the reasons why so great a number of ruined
Irish inundated foreign nations, especially Spain and
France

CHAPTER V.

THE IRISH CONQUERED NOT SO MUCH BY THE ENGLISH AS BY ONE ANOTHER.

THE Catholics might have been able to find a remedy for
all these evils, had it not been that they were destroyed
from within by another and greater internal disease   For
most of the families, clans, and towns of the Catholic chiefs,
who took up the defence of the Catholic Faith, were divided
into different factions, each   having different leaders and
following lords who were fighting for estates and chieftain-
cies.   The less powerful of them joined the English
party in the hope of gaining the chieftainship of their clans,
if the existing chiefs were removed from their position and
property, and the English craftily held out that hope to
them   Thus, short-sighted men, putting their private
affairs before the public defence of the holy faith, turned
their allies, followers, and towns from the Catholic chiefs
and transferred to the English great resources, but in the
end did not obtain what they wished for, but accomplished
what they did not desire   For it was not they, but the
English, who got the properties and rich patrimonies of
the Catholic nobles and their kinsmen ; and the holy faith
of Christ Jesus, bereft of its defenders, lay open to the barbarous violence and lust of the heretics   There was one
device by which the English were able to crush the forces

of the Irish chiefs, namely, by promising their honors and revenues to such of their own kinsmen as would seduce their followers and allies from them, but when the war was over the English did not keep these promises

This hope turned Con and Henry, sons of the chief Shane O'Neill, and Art, son of Turlough, against O'Neill. The same greed for chieftaincy prompted Niall O'Donnell, surnamed Garve, to effect the destruction of Tyrconnell by levying war against O'Donnell. The same envy drove Owen O'Sullivan against his cousin The O'Sullivan Bear. The same ambition set Thady O'Rourke against The O'Rourke, his brother. The same lust excited the English Maguire against The Maguire. Why should I narrate the dispute between Florence, Dermot and Daniel as to the chieftaincy of Clancarty ? Why should I recall how Earl James FitzGerald was stripped of his resources by the faction of the other James ? Why repeat six hundred examples of the same thing ? Assuredly, my countrymen, however high they may stand amongst the nations in the profession of, and devotion to, the Catholic faith and Divine religion, yet during this war, were far worse than Turks or heretics in faction, dissension, ambition and perfidiousness. Wherefore, it could not be otherwise than that by so many and so great distractions, Ireland should be utterly destroyed, for as the holy Evangelist has it, " Every Kingdom divided against itself shall be destroyed " Indeed my wonder is how it should have so long withstood so many divisions, so many wars, such incendiarism And, indeed, had it not been accomplished by God, I do not think that the few Catholics could have so often overcome the multitude of Protestants and their allies , that half-armed soldiers could have been able to defeat armies thoroughly equipped with all kinds of arms ; that the attenuated resources of the Catholics could have withstood during fifteen years the wealth and power of the Queen of England , that from small beginnings a war should have, beyond all expectation, swelled to such dimensions that the heretics were nearly on the point of losing all Ireland

---

CHAPTER VI.

WHAT WAS THE STATE OF IRELAND AT THE BEGINNING OF THIS WAR ?

AT this time Daniel MacCarthy, chief of Clancarty and Earl of Valencia, more anxious for peace than war, and growing old, tried in every way to retain the friendship of the English, and being given to sumptuous banquets and magnificent entertainments, he encumbered his ample patrimony with lavish expenses. The English having correctly gauged the man's disposition feared no obstruction from him to persecution, provided only they allowed him to live as a Catholic.

The truly brave family of the Munster Geraldines was nearly extinct. Two other powerful chiefs of Munster (with shame be it said) fell under the contagion of heresy. O'Sullivan, chief of Bear, and his kinsman Owen were quarrelling about property. In Connaught, Ulick Burke, Earl of Clanrickarde, after he had killed his brother John, was so odious to many of the Irish that he not merely failed to secede from the English, but even kept many Connaught men in obedience to them. Other Burkes quarrelled about the chieftaincy of the MacWilliam's country. The Leinster Irish chiefs who used most constantly take part against the heretics were for the most part extinct. The Earl of Kildare, brought up a heretic from his cradle, offered no hope to his country. The Anglo-Irish chiefs of Leinster and Meath seem never to have plucked up spirit. In Ulster, Turlough O'Neill, chief of Tyrone, and Hugh O'Neill, created Earl of Tyrone by the Queen, stood jealously out against one another, so that neither did any harm to the English. We have seen that hostages against rebellion had been wrung from Hugh O'Donnell, prince of Tyrconnell and other Ulster chiefs. The more powerful being thus divided and hampered, who would believe the weaker would venture anything ? Yet, although as we have shown above, there was little to hinder truculent persecution, a certain fear of the Irish chiefs haunted the heretics when they attacked the Catholic faith, after they had extirpated it in England.

THE THIRD TOME. BOOK II.

OF

DON PHILIP O'SULLEVAN OF BEAR IN IRELAND

ON THE FIFTEEN YEARS' WAR.

IN the foregoing book we have set out the champions of
both sides, and their warlike resources, and the state of
Ireland when the war began Now let us describe the
war itself, its source or causes, and here relate its first and
tentative stage

—— . o . ——

CHAPTER I.

ON THE WRECK OF THE SPANISH FLEET, ALFONSUS LEIVA,

O'ROURKE, MACSWEENY TUETH AND OTHERS.

PHILIP II., that most far-seeing King of the Spains, pitying
the misfortune and the darkened state of England, over
which, having married Queen Mary, he had reigned for a
short time, got together a splendid fleet and valiant army
under the command of the Duke of Mitina Sidonia, and
despatched them to that island, where undoubtedly they
would have destroyed the deadly pest of heresy in its very
cradle, if they had landed safely.   But our sins rising
against us, in the year of our Redeemer 1588, partly by the
skill of the heretics, but principally by a storm which arose,
the fleet was scattered far and wide and portion of it returned
to Spain ; part caught by the storm between England and
Belgium was carried round Scotland and Ireland , while
a great part of it was wrecked.   Some ships were driven
by the storm on the coasts of Ireland and Scotland, and
these striking on jutting rocks and sinking, had some of
their men drowned, while some narrowly escaped by swimming or scrambling. The English killed such of the
strangers as they caught. Alfonsus Leiva, a Spanish
nobleman, having sailed round these islands, became distressed for want of provisions, and took his ship, shaken

as it was by the storm, into an Ulster port in the country of MacSweeny Tueth. Three hundred other Spaniards, whose ship had been wrecked off Sligo, a part of Connaught, sought the protection of Brian O'Rourke, surnamed More, chief of Breffny, who was not far off. As soon as Elizabeth, Queen of England, and her Viceroy, John Perrott, had learned this, they required O'Rourke and MacSweeny Tueth to suffer the royalist ministers to try the Spaniards. To this requisition O'Rourke and Tueth replied that the Catholic religion, which they professed, would not allow them to hand over Catholics to death, and moreover that it would be incompatible with their honor to betray those who had fled to their protection. And hereupon O'Rourke provided a guide and provisions for the three hundred who had come to him and sent them to Tueth, with whom Leiva was staying while his ship was being repaired. Others also, who had been shipwrecked in different places in Ireland, flying from the English, flocked to him, the Irish supplying them with guides and provisions. Already there were with Tueth nearly 1,000 Spaniards under command of Leiva. Tueth, elated by the number of Spaniards, and relying on their valour, urged Leiva to declare war against the English in Ireland ; that he would arm his mercenaries ; that O'Rourke would do the same , that all the Irish would join in defence of the liberty of the Catholic faith , that the Queen had neither means nor sufficient forces nor fortified places ; that having first gained Ireland, England might then be easily conquered. Leiva replied that this would not be at all right for him, as he had not received orders to that effect from his own king, but that when he got to Spain he would urge the king to send a stronger army to assert the freedom of Ireland. And so, being supplied with provisions by Tueth, he embarked all his soldiers in his ship, now repaired. But scarcely had he set sail, when in the sight of the mourning Tueth, the ship, burthened with the multitude of men, went to pieces and sank with all hands.

The Spaniards who afterwards escaped from the ship-wreck to the Irish coast, were sent by the Irish to Scotland, to Earl Bothwell, commander of the Scottish fleet, and by him were sent to France or Belgium.

The Queen having ordered that O'Rourke's and Tueth's disobedience should be punished by force, Richard Bingham, an English knight, Governor of Connaught, proceeded to attack O'Rourke, and got together a few English and many Irishmen. Amongst others, Ulick Burke, Earl of

Clanrickarde, accompanied him O'Rourke had some
time previously hired Murrough MacSweeny, surnamed
Na-mart, with his band of two hundred Munster-men, and
had, shortly before, armed many mercenaries, and he had
no more forces when, in the village of Drumahaire, he was
surrounded by the enemy's cavalry and gunmen to whose
assistance a division of pikemen were coming up Murrough,
when it seemed as if he must not only suffer defeat, but
even perish unavenged, if he gave battle with such scanty
forces to so numerous an enemy, arranged his ranks and
evacuated the village, he, himself, bringing up the rear,
encouraging his men and sustaining the enemy's attack,
in which he received a wound from a leaden bullet, which
passing from the end of his nose across his cheek, put out
his left eye.   He suffered so much from this wound that
he was unable to discharge his functions, and a panic seizing
the rest, they seemed on the point of breaking their ranks,
when my uncle Roderic MacSweeny—a young man—
quickly assumed the command and taking up the colours
and arms from his kinsman Murrough rallied the panic-
stricken and brought off the rear ranks
     When Murrough's wound had healed and the war
seemed about to be renewed he was not able to do anything.
For he had lost his left eye and was still more blinded by
the beauty of Gorumplath O'Rourke, O'Rourke's niece by
his brother Conn, whom he abducted, violated, and then
dismissed   O'Rourke, indignant at this foul deed, ever
afterwards considered the author of this crime unpardonable.
O'Rourke being about the same time deserted by Murrough
and by his own mercenaries, was driven to Tueth, by whom
he was received not only with kindness but with great and
unheard of magnificence
     Tueth surrendered to his rule his towns and whole
country, transferring to him the entire legal administration, and himself serving in the army as a captain under
O'Rourke
     O'Rourke, having received this power, had two of
MacSweeny's most intimate followers hanged, and when
on account of so severe a punishment for a trivial offence,
Tueth's friends remonstrated with him for having given
all his authority to O'Rourke, " Do not be surprised," said
Tueth, " he is assuredly more worthy of a chieftaincy who
knows how to execute justice, than I who, perhaps, should
allow crimes to go unpunished." The royalist army
pursuing O'Rourke after he had been driven from his own
country, turned the entire weight of the war against Tueth.

This army was a large one, composed of some Englishmen but principally of Irishmen, who thought they would not be safe in disobeying the Queen when there appeared to be no means of resisting her. O'Rourke, worried and fretted by the loss of his possessions, went, against Tueth's wish and advice, to Scotland to hire Scots for the purpose of recovering his country. Here he was seized by James Stuart, King of Scotland, who afterwards became King of England also, and sent in chains to London, to Elizabeth Queen of England.

There he was brought before the Privy Council and asked by one of the Councillors, why he did not bend the knee, "I am not accustomed to do so," said he. "But," said the Councillor, "do you not genuflect before images"? "Certainly," said he. "Why then," said the Councillor, "not do the same now?" "Because," said he, "between God and his saints, whose images I respect, and you, I have ever thought there was a great difference." Shortly after he was put to death. When this became known, his son Brian was proclaimed O'Rourke, by the clansmen, and the war in Connaught being renewed, he endeavoured to recover his patrimony with the assistance of Tueth, in a successful campaign.

CHAPTER II.

DISTURBANCE IN LEINSTER AND OTHER EVENTS.

ABOUT this time the English Protestant oppressors of the Catholic religion putting into execution the royal commands and grievously harassing the Leinster-men, petty disturbances arose in Leinster. Walter FitzGerald, surnamed Reagh, of the Earl of Kildare's family, flying from this persecution, betook himself to the village of Gleran, amidst the dense woods adjoining the country of Fiach MacHugh O'Byrne, son of Hugh, whose daughter this Walter had married. This Fiach, like his father, was the bitterest enemy of the Protestants. He had joined Viscount Eustace's conspiracy against them, as we have seen above, and having returned to his allegiance, he afforded protection to Catholics who fled to him from Protestant oppression. Some he concealed; others he openly rescued. For this he was attacked by the royalists, but partly by valour and partly owing to the thickness of his woods, he kept himself safe until promised pardon and protection, which the English freely conceded lest he should create greater disturbance While Reagh was staying with Fiach he was often attacked by the English, and he, in turn, accompanied by a few armed men, attacked them.   As he was returning to Gleran after ravaging some outlying districts inhabited by English, he met Dudley Bagnal, an English knight, brother of the Marshal of Ireland, with a company he had garrisoning Leighlin A fight ensuing, Dudley and nearly his entire company were killed Not long afterwards, Walter with 60 foot, unexpectedly attacked Ormond, plundered it, and defeated and put to flight a superior number of horse and foot of the Butlers, who had given chase, killing some, especially their leader Peter Butler, nephew of the Earl of Ormond by a brother

Traversing, by unfrequented roads, large tracts of Leinster and Meath, he reached Lough Swedy, a town of Meath, in which lived many opulent Englishmen, the doors of whose houses were broken in by night, and he and his comrades entering slew the men and returned home laden with booty.   Finally, seeing he had done so much injury to the Protestants, and could not be easily captured, on account of his daring and the shelter of thick woods, and to prevent greater troubles, the English thought it best to pardon him and forgive all his crimes Negotiations being opened and having got a safe-pass he went to Dublin to John Perrot, Viceroy of Ireland.   When the brothers and relations of Dudley Bagnal heard of his arrival they surrounded the house in which he was with an armed band.   Reagh, putting on his helmet and a shield on his left arm, defended the door by himself, with a drawn sword, until the Viceroy coming up, put an end to the fight, and sent him home safe, with pardon for his deeds

---

CHAPTER III.

EARL TYRONE, SUSPECTED OF REBELLING AGAINST THE ENGLISH
IS CALLED TO ACCOUNT.

No sooner were the risings of O'Rourke and Tueth quelled than the Queen was distracted by greater events.   For Hugh O'Neill, surnamed Gavelock, (because of his being born while his mother was a captive in chains) the son of the Chief, Shane, returning from Scotland to Ireland reported to William Fitzwilliam, the English Viceroy of Ireland, that some Spanish noblemen of the Duke of Medina's fleet, had been laden by Hugh O'Neill with presents, and sent into Scotland with letters to the King of Spain, in which he asked protection against the Queen, promising his own co-operation ; and that the Spaniards had communicated all this to him—Gavelock—thinking he was in Tyrone's confidence, as he was allied to him by blood and was a Catholic in religion. The Viceroy and Irish Council set out from Dublin for Stradbally, a town in Ulster, and summoned Tyrone to explain. He unhesitatingly denied the charge, alleging that Gavelock was an enemy of his and unworthy of credit. Gavelock asserted that he was ready to prove the charge in single combat, but he and Tyrone were forbidden to enter the lists. Gavelock undertook to produce witnesses. A day was appointed on which the witnesses were to be produced, and Tyrone having given bail, and being dismissed, prevented Gavelock from prosecuting his enquiries, and kept him in custody. Disobeying the Viceroy's command to send Gavelock a prisoner to Dublin, Tyrone had him hanged, a Meath-man acting as executioner, on account of their loyalty and affection for the O'Neill family and the Chief Shane, no man out of all Tyrone, could by any means be brought to put Gavelock to death.

Tyrone then went to Dublin to the Viceroy, and thence to England to the Queen, seeking pardon, which he obtained, having, as it is believed, bribed some, and the Queen, perhaps, thinking it wiser to maintain him, even if guilty, as a rival to Turlough O'Neill, chief of Tyrone, for which reason he was supported and petted. And so returning to Ireland, bail was given by Earl Ormond and Christopher Hatton, Privy Councillor in England, that he would attend in Dublin before the Viceroy whenever called to account. A few days after the Viceroy summoned him to Dublin, that he might keep him in perpetual imprisonment. He preferred to risk himself rather than his sureties, and so he set out for Dublin, having sent before him his House-Steward who provided a splendid and magnificent banquet, to which he invited the leaders of the nobility and Queen's army. Tyrone himself dismounted at nightfall at the gate of Dublin Castle where the Viceroy was staying, and entered. The Viceroy greeted him, bid him refresh himself that night after his fatiguing journey , not to miss his banquet , and to wait on him (the Viceroy) next day. Tyrone on leaving the Castle turned his horse into the field, as if he

E

were going to return, and then accompained by a single
gentleman, fled into Ulster, considering as the fact was,
that his sureties were now discharged from any liability on
their bond.   When he had delayed for some time, the House-
Steward bid the guests sit down, saying Hugh was either
detained by the Viceroy in the Castle, or that he did not
rightly know where his master was.

CHAPTER IV.

THE ULSTER HOSTAGES FLY FROM THE ENGLISH.

A FEW days afterwards, some of the Ulster hostages, viz. :
Hugh O'Donnell Roe, Daniel MacSweeny Gorm, and
Hugh O'Gallagher, of whom we have spoken above, fled
from Dublin Castle.   Roe, however, fell into the hands
of Felim O'Toole, an Irish gentleman, and the Queen's
officers.   Felim desired to release him despite the Queen's
officers, and though he knew he would imperil his property
and get into difficulties.   Dreading this misfortune, Rosa
O'Toole, Felim's sister and wife of Fiach O'Byrne, persuaded
her brother to consider at once his own, and Roe's safety,
and to this end to detain Roe with himself that night
in Castlekevin until he should be liberated, against Felim's
wish, as it were, by her husband Fiach, coming with an
armed band, for she thought her brother should be more
cautious than her husband who was already used to rebellion, and had devoted his life to fighting against the
Protestants, and in support of their enemies.   This advice
being approved of, Fiach hastened with an armed band
to rescue Roe   The Viceroy being also informed in Dublin,
sent a company to bring in Roe in chains   That night
it rained so heavily that the waters of an intervening
river overflowed its banks and inundated the adjoining
country, so that Fiach could not possibly cross the ford.
Meantime the English, who were not obstructed by the
river, carried off Roe to Dublin, where he was more closely
guarded in the same castle, and even put in chains
     After some days had passed, he again planned a dash
for freedom with Henry and Art O'Neill, sons of the
chieftain Shane, who were confined in the same prison.
This plan he also communicated to a youth—Edward
Eustace a friend of his, and to Fiach the most inveterate
enemy of the Protestants. The lad Edward promised

to supply him for his flight with four horses Fiach promised a guide who would conduct him to his house in Glenmalure and that he would send him thence safely into Ulster. On the appointed night, Roe procured a file with which he cut the fastenings of his, Henry's and Art's chains He also procured a very long silk rope by which to let themselves down from the top of the high castle In the early part of a stormy night, they tied one end of the rope to the privy and first Henry clutching the rope with his hands and between his legs, descended down the privy sewer, and without waiting for his companions, took the road to Ulster and escaped safely. Roe followed and waited for Art Art in sliding down the rope too quickly was badly hurt by a stone which accidentally fell from the sewer and was scarcely able to pick himself up. The lad Edward, who had promised the horses had four fleet steeds saddled in stable the three previous days, but on this day they had been taken away by a friend without his knowledge. The guide sent by Fiach was waiting near the castle, and during that night and the following day conducted Roe and Art through bye-ways and lonely places, lest they be caught It was winter time, a few days before the feast of our Lord's Nativity, and the ground was covered with deep snow. Owing to this, Roe, who had worn out his shoes, by the long and hasty journey, lost the nails of both his big toes which were frozen off with the snow, his feet, now bare, being exposed to the action of the snow and roughness of the ground Art, although he had stronger shoes, was so seriously hurt by the falling stone, that being hardly able to cover the long and rugged roads, he was delaying Roe. Nearly worn out they arrived at night in a cave not many miles from Fiach's house, and leaving them there, as arranged, the guide set off to report the fact to Fiach

The two youths, who flying all day, had not taken any food were famished with hunger, but worn out with the journey, passed the night sunk in a deep sleep And now the second day had dawned and no one came from Fiach The third day of fast was running out, " Art," said Roe, " see how the brute beasts feed on plants and leaves, let us also, who though endowed with reason are nevertheless also animals, assuage our hunger in the same way until food is supplied by the faithful Fiach." And so he plucked leaves from the nearest tree and eat them, but Art refused those offered to him. Meantime Fiach left no stone unturned to supply them with food, but was

long prevented by those who observed his smallest act and
movement as that of a suspected man   At last on the
third night he sent food by four soldiers   Art, exhausted
by the wound from the stone and the long fast, could not
lift the food to his mouth, nor when put to his lips by Roe
and the soldiers could he eat it   Roe who was more robust,
and who had considerably sustained his sinking energies
by the leaves, refused to eat, for grief at seeing his comrade
breathing his last before his eyes. However, Art being
moved out of his sight, he was forced to eat by the soldiers.
After the excitement and fuss of those who were searching
for Roe had subsided, and Art being interred, Roe was
secretly brought foot sore, to Fiach's house and cured.
When he had been cured Fiach sent him by Walter
Fitzgerald Reagh to Ulster to the Earl of Tyrone ; Tyrone
sent him to Maguire, and Maguire delivered him to his
father, Hugh O'Donnell, Chief of Tyrconnell

———

CHAPTER V.

ROE COMPLAINS OF THE WRONGS INFLICTED ON HIM, AND BEING
ELECTED O'DONNELL, RESOLVES TO FREE HIS NATIVE LAND
FROM HERESY.

AT this time Willis, an Englishman with two companies,
was levying tribute in Tyrconnell, and was attacked by
MacSweeny, as soon as ever the latter had heard of
Roe's safe arrival. Willis betook himself to the monastery
which is called the fort of the strangers (*Donegal*) Being
surrounded there he surrendered to Roe by whom he was
dismissed in safety with an injunction to remember his
words, that the Queen and her officers were dealing unjustly
by the Irish , that the Catholic religion was contaminated
by impiety ; that holy bishops and priests were inhumanly
and barbarously tortured , that Catholic noblemen were
cruelly imprisoned and ruined , that wrong was deemed
right , that himself had been treacherously and perfidiously
kidnapped , and that for these reasons he would neither
give tribute nor allegiance to the English
    The O'Donnell being an old man, resigned the
chieftaincy, which he had held for nearly twenty years,
and asked that the government and command should be
entrusted to his son Roe, whom he named The O'Donnell,

and required all subjects of his country to admit Roe's authority, while he himself, after the manner of Irish Chiefs, devoted the seven years which he lived after this, to prayer and meditation on holy things

O'Donnell, by which name we shall henceforth call Roe, was inaugurated in the usual way, and then directed all his plans and thoughts to this one end, namely, to liberate his native land and the Catholic religion from the heresy and tyranny of the English, forming a confederacy with those who followed him either by custom or in right of his Chieftaincy

These were Owen MacSweeny, surnamed Oge, chief of Tuath, who had already rebelled in order to save the Spaniards, Donough MacSweeny, Chief of Banagh; Daniel MacSweeny, Chief of Fanad; John O'Doherty, Chief of Innishowen; O'Boyle, and others of lesser note, from whom should by no means be omitted, O'Rourke, Chief of Breifny in Connaught, who lost no opportunity of avenging the death of his father, who was killed by the Queen.

O'Donnell did not doubt but that Earl Tyrone would also take up arms for the Catholic religion, unless prevented by a great dread of Turlough O'Neill, his kinsman and Chief of Tyrone, who mindful of ancient feuds seemed unlikely to let pass any chance of injuring the Earl. And Turlough might be easily deposed as the leaning of the Tyrone-men was towards the Earl. Desirous of removing this obstacle, O'Donnell, first of all attacked O'Neill, and putting his capital—Strabane— in the hands of the Earl, drove Turlough into a small island in a lake. Here until his death, two years afterwards, O'Neill maintained himself midway between O'Donnell and the Earl, indifferent to the war, either because he was worn out by age, or because the clansmen would not side with him against the Catholics, or because he himself, a Catholic, did not wish to help Protestants.

CHAPTER VI

MAGUIRE TAKES UP ARMS AGAINST THE PROTESTANTS EDMUND, PRIMATE OF IRELAND, KILLED BY THE ROYALISTS: AND SUNDRY OTHER MATTERS

AT the end of the following autumn, Hugh Maguire, Chief of Fermanagh, was forced to take up arms against the

Protestants. For the Protestant bishop of Meath sent an heretical minister to the Abbey, called Clones This is in the chieftaincy of Oriel, near Maguire's country. Here the minister in various ways harassed not only the country people and farmers, subjects of the Abbey, but also the adjoining tributaries of Maguire's, who were Catholics and yet forced to attend heretical worship against their will, and on their resisting, the minister prosecuted them for offences under the Popery laws (as the Protestants call them), and for treason, and had them fined, pursuing with rapacity the wretched means of the poor. He very soon paid the penalty of this wickedness when he was burned one night in his house The English accused Maguire of being the perpetrator of this deed, and summoned him to a trial, and when he did not attend to take his trial on the appointed day, but on one excuse or another post-poned attending from day to day, they sent two armies to either bring him in in-chains, or strip him of his property. Meantime Maguire harried a few of the English who lived in Connaught.

About this time Edmund MacGauran, Primate of Ireland, Archbishop of Armagh, was conveyed from Spain by James Fleming, a merchant of Drogheda, bearing a message to the Irish from the King of Spain, to declare war on the Protestants in defence of the Catholic Faith, and informing them that he would very speedily send them aid The Primate going to Maguire who was already at war and a man of warlike propensities, had no difficultiy in persuading him to continue the struggle on the faith of his Catholic Majesty's assurances, and reliance on his sending assistance

Maguire with the Primate and slender forces crossed O'Rourke's country of Breifny and again attacked Connaught. On hearing this, Richard Bingham, an English Knight, Governor of Connaught, sent against him William Gilbert, an Englishman with a small force They met at a place anciently called the shield of miracles (sigeth na bhfeart). The cavalry of both parties preceded the foot battalions, covering the wings The day was very dark owing to a thick mist, so that they did not see one another until they came face to face. The trumpet suddenly giving the command, precipitated both into battle Maguire, who never in the least lost his presence of mind, ran Gilbert through with a spear, killed him, and routed and put his cavalry to flight. The foot closely followed Maguire. The Primate was mounted on horseback and accompanied by only two gentlemen—Felim MacCaffrey and Cathal Maguire. While Maguire was fighting Gilbert, another troop of royalist cavalry fell upon the Primate, who, as he was flying fell from his horse and was killed as he lay on the ground. Felim was also slain fighting. Some foot-soldiers of the Catholic army recognising the Primate's voice, although they could not see him on account of the thick mist, rushed up and thinking Cathal who with drawn sword was defending the Primate, was one of the Protestants, they killed him with many wounds, while the Protestants escaped unhurt, owing to the fleetness of their horses. Maguire was more grieved at the Primate's death than rejoiced at the victory, and laden with booty returned home. Subsequently O'Rourke and Maguire resolving to punish, not only the English Protestants, but also those Irish Catholics who aided them, laid waste O'Ferrall's country of Annaly in Meath. William O'Ferrall tried to rescue the spoils in a cavalry fight, but at the very first charge Maguire put an end to the combat, having by his dexterity and valour pierced William with a spear. On his death the others offered no further resistance, and O'Rourke and Maguire retained the booty.

CHAPTER VII.

MAGUIRE ENCOUNTERS WITH DISADVANTAGE THE ROYALIST ARMY AND LOSES ENNISKILLEN BY TREACHERY.

WHILE these events were in progress, the two armies which the Queen had ordered to be mobilised against Maguire, were got together. One was led by Henry Bagnal, knight, Marshal of Ireland, and Governor of Ulster, who had under him far from contemptible forces from Irish and English garrison troops and recent Irish levies. He had 700 horse, the greater part of which, as well as a considerable part of the foot, was commanded by Earl Tyrone, who thought it would be very unsafe for him not to assume the appearance of obeying the Queen's orders. Maguire, much alarmed at the impending danger, besought O'Donnell to help him. He got from O'Donnell a few Irish gallow-glasses and Scottish bowmen and armed some of his own mercenaries, of whom nearly 100 were cavalry, but he was still very inferior in strength to the enemy. Bagnal

with all his forces encamped on the south side of the river
Erne, intending to cross the ford called Belacooloon and
attack Maguire's mercenaries who had fled thither.
Maguire encamped on the other side of the river   The
battle began by hurling missiles on either side.   The
royalists had the advantage in numbers, in equipment,
and position, since they had a much larger number of foot,
700 horse against 100, and gunmen against archers, and
of course, the bow could not send the arrow as far as
the gun sent the leaden bullet.   Moreover the gunners
were able from a wood which adjoined the river bank, to
attack with impunity the Catholics who were standing on
open ground, while the archers could not well aim their
arrows against the royalists protected by the thickness of
the wood   When, in this way, the fight had been carried
on with great loss to the Catholics, Earl Tyrone, who commanded the royalist cavalry, set spurs to his horse and
forced the ford with all his cavalry and charging the
Catholics, totally routed them, but did not pursue them
far, as he was pierced in the thigh by an Irish foot-soldier,
and Maguire with his cavalry came to the rescue of the foot.
In this battle the Catholics lost under 200, and the royalists
very few.   The ancient enmity between Tyrone, who had
been seriously wounded, and Bagnal, was increased by this
victory, as each claimed for himself the glory thereof.
Bagnal because he was the commander of the army and
because as Governor of Ulster the others were under his
authority : Tyrone, because he had brought up the greater
part of the cavalry ; had crossed the ford with the horse ;
had put the Maguirites to flight ; had all the risk ; and had
been wounded.   Wherefore, when asked by Bagnal to
certify to the latter's valour in letters to the Queen and
Viceroy, Tyrone replied that he would tell them the truth.
O'Donnell, who was coming to Maguire's assistance with
a larger number of cavalry, gunmen, and gallowglasses,
arrived the night after the battle, and would have attacked
the enemy, were it not that he was privately asked by
messengers from Tyrone to have a care of the latter's safety,
and not surround the Protestants while he was in their
camp, which he would soon quit, as in fact he did, fearing
lest Bagnal would throw him into chains, and so send him
to the Viceroy (as it was believed he had orders to do).
That very night he fled, wounded as he was, from the camp
to his town of Dungannon, where he was soon cured under
medical treatment.   At this time Richard Bingham,
Governor of Connaught, captured Enniskillen rather by

the treachery in the garrison than by force. This is an island surrounded by the small Lough Erne, and on which Maguire had a castle fortified by a double ditch. Against this Bingham led fifteen companies of foot and four of horse collected in Connaught partly from the English, but chiefly from Irish Catholics, and marched through Breifny, O'Rourke's country, at this time wasted and ruined. Ferried over in pontoons and small boats, he for some days in vain assailed the castle, which was defended with great bravery by 80 men Seeing clearly that he was only wasting his energy, he sounded a parley with the defenders One who was not of noble birth, but in whom the defenders principally trusted their safety and the castle, on account of his intimacy and influence with Maguire, by whose munificence he had been enriched, came to Bingham's camp This man was not inaptly nick-named the boar's or sow's son, for besides being of ungainly build and ugly countenance, he had projecting from his mouth two huge teeth like a sow's or boar's tusks Corrupted and seduced by Bingham's promises and bribes, he arranged to betray the castle, and then returned to his own people as if resolved to defend the Castle to the death When the truce had expired Bingham attacked the Castle in the usual way The defenders each defended his own post. The boar's son, as if fighting bravely and stoutly, showed himself to the enemy on the outer ditch They bore down on him in great numbers He, as arranged, fled and left the place undefended, and as soon as he got within the second ditch quickly turned about. Thither also the enemy following, he allowed them in, and fell back on the Castle gate, which, upon his entry, the soldier there stationed hastened to close and fasten against the advancing enemy, but the sow's son with a blow of his drawn sword felled him to the ground and throwing open the gates let in the enemy who slew all the defenders except the traitor. Even the old men, children and women who had fled to the castle were thrown headlong from the top of the bridge which connected the island with the mainland. Having placed a garrison in the Castle, Bingham and Bagnal beat a hasty retreat, already distrusting Tyrone, and fearing O'Donnell and Maguire would be reinforced by large forces

CHAPTER VIII

O'DONNELL BESIEGES ENNISKILLEN AND SENDS A MESSENGER
TO SPAIN TO BEG ASSISTANCE FROM HIS CATHOLIC MAJESTY.

AFTER the retreat of the royal armies, O'Donnell determining to avenge Maguire's losses, without delay, and being
especially incensed by the cruel slaughter of the old men,
women and children, hastened to besiege and storm Enniskillen As he had no brass cannon to batter the Castle
it was easily defended by the English O'Donnell perceiving this, and thinking within himself that it would be
hard to liberate Ireland and the Catholic religion from the
heresy and tyranny of the English without the help of
foreign princes, he sent James O'Healy, Archbishop of
Tuam, a man of approved learning and innocence of life,
as ambassador to lay before Philip II., Monarch of the Spains,
the state of affairs in Ireland, to beseech him to send to the
well nigh failing Catholic faith in Ireland, the succour he
had promised through the Primate of Ireland, and to assure
him of the co-operation and allegiance of O'Donnell and
other Irish chiefs. The bishop was most graciously and
with more than royal generosity, received by the King, to
whom he explained the feelings of O'Donnell and other
Irish chiefs towards the Spaniards ; their faith ; constancy ;
bravery and military skill. Also the island's climate,
salubrity, fertility, harbour accomodation, rich cities and
towns, beauties of river and lake and many other advantages, adding, what now no one who knows the island
doubts, that Ireland once possessed, Scotland, England,
Holland or Batavia, and all Belgian France might with
little difficulty be assailed and conquered He then begged
the king (as was the end and object of his mission) to help
the Catholic religion The King could at first scarcely
credit the bishop's speech because of the contradictory
reports on Ireland spread by the English who hid its glories
in a cloud of lies, lest that most promising island celebrated
for its many indigenous charms, and from which England,
the nurse of error, might be destroyed, should be sought
after by the Spaniards. He therefore summoned to his
presence, Richard Stanihurst, who, to curry favour with
the English, had published a book in disparagement of
Ireland, but he would not contradict the Bishop in anything
he had said, for it was entirely true, and the King then
believing the Bishop's account began to admire and pay

greater attention to Ireland, and dismissed the Bishop, in a ship himself provided, loaded with presents, and with an answer to his message After the ship had left the Spanish shores, it was again driven into port by the violence of wind and weather, and whilst waiting for settled weather and a favourable wind, the captain of the ship, appointed by the king, happened in a quarrel in a town called Sant Ander to kill a man, and to avoid arrest by the magistrates of that place, he embarked the Bishop and others and set sail in bad weather with the result that the ship was wrecked and all hands perished in the storm. A few years subsequently His Catholic Majesty ordered a fleet with 17,000 men to sail for Ireland, but this was wrecked off a port of Gallicia called Corcuvion, with the loss of 10,000 men

Meanwhile O'Donnell, confident that his Catholic Majesty, the greatest bulwark of Christianity, would send help to the Irish in good time as he had promised by the Primate, made no delay in enrolling Irish and Scotch troops and cut off Enniskillen from supplies

CHAPTER IX.

DISTURBANCE IN LEINSTER RENEWED   SUNDRY MATTERS DETAILED

PETTY risings of Leinstermen again took place, occasioned by Peter FitzGerald, a heretic.   This man was, on account of his inhuman cruelty, made a magistrate by the English, and put to death not only men but, such was his brutality, even women and children He especially thirsted for the blood of Walter Reagh FitzGerald and suddenly surprised the latter's town of Gleran with a band of assassins, but to no purpose as Reagh was at the time from home and his wife who was there fled for safety. Shortly after this, Reagh with Turlough, Felim and Raymund O'Byrne, sons of Fiach, his kinsmen, with 12 horse and nearly 100 foot unexpectedly attacked Peter's castle, and having first set fire to the doors and then to the rest of the house, burned him and his family Meantime the English neighbours with a troop of horse and some foot surrounded Reagh, but he charging and wounding a few of them, put the rest to flight Hereupon Reagh and the sons of Fiach were proclaimed enemies and were diligently and closely pressed by the English. Reagh being unexpectedly surrounded in his town of Gleran by Protestants and Irish auxiliaries, especially Butlers, betook himself with a few armed men into a small fort which in anticipation of sudden emergencies he had surrounded with a trench and ditch. This the enemy attacked. He endeavoured to repulse them. The enemy in great numbers pressing in on all sides, Reagh's brother Gerald was killed by a leaden bullet, fighting bravely. Most of the others were wounded. Reagh, when he could no longer hold the fort and was short of provisions, broke through the midst of the enemy's serried ranks and escaped with a few men. Not long after when at dusk he had distributed his soldiers in the village, he himself with two comrades entered a house some distance from the others and stumbled on 16 of the enemy's soldiers Swords were drawn on both sides, five of the royalists were severely wounded, one of Reagh's two comrades was killed and he himself was thrown down with his thigh almost broken by a blow of a mallet His second comrade, one George O'More, lifting his fallen leader from the ground and putting him on his back endeavoured to rescue him from the enemy's hands by flying to his comrades who were staying in the nearest hamlet. When his pursuers gained on him he let Reagh down and fought with four or five until his comrades came to the rescue. Reagh was concealed by these, but while under treatment was betrayed by his guardian who had been captured by the English, and was afraid of his own head Being brought to Dublin he was impaled on a long sharp iron spike and so perished After Fiach heard of Reagh's death he successfully attacked the royal troops four times. After these victories, fortune, seldom long favourable to the Catholics, turned the die It was pretended that Turlough, at once the first in birth and valour of Fiach's three sons, had arranged to betray his father to the English. Fiach believed this the more readily, because Rosa O'Toole, his wife and Turlough's step mother, who was imprisoned in Dublin by the English, sent him the warning, whether merely fearful of her husband's life or deceived by the craft and treachery of the English, is uncertain Turlough therefore was seized "Because," said Fiach, " paternal love will not allow me to inflict fitting punishment on your perfidy, I will give you up to those to whom you would have betrayed me, that as you have experienced paternal affection, so you may test the humanity of the enemy." Turlough was sent in chains to Dublin and not only expiated his imaginary crime but shed a lustre on his entire house by his noble death, for though often pressed by the English and offered bribes to subscribe to the royalist sect, he preferred to die a cruel death professing the Catholic creed of Christ, than to live denying it. He was a sad loss, especially to his father, who shortly after was betrayed by one in whom he had complete confidence and who guided the enemy to where they surprised him with a few retainers, and beheaded him. However Felim and Raymond, his sons, did not, on this account, fail to carry on the war their father had started

---

CHAPTER X

TYRONE FOR VARIOUS REASONS BECOMES INCENSED AGAINST THE PROTESTANTS, AND SUSPECTED BY THEM.

MEANWHILE O'Donnell continued the siege of Enniskillen, and Earl Tyrone became daily more irritated against the Protestants and suspected by them In the first place the Queen's thanks were sent to Bagnal for the victory obtained over Maguire at the ford of Belacooloon, but no acknowledgments were offered to Tyrone, at which he was indignant, nor was he so vexed at being defrauded of his due as at Bagnal's reward, exultation and triumph therein. Indeed for many reasons these men hated one another with inextinguishable hatred. As Governor of Ulster, Bagnal was regarded by Tyrone as encroaching on the clansmen's rights and to be resisted. Tyrone captivated by Bagnal's sister, a remarkably fine and beautiful woman, had abducted and married her and converted her from the Protestant to the Catholic faith, and he complained that her allotted dowry was withheld from him by Bagnal. Bagnal had often said that his sister and family were not as ennobled by the illustrious rank of her husband as disgraced by the rebellion and recent perfidy of the Papist, and that he had step-children to whom, and not to his sister's issue, in case she had any, should his vast estate descend On this and other accounts they challenged one another to single combat in Dublin, and probably would have fought had not friends prevented them Hence Bagnal omitted no chance of harassing Tyrone, and of exciting the Queen's jealousy against him. Moreover Tyrone reflected on the recent cruel death of MacMahon and his name attainted by act of Parliament, and he recalled the destruction of other Irish chiefs But to a Catholic, the liberty of the Catholic religion especially appealed. To these other misgivings were soon added.

When Shane O'Neill, Chief of Tyrone, was treacherously destroyed by his own Scottish soldiers (as we have shown above), his possessions were forfeited to the Queen, although ineffectually, because Turlough O'Neill retained them. Amongst these, Farney, a town of Ever MacMahon's, was specifically forfeited to the Queen as it had belonged to Shane and been given by the Queen to the Earl of Essex, an Englishman. But up to now neither the forfeiture nor grant had been enforced as Ever withheld possession of his property. Subsequently, after this Earl's death, his son granted Farney to one John Talbot, an Anglo-Irishman, and Talbot was put into possession of the castle and patrimony of Farney by decree of the Queen, the Catholics vainly protesting against his having unjustly procured from the heretics in his iniquitous action the property of Ever a Catholic. Now Ever's sons, thinking it a suitable opportunity while O'Donnell was up in arms, got together a company of friends and attacked Farney Castle by night. They unexpectedly applied fire to the doors, Talbot who was within the castle was awakened by the smoke and clad only in his shirt slipped out of bed and threw open the doors Having hid behind the door, he escaped naked, when Ever's sons and their band rushed in, and fled for safety. His family, also, stripped and turned out, followed him. The English blamed Tyrone for this act, asserting that without his connivance Ever's sons would not have dared to do it. About the same time the English who had garrisoned Armagh, the seat of the Primate of Ireland, determined to enter the Church and threw into chains the Sacristan, who resisted them, and other priests. Brian O'Neill who chanced to be in the town at the time, took up the quarrel and liberated the priests, and ordered twelve of the English soldiers to be hanged The rest of the garrison fled, and the Protestants felt perfectly certain that Tyrone was the instigator of this action.

CHAPTER XI

THE ROYALIST ARMY ROUTED BY MAGUIRE AND CORMAC O'NEILL
AT THE FORD OF THE BISCUITS. ENNISKILLEN SURRENDERED
TO O'DONNELL, BY WHOM THE ENGLISH OF
CONNAUGHT ARE RUINED.

IN this state of things, the garrison of Enniskillen castle, surrounded by O'Donnell, was pinched with hunger, so much so that the Sow's son, the betrayer of the castle, and who had been left in it by the English, and was now like a ravenous pig labouring under the pangs of an empty stomach, was sent in a boat with five comrades over the lake, because he knew the district and roads, to tell in what straits the castle was. But, being intercepted by the Catholics, was, together with his comrades, slain with many wounds. Nevertheless, the English being well aware of the castle's difficulties hastened to throw in supplies, corned meat, cheese and a large supply of biscuits were got ready. Soldiers were drawn out of the garrisons; a hosting of Irish made; 2,500 men, of whom 400 were cavalry, were got together out of the recent Irish levies and English garrison. Henry Duke, an English knight, and Governor of Offaly, was appointed commander, and Fool (*Fuller*), also an Englishman, was marshal. O'Donnell being informed of their designs sent messengers to Tyrone, to inform him that the Protestants were coming to relieve Enniskillen, that he would resist this to the death, to point out the critical situation of affairs, and that he must consider Tyrone his enemy, unless he came to his aid in such a pinch. On receipt of this message, Tyrone was perplexed with conflicting anxieties, thinking in his own mind that O'Donnell had started this war in an uncertain hope of aid from Spain, and before seeing the Spanish colours in Ireland, and thus put the fate of the Catholics in great peril, even should O'Neill himself come to the rescue. On the other hand, if he did not assist the Catholics, although he was already suspected by the Protestants, he would be regarded as an enemy by both parties. However, when the Queen's army was coming up, Cormac O'Neill, brother of Tyrone, arrived in O'Donnell's camp with 100 horse and 300 light armed musketeers, but whether sent by Tyrone, or on his own motion, is not generally agreed on. Maguire and Cormac with a thousand foot, advanced from O'Donnell's camp to meet the enemy, and obstruct their advance, and by keeping them from sleep and rest render them less vigorous when encountering O'Donnell himself later on. Meantime, Duke halted, about nightfall, not more than three miles from a ford on the river Farney. Here, as soon as it was dark, gunmen sent by Maguire and Cormac, suddenly poured in upon him a close and heavy fire of leaden bullets. Duke sent his musketeers against these gunmen, and, so both sides fought throughout the whole night at long range, and the royalists were rendered sleepless by reason

of the danger and the noise of the guns.   On the next day,
after dawn, Duke drew up his entire army in three divisions,
supported by wings of cavalry and gunmen.   He had a
large quantity of baggage, and beasts of burthen carrying
supplies, asses, attendants, and hangers-on, which he divided
into two parts, placing one portion between the first and
second division, and the other between this and the rear
column.   Having arranged his troops in this position he
moved them, half asleep with the vigil of the previous night,
out of his camp, and as he advanced was continuously
attacked by the Catholics, hurling darts and compelling
him to halt frequently, while he in turn drove them back.
At 11 o'clock he came within gunshot of the ford on the
Farney.   Here he ordered the cavalry to dismount because
the ground was unsuitable for a cavalry fight.   Maguire
and Cormac with 1,000 foot now attacked in full force
Their musketeers resisted the first division rather stoutly,
and not only their musketeers but also their pikemen
pressed the rear division   The first division cleared the
way with the sword, and driving the Catholics back gained
the ford.   Meanwhile the Catholic musketeers, who were
attacking the rear division, drove the wings of Protestant
gunmen in on the column and staggered it with an incessant
fire of leaden bullets.   The ranks being now disordered, the
Catholic pikemen, charging through, put them into confusion and drove them into the second part of the baggage,
and finally back on the second division.   Thereupon the
middle division was involved in a double struggle—to rally
the rear division, and to resist the Catholics.   But the
Catholics, pressing on, routed both, and driving them
through the other division of baggage, threw them into the
first division.   Thus the whole army, in a confused and
disordered   crowd,   crossed   the   ford   abandoning   the
provisions and all the baggage, saving only those horses
which were especially required by the cavalry.   Thereupon,
Duke held a council of war as to what was to be done.
George Oge Bingham thought they should retreat, lest
having lost their provisions all should perish from want,
and share the fate of the defenders of Enniskillen, whom
they could not assist.   On the other hand, Marshal Fool
(*Fuller* ?), whose name signifies stupid, foolishly protested,
and maintained that they should relieve the Queen's Castle.
The place where the Protestants had halted was marshy,
and their horses sinking in this bog could not be brought
into action, so that they were shot down by the Catholics
with impunity   Fool, therefore, advanced his wing

of gunmen against the Catholics to drive them back, whilst he re-organised the ranks of the army. However, he soon gave up this attempt, being pierced by a javelin and killed. The entire Protestant army was thereby panic-stricken and abandoning, even the horses fell back without any order or discipline upon the ford, which it had a short time previously crossed It was obstructed in this by the Catholic sharp-shooters, some of whom rifled the baggage whilst others defended the ford. Doubtful what was best to be done, the army rushed to another more difficult ford, which it perceived an arrow shot higher up the river, and plunged in before the Catholics occupied it. However, such was the haste and panic, and the depth of the ford, that about 100 soldiers were lost, over whose bodies the rest crossed. A few of the Irish followed the Protestants, who, despising their numbers, halted for a moment, whilst Duke, the General of the English army, and other captains, threw away their arms and clothes except their shirts, but even when so stripped, he was not sufficiently light nor able to run without being supported between four of his Irish soldiers The Catholics intent on rifling the baggage, allowed the flying and terror-stricken enemy to slip through their hands. The few Catholics who had pursued beyond the ford returned immediately In this way, little over four hundred of the English Protestants and Irish Catholic mercenaries in their service perished in the river and by the sword The horses, a huge pile of arms, the provisions and all the baggage were captured, amongst these, an immense quantity of biscuits scattered in the very ford gave this place the new name of Beal antha nambrisgi. On hearing of the royalist army being routed and put to flight, the castle of Enniskillen, blockaded by O'Donnell, was surrendered, the defenders being dismissed as agreed, and Maguire was completely restored Shortly after this surrender of the Castle—MacSweeny Tuath, one of the prime movers of this war and who was present at the siege, paid the debt of nature—a sad loss to the Catholics. He was succeeded by Maelmurray MacSweeny, the son of Murrough Mall (Mac Muracha M bhuill), whose constancy was not at all equal to that of his predecessors, as will appear later on The siege being over, O'Donnell remembering the cruelty with which the English had thrown women, old men and infants, from the bridge of Enniskillen, with all his forces invaded Connaught, which Richard Bingham held ground down under heretical tyranny In his raids extending far and wide he destroyed the English

F

colonists and settlers, put them to flight, and slew them, sparing no male between 15 and 60 years who did not know how to speak the Irish language. He burnt the village of Longford in Annaly, which Browne, an English heretic, had wrested from O'Farrell and now occupied. He returned to Tyrconnell laden with the spoils of the Protestants. After this incursion into Connaught, not a single farmer, settler, or Englishman, remained except those who were safely inside the walls of the castles and fortified towns, for those who had not been destroyed by fire and sword, being stripped of their goods, retired to England, railing with bitter curses against those who had brought them into Ireland.

CHAPTER XII

NAᵉG-CEANN WITH O'DONNELL'S ASSISTANCE REDUCES BELLEEK CASTLE ; SUCCESSFULLY ENCOUNTERS THE ENGLISH ; AND IS INAUGURATED THE MACWILLIAM

AT this time O'Donnell honorably entertained a Connaught nobleman, Theobald Burke, surnamed The Bald (Theobald na-gCeann), the son of Walter, and nephew of The MacWilliam, and who having been despoiled of his ancestral estates by the English and imprisoned in Athlone had escaped a few months previously. O'Donnell persuaded him to attempt the recovery of his father's estates by force of arms, and Na-gCeann, having got from O'Donnell a few soldiers, returned to Connaught and besieged the castle of Belleek This was held by a garrison under John MacKinnily, an Irish Catholic, but loyal to the Queen, and when it seemed as if he must soon perish from want of provisions, the Protestants resolved to come to his aid. Between those of Duke's army who did not desert after the defeat at the ford of Biscuits, garrison troops summoned from the town of Galway, and recent levies in Connaught from the village of Clonacastle, there were in all fourteen companies of foot and three troops of horse, over which Fullerton, an Englishman, was placed in command. The principal captains were Tuite, an Anglo-Irishman ; Hugh and William Moystyn, sons of an English father and Irish mother ; and George Bingham Oge and Minch, English-men. These were ordered to throw supplies into Belleek castle. Na-gCeann being informed of this, and having got further forces from O'Donnell, marched with a thousand men to meet Fullerton and attack him in the passes on his road and so fight him at advantage. Fullerton set out from Cloonacastle and having advanced about twenty miles proceeded to ravage the country and drive off his prey. Na-gCeann's advance guard fell in with the scattered and dispersed royalist plunderers and slew about sixty of them. Fullerton, however, getting the prey together crossed the ford of Ballylahan and divided his forces into two columns between which he placed the booty, prisoners, and other baggage. Himself accompanied by his body guard marched in the middle, protected as if by a fort The natives incensed at the plundering, and the soldiers sent on by Na-gCeann, suddenly coming up attacked the baggage on the march, drove off the cattle, scattered the baggage, carried off almost all the provisions, slew Fullerton with many wounds, and got off themselves safely despite the efforts of those who ran up from the columns Hereupon the royalists deprived of their general and supplies, dejectedly betook themselves to Inishcoe, a large but then deserted village There they rested after their march for three days, during which time they suffered from want, living on scanty rations of biscuit and water Meantime John MacKinnily having used up all his provisions, essayed to relieve his hunger on herbs and cabbages, but being at last unable to subsist on these and worn out with want, he surrendered to Na-gCeann's mercy. The royalist captains hearing of this, returned by another route to the country of Theobald Burke, surnamed Na-long, claimant to the chieftaincy of MacWilliam's country, and who more on account of this claim, and of enmity to Na-gCeann than of love for the Protestants, ever adhered to the Queen As they were returning by Mount Nephin, Na-gCeann attacked them about 7 o'clock in the morning, and pursued continuously attacking them, sometimes at close quarters and sometimes at long range until about five o'clock in the afternoon. The Catholics were inferior in numbers, but the Irish gunmen and Scottish archers sent by O'Donnell were great marksmen. The English weak with hunger were hardly fit to carry their arms, and so the Irish killed those who fell out of the ranks in sight of their comrades. Hence the Irish mercenaries in the Queen's army were engaged in the double task of defending themselves and their English associates. On that day 400 of the royalists were slain including Tuite the Irishman, and Minch, the

Englishman.   The Catholics did not suffer any considerable loss.   Shortly after this Na-gCeann was, at O'Donnell's instance, inaugurated The MacWilliam, by which title we shall hereafter call him.

CHAPTER XIII.

THE ENGLISH GARRISON DRIVEN OUT OF PORTMORE AND BESIEGED IN THE CASTLE OF MONAGHAN

THESE risings increased daily   There is in Ulster a river which the Irish call the Abhainn-mhor, and the English the Blackwater, either because it is more turbid than other Irish rivers, which are usually clear and pellucid, or because the English often met with defeat and disaster on its banks   On this river there was a fort. famous on many occasions in this war, as will appear later on, called by the English, the Blackwater fort, and by the Irish, Portmore, that is to say the great fort   It was situated three miles beyond Armagh, the seat of the Primate of Ireland, and seven miles south of Dungannon, Earl Tyrone's chief town. From this fort the Queen's English garrison and heretical minister were expelled by certain Irishmen.   Moreover, some of the MacMahons besieged Monaghan castle, the capital of Oriel, unjustly taken, as we have seen, from that family by the Viceroy's decree and fortified by an English garrison.   The besiegers cutting off all supplies, it seemed as if the garrison must surrender from want.   A quarrel having broken out in Armagh, as we have seen, between the Catholic priest in charge of the principal church and some English soldiers, a certain Irish nobleman, who at the time chanced to be there, cleared the town of all the Queen's garrison who were well punished, some severely wounded and some killed.   For all these things the English laid the blame on O'Neill.

TOME III. BOOK III.

OF

DON PHILIP O'SULLEVAN OF BEAR IN IRELAND.

ON THE FIFTEEN YEARS' WAR.

WE have seen the first irregular and preliminary stage of the war. And now follow greater events, more memorable and interesting. We shall in the present book relate the fierce and bloody contests between O'Neill, the great leader of the War : O'Donnell, and other Irishry on the one side ; and on the other, John Norris, a most distinguished English general ; Russell, and the proud Borough, Viceroys ; the Earl of Kildare ; Bingham and other champions of the Queen's party.

CHAPTER I.

THE EQUIPMENT AND LEADERS OF BOTH PARTIES. EARL TYRONE INAUGURATED THE O'NEILL.

BY these risings of the Catholics, commotions, and defeats, Elizabeth, Queen of England, was sorely worried, and strained every nerve to quiet Ireland and break down the Catholic forces. In the year 1594 she appointed William Russell viceroy instead of William Fitzwilliam, who had held that office but had resigned She recalled from France the English veterans who were employed there against His Catholic Majesty, Philip II., and ordered a levy in England and Ireland. John Norris, an English knight, with 1,800 English veterans from France, speedily landed in Ireland. Such royalist troops as he found in Ireland —veterans and raw recruits alike—he summoned to his standard, and hastened into Ulster as if to relieve Monaghan castle which, as above mentioned, was surrounded by the MacMahons.

At this time died Turlough, who had been The O'Neill, and who was regarded as the impediment to the Earl of Tyrone's making war on the English. On his death

Tyrone was after the Irish fashion declared The O'Neill
by the clansmen and by this title we shall henceforth call
him.   However, he wrote to Norris asking him not to take
extreme measures and stating that he would prefer to
preserve the Queen's friendship than to be her enemy; that
he had never conspired against the Queen's crown ; and
that he had been unjustly accused by envious persons.   He
sent a similar letter to the Queen.   But Bagnal, the Governor
of Ulster, and O'Neill's bitterest enemy intercepted and
suppressed both letters.   O'Neill when he saw that an
answer to his letters was too long delayed and that the
enemy was approaching, prepared to meet him and prevent
him relieving Monaghan, which MacMahon's people with
the slender force at their command, could not do.   Maguire,
a most redoubtable hero and Chief of Fermanagh, who was
captain of the horse , O'Kane and other chiefs at the head
of about 2,000 horse and foot, accompanied him.   Norris
is said to have increased his army to 4,000 horse and foot
splendidly armed.   Some were English veterans trained
in France, some Anglo-Irish, others old Irish, especially
O'Hanlon, Chief of Orior in Ulster, who by hereditary
right was royal standard-bearer beyond the river Boyne.
Bagnal, Governor of Ulster, was in attendance, and Norris
himself, who had displayed the greatest courage and
military skill in fighting the Spaniards during the French
and Belgian wars, in which he had deservedly earned glory
and fame, for in truth he was the greatest of the English
generals of his time, although in this war fickle fortune or
rather Divine Justice showed him little favour.

––––

CHAPTER II.

O'NEILL AND NORRIS ENCOUNTER FOR THE FIRST TIME AT
CLONTIBRET, AND MONAGHAN IS SURRENDERED TO THE
CATHOLICS.

THE great General Norris, with his army, entered Oriel in
MacMahon's country and came to a place not far from
Monaghan which is called Clontibret (Cluoin Tiburuid),
where he displayed his forces to the enemy.   O'Neill, not
less skilful as a general, but very inferior in strength, came
against him.   Here for the first time the two far-in-a-way
most illustrious Generals of the two most warlike islands

faced each other. The ground here was an open and level plain, but somewhat heavy with moisture. The waters flowing from the surrounding bog formed a ford over which the English might most conveniently cross. O'Neill blocked this ford; Norris tried to force it. O'Neill endeavoured to drive him back. A cavalry fight and musketry skirmish commenced simultaneously round the ford. The Royalist horse were better armed, the Irish troops were more nimble. The Irish sharpshooters were far better marksmen. This advantage was often common to both parties since there were generally more Irish than English in the Royalist army. The Queen's musketeers were twice worsted by the Catholics, and recalled by Norris, who was always the last to leave the fight, and had even a horse shot under him by a leaden bullet. All of both parties justly admitted the superiority of Maguire's cavalry. Norris being annoyed at his men having been twice repulsed and unable to hold their ground, James Sedgreve, an Irish Meath-man of great size and courage, thus addressed him and Bagnal—"Send a troop of cavalry with me and I promise you I will drag O'Neill from his saddle." O'Neill was stationed on the other side of the ford supported by forty horse and a few musketeers surveying the battle thence and giving his orders. For the third time the cavalry and musketeers renewed the fight and Sedgreve accompanied by a troop of picked Irish and English horse charged the ford. In the ford itself a few horse fell under the fire of O'Neill's bodyguard, but Sedgreve rushed upon O'Neill and each splintered his lance on the corslet of the other. Sedgreve immediately seized O'Neill by the neck and threw him from his horse. O'Neill likewise dragged Sedgreve from his horse and both gripped each other in a desperate struggle. O'Neill was thrown under but such was his presence of mind, that prostrate as he was, he slew Sedgreve with a stab of his dagger under the corslet between the thighs and through the bladder. Eighteen illustrious cavaliers of the Royalists fell round Sedgreve and their colours were captured; the rest sought safety in flight. With them all the Queen's forces were likewise compelled to retreat, having lost seven hundred more or less, whilst the Catholics had only a few wounded, and no number of killed worth mentioning. On the following day as Norris retreated, being short of powder, he was followed and attacked by O'Neill at Bealach Finnuise, where O'Hanlon, Chief Standard Bearer of the Royalist Army, was wounded in the leg and others were shot down by leaden bullets.

Hinch, an Englishman, who held the Castle of Monaghan
with three companies of foot and a troop of horse, was
obliged to surrender it for want of provisions.   He, himself, was let go scot free as agreed

———

CHAPTER III.

THE CATHOLICS FORTIFY TWO CASTLES TAKEN FROM THE ENGLISH IN CONNAUGHT.

WHILE this campaign between O'Neill and Norris was in
progress in that part of Ulster which adjoins Meath and
faces England there was no lack of activity between
O'Donnell and Richard Bingham in that other part of
Ulster which adjoins Connaught and in Connaught itself.
In Connaught George Bingham Oge held Sligo Castle
with 200 foot, of whom some were Irish.   Leaving this in
charge of Ulick Burke, son of Raymond, an Irish chief,
with some of the soldiers, Bingham himself with the rest
sailed round to Ulster in two ships and raided Rathmullan,
the chief town of MacSweeny Fanad who was then absent ;
dismantled the Carmelite Convent and forced the monks to
fly to the castle.   Laden with booty, he returned to Sligo
Ulick thought that the Irish soldiers were defrauded in
the division of the booty and took council with them as
to how they should be revenged on Bingham and the
English   He arranged to wrest the castle from them on
a certain day, and when it came round the Irish attacked
the English.   Bingham was poniarded by Ulick and
the others were either killed or seeking safety in flight,
paid the penalty of their sacrilege in raiding the home of
the holy Carmelites.   The castle was surrendered to
O'Donnell, who appointed Ulick commander of it   About
this time Tomaltagh and Cathal MacDonough took
Ballymote castle from George Bingham the Elder
In the following autumn, about the time of Norris's
defeat by O'Neill, Richard Bingham made an incursion
to recover Sligo and take vengeance on Ulick for the
slaughter of his kinsmen.   He besieged Ulick locked up
in Sligo castle.   Ulick sallying out every day with the
defenders fought before the walls   O'Donnell hastened
with 1,600 troops to raise the siege.   He pitched his tent
at Duraran within view of the enemy.   On the first two

days the cavalry of both sides riding up to the river which flowed between them, skirmished with javelins. On the third day Roderic, brother of O'Donnell, with Felim MacDevit and anothe gentleman, having crossed the river, reconnoitred the camp. Against him came Martin, an Englishman, who was accounted the best horseman in Bingham's army, accompanied by his troop Roderic giving reign to his horse fled to his own people Martin followed and was the first of his troop to rush the ford when Felim turning round pierced him with a spear and knocked him dead from his horse, into the stream, while Roderic and Felim and their comrade got off safely. On the following day, the fourth of the siege, Bingham raising the blockade, returned home, O'Donnell following and harassing him with missiles

CHAPTER IV.

RUSSELL, THE VICEROY AND NORRIS, WORSTED BY O'NEILL, BINGHAM VIGOROUSLY BUT FRUITLESSLY ATTACKS SLIGO CASTLE.

IN the following year the English proclaimed O'Neill an enemy and traitor to his country, and now, thoroughly incensed against him, Russell the Viceroy and Norris, commander of the Queen's army took the field.

There is in Ulster a town called Newry, which the English always kept strongly garrisoned. Thence the royalists with all their forces sallied forth, fully determined to capture the city of Armagh, the seat of the Primate of Ireland However, they had gone scarcely eight miles when at Kilcloney, O'Neill met them with half as numerous forces, and accompanied by Maguire, O'Kane, the sons of O'Hanlon and other noblemen. Here a battle commenced after midday, and the royalists having suffered severely, were forced to retreat to Newry On this day the Catholics had 200 and the Royalists 600 killed.

Bingham on his side was by no means asleep He summoned the Irish earls of Thomond and Clanrickarde, and made a levy in Connaught. He collected the garrisons and Anglo-Irish gentry of Meath, and with 24 standards attacked and blockaded Sligo. Ulick Burke and his garrison advancing outside the ramparts fought stoutly, but at last

was shut up in the castle by the overwhelming numbers
of the besiegers and kept off the enemy by hurling missiles
from the towers, battlements, windows, and other fortifications The Royalists advanced a sow* under the walls
of the castle and began to bore and undermine them.
Ulick pounded the roof of the sow and the soldiers in it
with a beam of great size fastened by ropes to the battlements and alternately raised and dropped O'Donnell
advanced to the rescue of the besieged, and Bingham fled
Six hundred Royalists perished in that siege. However
the castle was so troublesome to defend that O'Donnell
demolished it

CHAPTER V.

THE ROYALISTS TREAT FOR PEACE WITH THE CATHOLICS ; OCCUPY ARMAGH , AND UNSUCCESSFULLY ASSAIL O'NEILL.

SINCE the Royalists were unsuccessful in the field, they
made truces with O'Neill and O'Donnell and opened
negotiations for peace.   Henry Wallop, Treasurer of
Ireland, and Robert Gardner, Chief Justice, came to them
to ascertain with what terms they would be satisfied.
O'Neill complained that the reward of his labours and
merits had been intercepted by Bagnal, and that he had
been falsely accused of crimes, and also complained bitterly
of other wrongs.   Amongst other terms he asked a full
pardon for all offences and that he and his people should
be allowed to profess the Roman Catholic faith, and that
the Queen's judges and ministers should never enter his
country   O'Donnell and others made the like demands,
first complaining much of their wrongs.
    Meantime 1000 English foot who were hired in Belgium
by the Batavians against the Spaniards, were recalled and
sent into Ireland.   Russell the Viceroy and Norris
quickly marched into Ulster these and the veteran
English and Irish troops from France and Ireland,
as well as the English recruits in Munster, Leinster
and Meath, and so called Anglo-Irish :—a regular
army three times the size of O'Neill's.   Without
any resistance they entered Armagh, the most celebrated
and holiest metropolitan city of Ireland, expelled the monks,
priests, and holy nuns, and other townspeople, the town
being without natural protection and entirely defenceless.

* Sow—A military engine. See note " Irish Arms " in appendix.

They entered and profaned the churches, turning them
into stables and to profane uses They fiercely destroyed
images of the saints and in the height of their delight went
on not doubting but that with so strong an army they
would on this single expedition crush O'Neill and all the
Catholics and cow their resolution. However, they had
not gone more than a mile and a half from Armagh when
O'Neill at the head of his slender forces met them, later
than, perhaps, he would have wished, as he would have
desired to keep them out of Armagh. At Beal antha
Killotir (*Kilcreevy Otra?*) O'Neill blocked the road and
vigorously attacking the English veterans from France
and Belgium in the midst of their triumph, he threw them
into confusion and drove them before him, and pursued
them as with broken ranks they retreated to Armagh,
killing and wounding many. The Catholics lost only forty,
amongst them two noblemen, Farmodirrby O'Hanlon and
Patrick MacGuilly The Royalists leaving 500 soldiers
under Francis Stafford, knight, at Armagh, returned and
halted not far from Dundalk, whence the Viceroy leaving
the entire management of the war against O'Neill to Norris,
returned to Dublin to look after affairs in Leinster and
Connaught

CHAPTER VI.

THE SPANISH AMBASSADORS PREVENT THE CONCLUSION OF
PEACE. THE GARRISON OF ARMAGH STRANGELY CHASTISED
BY SAINT PATRICK.

NEGOTIATIONS for peace were again opened. The Queen
offered fair and honourable terms to the Catholic clergy
and laity. Hostages were given by O'Neill and O'Donnell
and other Irishmen that they would agree to fair and honorable terms and not prosecute the rebellion any further.
But before peace was concluded or arms laid down Cobos
and other ambassadors of Philip II., King of Spain, reached
O'Neill and O'Donnell, bidding the Irish in the King's
name to be of good heart, that an army would be sent to
their assistance by His Catholic Majesty without delay. The
result of this embassy was to break off negotiations for peace,
and the war was renewed on both sides. O'Hanlon,
Magennis, and all Ulster except the Royalist garrison
towns and the Anglo-Irish of Louth, joined the Con-

federation. The war spread in Leinster, and Connaught
was very unsettled

O'Neill was so sorely vexed at the holy city of Armagh
being contaminated by heretics, that he determined to cut
it off from provisions, not daring to assault it while so
strongly garrisoned.   St. Patrick, however, the Patron
and Guardian of Ireland, and who was the first to consecrate
this city to God, would not put off the punishment of the
crime which impiously defiled the sacred town with heretics.
It is believed that he was the Bishop who, clad in pontificals,
frequently and plainly appeared to the English at night
and threatened them , took away the iron tips
of their spears , and extracted the bullets and powder
from their guns.   Rowley, an English captain, was so
terrified by these portents, that he became almost insane ,
and Baker, an English adjutant, being carried by the Bishop
to the pinnacle of the church, swore he would never again
profane churches and dreading Divine vengeance, he
abandoned the army, was converted to the Catholic faith,
and began to do penance   Meditating on this incident,
I cannot restrain my tears or refrain from deploring the
state of things in these times and the perverse behaviour
and madness of not merely the new, but even of many of
the ancient Irish who, although they were Catholics,
assisted the English heretics who had placed a garrison in
the holy city of Armagh and defiled it, laying impious
hands on the images of St Patrick, the Patron of Ireland,
and of other saints and expelling God himself as present in
the Holy Sacrament of the Eucharist, trampling them
under foot or hacking with their swords when pursued.
Nor do I bewail so much the folly of laymen as the crass
stupidity of our parochial guides and masters and other
clergy who during this war yielded obedience and afforded
assistance to the heretics.   Baker, an English heretic soldier,
swears to Saint Patrick that he will never again violate
churches in Ireland, and, lest he be compelled to break his
oath, he gives up the army, his pay, rank and glory, and
(O shame!) the Anglo-Irish Catholic priest will not influence
Irish Catholics against assisting the English heretics who
have desecrated the Church of Saint Patrick and attacked
its defenders.

CHAPTER VII.

O'NEILL INTERCEPTS THE SUPPLIES SENT TO ARMAGH AND BY
STRATAGEM CUTS OFF MANY OF THE GARRISON.   ARMAGH
IS   SURRENDERED   TO   HIM.   HE   VAINLY   ATTACKS
CARLINGFORD CASTLE

To return to our subject   A great swarm of lice afflicted
the garrison of Armagh and many perished of this plague.
Famine soon followed.   The Royalists, exercised by this
circumstance, sent three companies of foot and one troop
of horse with supplies.   O'Neill with eight companies and
some horse intercepted these at Mount Bued, routed them
in a night attack, and captured the provisions.   At dawn
the next day he dressed some of his own cavalry and foot
in the English uniform and ordered them to go towards
the city carrying the captured standards and the provisions
He, himself, followed with the rest and commenced a
feigned attack.   The cavalry on both sides dexterously
encounter   and   break   their   spears   on   one   another's
cuirasses .   guns are briskly fired at the report and flash
of which soldiers fall as if wounded.   Stafford the Governor
of Armagh garrison, seeing this,   sent half of the garrison
to assist those conveying the supplies   There is a monastery
within a gunshot of Armagh, having passed which the
garrison were attacked in the rear by Con, son of O'Neill, who
had been placed in ambush in the monastery with some foot,
and in front O'Neill with all his men who had been engaged
in the feigned fight bore down and destroyed them under
Stafford's eyes.   Not long after this Stafford was compelled by want of food to surrender Armagh to O'Neill,
and as agreed, was sent to his own people.

Twenty-four miles from Armagh and eight from
Newry is Carlingford castle, overhanging the river and
fortified by nature and art.   It was now held by half a
company of English with whom were Thomas Kellody
and eight other Irishmen   Thomas and the eight
Irishmen, as arranged with O'Neill, suddenly attacked the
English and killed six and drove the rest out of the castle.
O'Neill had promised Thomas that he would be at the
castle at cock-crow that night and Thomas waited for him
in the castle until near dawn, but O'Neill delaying too long,
Thomas left the castle and fled   At break of day O'Neill
halted with his men before the castle, and fearing lest it
was held by the English did not venture too close, until

Thomas should give the signal The English who had
been expelled from the castle, seeing O'Neill halting and no
signal given from the castle, guessed that it had been
abandoned by Thomas, and themselves entered the empty
fort and defended it O'Neill disappointed in his expectations returned home.

— — —

CHAPTER VIII.

NORRIS OCCUPIES ARMAGH A SECOND TIME : ERECTS MOUNT-NORRIS ; LOSES BOTH · AND UNSUCCESSFULLY ENCOUNTERS O'NEILL.

AGAIN Norris with all his forces seeks Armagh deserted by
O'Neill, and places there a garrison of four companies under
Henry Davers, a knight   Thence he makes for Portmore
and occupies that place also , the fort having been dismantled and the buildings burned by O'Neill He was
prevented advancing further by O'Neill's appearance
with his army, encamped on the road where he could not
be attacked with advantage.   Norris commenced to erect
a fort which he called after himself Mountnorris O'Neill
endeavoured to obstruct him.   Fighting went on for some
days, some falling on both sides but the Royalists suffering
most   At last Norris retired, leaving a garrison under
Williams in the new fort   After his retirement O'Neill
soon reduced this fort and Armagh into his possession by
cutting off the garrisons from supplies He sent the
garrisons safely away as agreed. Norris again set out in force
to recover Armagh.   At Mullaghbrack, in Orior, O'Neill
ventured a battle and routed and scattered the enemy, who
reorganised by Norris, renewed the fight. Again they
were defeated by the skill and valour of O'Neill's gunmen
and of Maguire, his master of the horse For a second
time reanimated by Norris they renew the combat, and
for the third time are compelled to retire before the fierce
attack of the ¿Catholics, and to retreat, Norris himself
receiving a bullet wound, according to many.   The gentlemen of both parties justly conceded the honours of this day
to Maguire.

CHAPTER IX.

NORRIS VAINLY TREATS WITH O'DONNELL FOR PEACE IN
CONNAUGHT AND CARRIES ON AN UNSUCCESSFUL WAR.

I DO not find that after this day Norris again faced O'Neill.
Setting out for Connaught he halted at Athlone and
assembled all his forces. Thither came the Earls of
Thomond and Clanrickarde ; Na-long , and other Irish
chiefs of the English party ; The Anglo-Irish ; the levies
of Munster, Leinster and Meath ; Irish and English veterans,
and the reinforcements recently sent from England. He
is said to have had about 10,000 horse and foot. O'Donnell
mustered his forces of 5,000 against him At this time
there accompanied O'Donnell out of Ulster, the three
MacSweenys and O'Doherty, bound to him by ancient ties
of fealty, and the ever valiant Maguire ; out of Connaught
came O'Rourke, MacWilliam, O'Kelly, MacDermott,
O'Connor Roe, O'Dowd. With him came also Murrough
MacSheehy, a Munster gentleman of birth, with 300 men,
who had been for about two years lurking in the woods
in Munster and there raiding the heretics as opportunity
offered and going through many trials in harassing them
There were also some ecclesiastics, especially Raymond
O'Gallagher, Bishop of Derry, and Vice-Primate of Ireland,
who absolved from the ban of excommunication those who
went over from the Royalist army to the Catholics. Norris
advancing from Athlone with his great and well-ordered
army came to the village of Ballinrobe in MacWilliam's
country and halted there to the south of the river as
O'Donnell was encamped on the other side thereof. On
the first day and following night a brisk fire was kept up
on both sides. On the following day Norris beat a parley,
to which O'Donnell agreed. Out of the conference arose
negotiations for peace. Every day under truces terms
of peace were discussed, and the entire nights were spent
in fighting, making attacks on one another's camps,
capturing outposts and scouts and fighting hand-to-hand
and at long range It happened that on one night when
Na-long was on sentry, three hundred Royalists were killed.
Some fled from Norris to O'Donnell, especially Thady
O'Rourke, The O'Rourke's brother, who had lived with
his kinsman the Earl of Ormond from his childhood In
treating for peace Norris offered O'Donnell, O'Rourke,
MacWilliam and others, great advantages if they would
return to the Queen's allegiance. The treaty was delayed
by the arrival at this time in Donegal of a Spanish ship

urging O'Neill, O'Donnell and the other Irish chiefs in the name of his Catholic Majesty not to abandon the course they had begun, and assuring them of Spanish aid. And so when the negotiations had wasted a whole month, Norris being about to return, shifted his camp. O'Donnell followed him and seriously harassing his rear ranks and outside wings with missiles Norris, however, decided not to help his distressed followers until the Catholics who were attacking them crossed the nearest hedge, thinking, indeed, that those who should cross the hedge might easily be cut off by his men. O'Donnell also seeing this, and being mounted on a fleet horse, rode up to the hedge and recalled his men who were eager to cross it. Norris baulked in this plan, railed with terrible imprecations against the fate which condemned him to lose in Ireland, the smallest speck of the wide world, that fame which his great valour and military skill had earned for him in France and Belgium, and complained sorrowfully that the enemy's generals were not to be surpassed by him in military skill nor their troops to be excelled by his in stoutness and steadfastness. And fairly, indeed, might so great a general launch complaints against the fickleness of fortune. For in the opinion of all whom I have consulted in this matter, Norris was of all the English who flourished at this time, first alike in military skill and in valour, and in France and Belgium earned a great name by the success of his campaigns. Therefore I do not doubt but that it was Divinely ordained the Catholics should have most luck, but the Royalists, although stoutly and courageously fighting, should nevertheless be unfortunate. Nor is this strange, for I have no doubt but that the Irish Catholics in the Royalist army must have fought with a heavy conscience against the Catholic religion, and the English were not as strong and as suited for sustaining the burthens of war and battle as the Irish, and O'Neill studiously chose ground suitable for himself to meet Norris upon and where he fought at an advantage which seemed necessary to him, as he was inferior in point of numbers.

CHAPTER X.

RELATES SOME EVENTS IN LEINSTER. THE EXTRAORDINARY DEATH OF NORRIS.

Now I must notice events in Leinster which, although provided with meagre resources, yet joined the Catholic

confederation with great resolution and valour. After
the removal by treachery of that resolute hero and relentless
enemy of heretics, Fiagh O'Byrne, his sons Felim and
Raymond took up their father's arms. While Raymond
headed risings against the heretics, started in Leinster,
Felim went into Ulster, to O'Neill, to ask help, and having
got from O'Neill nearly 300 foot under command of Brian
O'More, surnamed Reagh, a Leinster chief, most opportunely
came to the assistance of his struggling brother and after
some successful forays recovered his entire patrimony, at
this time nearly altogether lost. Thence Brian harassed
with sudden raids those English who inhabited Wexford,
and the Irish of the English party. As he was driving
off a prey, four English companies with 400 Irish auxiliaries
overtook him in an open plain. Brian having drawn up
his column of 400 Irish foot (he had no more), hazarded a
battle and by the Divine assistance conquered. The English
were slain to a man, and not a few of their Irish auxiliaries
were missing. The rest sought safety in flight. The
risings in Leinster swelled when Owny O'More came of
age. He was the son of Roderic, of whom we have made
mention above, and having been concealed and reared by
Fiagh O'Byrne was, with his brother Edmund, sent by
Fiagh's sons into Leix before he was of an age for war.
Here, with the aid of some kinsmen and of some of his
father's tenants in Leix, he endeavoured to recover the
patrimony of his ancestors from the heretics. Wareham
St Leger, Governor of Leix, endeavouring to suppress his
young efforts, was defeated with the loss of about 50 men.

I have detailed these out of many incidents of the time
of Russell and Norris, who were deprived of their government for their unsuccessful management of the war, and
a successor was appointed The Presidency of Munster
was left to Norris, and he filled this office for three years
until he met a most extraordinary death. It is said that
as he was amusing himself by night at Mallow, a person
of black visage and garments suddenly entered the room,
with whom Norris, leaving his game, retired into his
bedroom, whence all witnesses were excluded except one
boy, who concealed himself near the door and heard the
conversation which is said to have been somewhat as follows ·
" It is time," said the black one, " for us to put the finishing
touch to our plans " " I don't wish to do it," said Norris,
" until we have wound up the Irish war." " On no account,"
said the other, " will I wait longer than the appointed day
which is now come." Suddenly a great uproar was heard,

G

attracted by which, those at play and the servants forced the door and burst into the room, when the Black one, who undoubtedly was the Devil, was nowhere to be found, but Norris was on his knees with his neck and shoulders so twisted that the top of his chest and his face were over his back He was, however, still living and ordered the trumpeters and drummers to be called to sound his death-knell, and whilst they were clamouring, he died about midnight His body was embalmed with aromatic and fragrant perfumes, and sent into England A propos of this incident, I am amazed at the folly of the heretics in bestowing this great honor on the corpse of an impious man, while they scatter the relics of saintly martyrs It may, however, be seen how much the Good God helped O'Neill in not only often defeating Norris, the most skilled of the English generals and superior in every warlike equipment, but even in conquering the Devil himself, who it is thought agreed to help Norris.

CHAPTER XI.

BOROUGH THE VICEROY AND THE EARL OF KILDARE WAGE AN UNSUCCESSFUL WAR ON THE CATHOLICS

AT the close of the year of Our Lord 1597 Thomas Baron Borough, a man of generous disposition and open hand, inured to war and of gracious manners, was sent as Viceroy to Ireland and on his arrival won over some of the Leinster-men and other Irish by his courtesy and graciousness He effected a month's truce with O'Neill, O'Donnell and others, but being unable to agree on terms of peace, commenced a more vigorous campaign against O'Neill He had a large army composed of the troops formerly serving under Russell and Norris and those lately sent from England, with which he invaded Ulster. He was followed by the Meath Anglo-Irish and regular troops under Barnwall, Baron of Trimblestown These latter were met at Crickstown by Richard Tyrrell with 400 foot, sent by O'Neill to spread disaffection in Leinster or promote it in Meath This Tyrrell was an Anglo-Irishman, but a Catholic, like the rest, and incensed by English injustice, had escaped from prison to O'Neill When Barnwall saw the small forces Tyrrell had, he sent against him his son with 1,000 foot, not doubting but that the youth would achieve a glorious victory, by the *eclat* of which he himself would gain the good graces of the Viceroy. Tyrrell, a veteran soldier, well skilled in war, defeated the Meathmen and put them to flight, and having killed many of them, carried off Barnwall's son a captive to O'Neill, by whom he was afterwards liberated on ransom.

Borough occupied Armagh and Portmore, which O'Neill had deserted. He unsuccessfully tried to advance, but was stopped by O'Neill, who blocked up the roads with two camps In one was MacMahon and Cormac, brother of O'Neill and Art, encamped on Drumflugh within two gunshot's of the enemy's road to Benburb. In the other camp O'Neill himself and James MacDonnell of the Glens pitched their tents at Tobermesson. The Viceroy being blocked on his march began to reconstruct fort-norris, which O'Neill had dismantled and in order to obstruct this work there were fought by day and night many skirmishes of cavalry and infantry, and especially with missiles both at long range and close quarters. O'Donnell came to O'Neill's assistance and his cavalry had the better of the enemy's horse and of Turlough O'Neill son of Henry and uterine brother of O'Neill, but who espoused the Queen's side. On a night in which the Catholics had attacked the Royalist camp there was a rumour that the Viceroy had been wounded, which I will not take on myself to say was true or false, but, leaving the Earl of Kildare in command he retired from the camp and died in a few days

Kildare, delighted and flushed with his authority, endeavoured to effect what the Viceroy had been unable to do, namely to advance further

Proceeding through a wood and bye-ways with his leading gentlemen and best soldiers, he had got over the worst of his road when the Catholics heard of his move and coming up attacked him and slew 60 royalist gentlemen including Turner, the Paymaster-General of the Queen's army, Francis Vaughan, the Viceroy's brother-in-law, and Thomas Walen, all Englishmen. Kildare thrown from his horse by a stroke of a lance and again mounted by two brothers—O'Hickey, Irishmen, sons of his foster-mother, was badly bruised and fled wounded and died in a few days after The O'Hickeys while mounting their master, were themselves surrounded and slain. Many royalists were wounded, and as many as had come thither out of the camp were killed, routed, or driven back. The royal army immediately retreated, having faced the Catholics between Portmore and Benburb from the end of Spring for about four months, and leaving garrisons at Armagh and in Portmore under Thomas Williams, an Englishman Hereupon the Irish whom Borough had conciliated, immediately broke out into rebellion again

TOME III. BOOK IV.

OF

DON PHILIP O'SULLEVAN OF BEAR IN IRELAND.

ON THE FIFTEEN YEARS' WAR.

WE have seen the campaigns of Russell, Norris and Borough. These were fierce enough, but fiercer followed. In this book are contained the events which occurred while Earl Ormond commanded the royalist army down to the death of Marshal Bagnal

---

CHAPTER I

HENRY BAGNAL RELIEVES ARMAGH AND ATTACKS O'NEILL'S CAMP

ON Borough's death, Thomas Butler, surnamed The Black, Earl of Ormond, an Irishman, was appointed commander of the royal army. Adam Loftus, Chancellor of Ireland, and Robert Gardiner, a judge, discharged the functions of Viceroy, and in their time occurred many memorable incidents.

O'Neill, understanding that the garrison of Armagh were in want of provisions, resolved to cut them off from supplies   In the Spring he called out his men from their winter quarters to Mullaghbane, fifteen hundred paces from Armagh and pitched his camp over against Newry, believing the royalists would go that way to Armagh. He stationed his brother Cormac at Armagh with 500 soldiers to prevent the garrison sallying out.   Henry Bagnal, an English knight, Marshal of Ireland, and Governor of Ulster with 24 companies of foot and 10 troops of horse, left Newry to relieve the besieged, and O'Neill did not doubt but that he would meet him on the road.   However, Con, an illegitimate son of O'Neill's who had been vexed by his father a few days previously, fled to the English, and Turlough O'Neill, son of Henry, and uterine brother of O'Neill's, who was already with the English, being both well acquainted

with the locality, secretly conducted Bagnal with all his
forces and baggage through unused roads and bye ways
past O'Neill's army   Bagnal immediately sent 1,300 foot
and three troops of cavalry with provisions on to Armagh
Cormac attacked them as they were bringing up the
provisions and also on their return, but could not keep such
superior numbers from entering the town   Meantime
Bagnal, with the rest of his forces, attacked O'Neill's camp.
Now Turlough and Con O'Neill led the way and because
they did not seek O'Neill's life, although irritated against
him, and because for personal reasons they bore a stronger
hatred to O'Hanlon who always sided with the Catholic
party, they endeavoured to bring Bagnal to that wing of
the camp where O'Hanlon was.   But it turned out quite
contrary to their intentions, for O'Neill was stationed
where they expected O'Hanlon to be, and the royalists
surrounding unawares twenty-four gentlemen placed by
O'Neill on guard outside the camp, either killed or seized
them , broke into the camp and surrounded the tent of
O'Neill who with those on that side of the camp fled half
asleep.   The royalists pillaged the abandoned tents and
slew some camp-followers in their sleep.   O'Neill getting
his forces together drove out the enemy and for a great part
of the day hung on their retreat, firing upon them   On
this action Bagnal plumed himself on having got the provisions into Armagh ; spoiled part of O'Neill's camp, and
suffered little.

CHAPTER II

THE ENGLISH GOVERNOR OF CARRICKFERGUS, CUT OFF BY
THE CHIEF OF THE GLENS, AND BARNWALL, GENERAL OF
THE MEATHMEN, IS ROUTED BY MACMAHON.

WINTER ensuing, John Chichester, an English knight, who
held Carrickfergus with a strong garrison sallied out to
forage, with 500 foot and a troop of horse.   At Aldfreck
he fell in with James MacDonnell, Chief of the Glens, with
400 foot and 60 horse.   The gunmen on each side attacked
one another   The royalists were driven back by the
Catholics   John coming to the rescue with his cavalry,
his gunmen renewed the fight and forced the Catholics to
retire.   James then brought up his horse, rallied his
musketeers and charged John   He was struck by three
lances but saved by his corslet   John was killed and fell

from his horse and his cavalry and foot turned tail. James pursued for about three miles up to the fort and slew all of the royalists he overtook so that barely messengers of slaughter escaped. Baron Barnwall, with his Meath Anglo-Irish troops and some companies of English was routed and put to flight by MacMahon, Chief of Oriel as he was ravaging that country (*Monaghan*).

CHAPTER III

O'NEILL AND O'DONNELL MAKE A FRUITLESS ATTACK ON PORT-MORE. BRIAN O'MORE SUCCESSFULLY ENCOUNTERS THE ROYALISTS.

FOILED in his attempt to cut off supplies from the garrison of Armagh, O'Neill at once set about reducing Portmore by starving it out.   During the siege O'Donnell, who had come to his assistance, persuaded him to try an assault on the fort   Having calculated its height scaling ladders of proper length and wide enough for five men to mount abreast were made and advanced to the fort   The besieged hastened to drive off the assailants at first with a heavy discharge of artillery and as they came closer the musketeers opened fire, which was returned by the assailants.   The ladders were brought forward to the Castle, but the besieged, who had learned that these ladders were being made, had deepened the ditch which surrounded the castle so that most of the ladders did not reach to the parapet and those who got to the top of them and could not get farther on account of the shortness of the ladders fruitlessly attacked the besieged.   Those ladders which did reach to the top of the fort were so few that the first to ascend were easily slain before they could be succoured by their comrades   One hundred and twenty Catholics perished, and amongst them Murrough Kavanagh, a Leinster nobleman and stout soldier who had distinguished himself in Belgian wars.   The others being tired out abandoned the assault and besieged the fort in the old way

At this time Owny O'More seeing that he was unable to withstand the enemy's forces, came to Ulster and asked O'Neill to aid Leinster   Meantime Brian O'More took on the conduct of the war in Leinster and seven times successfully encountered the English and their Anglo-Irish allies from Wexford, capturing seven standards and fourteen military drums.

CHAPTER IV

THE EARL OF ORMOND DRIVEN OUT OF LEIX AND OWNY COMES TO THE RESCUE OF THE CATHOLICS.

THE double anxiety of the insurrections in Leinster and the failure of provisions in Portmore, in addition to other matters oppressed Elizabeth, Queen of England, and she earnestly commanded her men to prevent a double mishap and to quell the risings in Leinster and relieve Portmore For these purposes recruits were sent from England, the garrisons were called out, a muster was made in the Irish provinces, and about 8,000 horse and foot of every kind were got together   Of these those who were decrepid with age or appeared too young for war were dismissed   The English recruits lately raised were placed in garrison towns. Of the remaining Irish and English 4,500 foot and 500 horse were selected for their stoutness and skill to relieve Portmore   Two thousand of the Irish allies and some regular Irish troops and the English, of whom few were cavalry, were entrusted to Ormond to quell the Leinster rising.   With these Ormond was confident he could reduce Leix and put down all insurrections in Leinster.   Leix, in which there appeared to be most difficulty, was first attacked. Brian O'More, who had but 300 foot, was placed in the greatest peril, but did not hesitate to harass Ormond by blocking the narrow passes.   Ormond sent against him 1,000 foot, English and Irish, under James Butler, his nephew, son of his brother Edward.   Brian, relying on the nature of the ground, did not hesitate to fight   James, dividing his forces into two divisions, advanced.   In this way Brian was forced to quit his advantageous position and encountered the division in which James himself was, on the level ground with missiles and especially with musketry, and being wounded by a bullet his spirit became rather heightened than cowed and he all the more zealously encouraged his men to fight   James, pierced by two bullets, perished miserably—a Catholic of illustrious birth fighting for heretics   On his fall the rest fled, and the other division was also routed as it was coming to the rescue. Brian, pursuing the fugitives effected a great slaughter, and would have done greater execution had not Ormond come up and shielded the panic-stricken, and leaving the rebellion unsettled, departed out of Leix   Brian died of his wound within four days and on his death all Leinster might, perhaps, without much difficulty have been reduced, were it not that the very opportune arrival of Owny O'More encouraged the insurgents When O'More was looking to O'Neill for aid there was with the latter Raymond Burke, Baron of Leitrim, who had been deprived of his estates

We have already shown how John Burke, Baron of Leitrim, when slain by his brother Ulick with the sanction of the English, left an infant son Raymond, and the government of the Barony was adjudged to the Queen because according to English law the wardship of chiefs during minority vests in the Queen The government of the barony was, however, bestowed by the Queen on Fenton, an Englishman and secretary of the Irish Privy Council, and from him Ulick, Earl of Clanrickarde, uncle of Raymond, had purchased the barony and thus getting into possession he refused to restore the barony to Raymond who was now of age and out of wardship. Raymond went to law and got judgment from the English and the Queen, but on account of the war breaking out before Raymond got possession, the English failed to carry their judgment into execution lest in such dangerous times they excite the ill-will of so powerful a man as the Earl Raymond therefore turned to O'Neill for assistance to recover his pátrimony O'Neill was so engaged in the defence of Tyrone that he put off helping him and with faint hope of success Raymond set out for Leinster with Owny, who was also accompanied by Dermot O'Connor, a Connaught Chief These were followed by all the Connaughtmen who having been driven from their homes were staying with O'Neill. Richard Tyrrell, also, of whom we have made mention already, was brought along by Owny who with these entered Leix on the same day on which Brian had fought the enemy, but not able to assist in the battle or come up with Ormond on his retreat.

CHAPTER V.

THE CATHOLICS AND ROYALISTS COME TO A FIERCE GENERAL
ENGAGEMENT WITH ALL THEIR FORCES   BAGNAL IS SLAIN.
ARMAGH AND PORTMORE ARE RECOVERED BY THE CATHOLICS.

WHILE these events were taking place in Leinster, Henry Bagnal, an English knight, Marshall of Ireland, and President of Ulster, arrived in the town of Newry, in the

province of Ulster, and which was held by a strong garrison
of heretics, and situated not more than nineteen miles from
the fort of Portmore which he was going to relieve with a
rather large army of Royalists   Thence after three days
march he halted in the city of Armagh   Bagnal was skilled
in the art of war, and what you rarely find in a general,
he was equally pre-eminent in council and in courage,
cautious in prosperity, courageous in adversity, and not
so insolent towards the vanquished or those who surrendered
as most of the English, who are never sparing of gibes.
And so I would venture to compare few of his people's
generals with him and to prefer still fewer.   He was bitterly
incensed against O'Neill not only on the general ground of
religion and loyalty, but also on account of private quarrels.
He commanded 4,500 foot, under forty colours and a like
number of captains, lieutenants, ensigns, sergeants, and
500 horse under eight colours, of whom Montague, an
Englishman, was master   Of the whole number, there
was a slight majority of Irish in the pay of the English All
were veterans, the Englishmen being either the survivors
of those who, under John Norris, had fought in France, or
who had been picked from the Belgian garrisons, or who,
from the beginning of this war, had learned military tactics
in Ireland.   The Irish, also, who, formed into corps under
regular military discipline, fought as mercenaries in the
Royalist army, had often given proof of their valour.
Amongst them were some Irish young men of illustrious
birth, especially the O'Reilly's son, Maelmurray, who from
his singularly fine figure and wonderfully handsome countenance, was surnamed the Fair, and Christopher St.
Laurence, son of the Baron of Howth   Here was no tyro
Here was none unskilled in military science   All were
exceedingly well furnished with all kinds of arms.   Foot
and horse were sheathed in mail.   The musketeers were
equipped for the fight, some with heavy and some with
light guns, girded with sword and dagger and having their
head protected with helmets   The whole army gleamed
with crested plumes and silken sashes, and other military
ornaments   Brass cannon mounted on wheels were drawn
by horses.   There was a large supply of gunpowder and
iron and leaden balls.   Pack horses and oxen carried a
quantity of biscuits, corned meat, cheese, butter, and beer
sufficient both to victual the army and provision the fort
of Portmore   Drivers accompanied the baggage, and a
large number of suttlers and foragers followed.   The fort
of Portmore was three Irish miles from Bagnal and being

besieged by O'Neill, was suffering from want of food. When O'Neill heard of Bagnal's arrival he moved his camp a mile from the fort and pitched it against Bagnal within two miles of Armagh, leaving a few men to prevent the besieged sallying from Portmore.

On this day the Catholics numbered 4,500 foot and about 600 horse, amongst them O'Donnell, who brought about 1,000 Connaught mercenaries under the MacWilliam Burke, and 2,000 of his own men of Tyrconnell and others. The rest were followers of O'Neill, his brother and kinsmen, and chiefs who were bound to him by ancient ties. In a word, there were assembled here nearly the entire youth of the nobility of Ulster and many young Connaughtmen of by no means ignoble birth. They were, however, very inferior in equipment, for both horse and foot were light armed, except a few musketeers, who had heavy guns. For this reason O'Neill being informed of the enemy's equipment, the strength of their army, and the resolution of their general, was in doubt whether a wise man would give ground until Fearfeasa O'Clery, an interpreter of Irish Prophecies, assured him, the holy prophet Ultan had foretold that in this spot the heretic would be routed, and showed him the prophecy written in Irish verse in a book of holy prophecies. Reassured by this prophecy O'Neill stimulated his men to the fight with this speech .—" Most Christian and fearless men, the Great and Good God has this day in His Divine generosity more than granted our most earnest and frequent prayers and petitions. We have ever been praying to God and his Saints to grant us to fight the Protestants on equal terms. For this have we offered up our prayers ; for this have we made our offerings, and now we are not only equal, but actually superior in numbers. Therefore, you, who have, when inferior in numbers, routed the heretical columns, are now in superior numbers pitted against them. I, for my part, hold that victory lies not in senseless armour, nor in the vain din of cannon, but in living and courageous souls. Remember how often when you were not so well equipped or disciplined you have overcome greater generals and forces, and even Bagnal himself. The English never could compare with the Irish in spirit, courage or steadfastness in battle, and the Irish who will be fighting against you will be dispirited by the consciousness of their crime and schism in fighting against the Catholic faith. This very Catholic faith will stimulate your valour. Here you are to defend Christianity, father-land, children and wives. Here must well-deserved chastisement be meted out to Bagnal, of all heretics, your bitterest enemy, who assails your properties, who thirsts for your blood, who impugns my honour. Here must be avenged the insult put upon me by Bagnal when I was deprived of part of my camp at Mullaghbane. Here must we get satisfaction for the deaths of your comrades whom we have lost in the attack on Portmore, and that fort itself which you have so long besieged, and have now cut off from supplies, must be captured. Here is to be obtained that victory which the Lord has promised in the prophecy of St Ultan. On then, with good heart and with the help of God and his Saints."

Bagnal on the other side then addressed his men :—
"Trusting in your valour, my most invincible comrades in arms, I have chosen you as my associates, and that the glorious victory I have promised myself might be accounted your work, I have stationed the unskilled and untrained in the garrisons and left to the Earl of Ormond the base and the infirm through whose degeneracy I thought this campaign might be imperilled. Indeed I have ever had such proof of your spirit and valour that I cannot but feel assured and most confident of victory this day. And I believe you have escaped safely with such providential good hap so many misfortunes, so many trials, that on this day you should crown your whole lives with a happy victory and avenge the misfortunes and deaths of your comrades, of Norris and Borough, cut off by rebels and traitors. What! Dare they, unless mad, encounter with naked bodies, armed men, men superior both in bodily strength and stoutness of spirit? I am a fool if they abide the bare look of you, and if you do not this day reduce all Ulster to your sway and subdue all Ireland to the Queen and yourselves reap an immense spoil. Remember your valour who under my command succoured Armagh and stripped O'Neill of a considerable part of his camp at Mullaghbane. Whoever brings me, before evening, the head of O'Neill or O'Donnell, I promise a thousand pounds of gold, and to everyone I will give according to his deserts thanks and acknowledgments both on the Queen's and my own behalf. Come, then, let us make haste and not delay our victory."

Having finished his harangue Bagnal raised his camp at Armagh, before sunrise about the fifteenth day after Lord Ormond's defeat by Brian O'More.

The pikemen were divided into three columns which were preceded and followed by the wings of horse and musketeers

It was a fine pleasant day when unfurling their banners they marched without opposition over the smiling plain, to the sound of the trumpet, the music of pipes, and the beat of military drums, stimulating man and beast to combat. Presently the road became more difficult, lying between shrubs, which, however, were low and thin   Bagnal having entered this road about 7 o'clock a.m. was assailed with a close fire kept up along the entire cover by 500 beardless youths armed as musketeers and sent by O'Neill. These skirmishers, standing beside the shrubs and shifting amongst the trees,* brought down horse and foot at long range and this with all more impunity in that the royalist cavalry on account of the shrubs could neither assist their own men nor resist the Catholics, and because the ground was more favourable to the skirmishers already in possession than to the approaching royalists   From these straits Bagnal, with much difficulty, at last extricated his forces, severely harassed by the sharp skirmish and annoyed at seeing themselves attacked with impunity by the skirmishers who seemed such a boyish and silly sort of men   An open plain extending to the Catholic camp came next and as soon as Bagnal gained this the royalist cavalry charged the Catholic skirmishers at full speed   However, O'Neill had dug numerous pits and trenches in the first portion of the plain, especially on and around the road itself, and covered them in with brambles and hay   Into these the mailclad and incautious cavalry tumbled and in this pell-mell fall the legs of the horses and riders were broken and the Catholic skirmishers did not allow them to be relieved by their comrades without a struggle   By this stratagem the royalist army reached the less obstructed plain not only dispirited but having some of their cavalry and foot lost and wounded.   Here O'Neill's wearied skirmishers were supplanted by fresh and sound troops and Bagnal also advanced to the fight his skirmishers and heavy armed musketeers.   These the Catholic light cavalry charged. The mailclads, too secure in the protection of their armour, held the field.

The light-armed excelling in dexterity and speed and

---

* " Juniper " is the word in the text, but I do not know if that plant grows in Ireland, I imagine the trees were hawthorns   The English speak of these trees as a wood or underwood   See life of Hugh Roe O'Donnell, translated, etc , by Rev Ds. Murphy, S J., xciv and description of Ireland in 1598, edited by Rev. Ed. Hogan, S.J ; p. 20

wheeling their horses again and again returned to the fight inflicted many wounds but giving ground, however, all the time.

The mail-clads fought at close quarters with lances about 6 cubits (9 *feet*) long, resting on their right thighs. The light-armed, having longer lances which they grasped in the middle and held above the right shoulder, rarely struck except at advantage, at other times hurling wooden darts tipped with iron and about four cubits long.   Thus Bagnal advanced often compelled to halt by O'Neill's light-armed, and as often repulsing them, until about eleven o'clock he halted not far from the Catholic camp   Now the plain was here bounded on both sides by a marsh and between these bogs O'Neill constructed a low light ditch four feet high and a quarter of a mile long with a rather deep trench inside more to impede the enemy than assist himself.   Midway between the ditch and royalist army oozed the discoloured waters flowing from the bogs, whence, perhaps, the place was called according to many the Yellow Ford (Beal atha bui) although according to others it is called the Ford of Saint Buianus.   The fight was renewed at the ditch with great vigour by the cavalry and gunmen of both armies.   In the heat of the fight an English gunman who had used up all his powder was taking some more from the barrel in which it was and accidently put in the hand which held the lighted tow match ; the light being put into the barrel ignited it and the two nearest barrels also full of powder and blew up some of the soldiers   Meanwhile Bagnal had got into position against the Catholic's ditch and columns his brass cannon, one of which when charged with powder and ball and fired off burst in pieces with the charge of powder and killed some who were standing round.

With the rest Bagnal broke down the ditch and the Catholic cavalry and musketeers exhausted from their defence of the ditch offering no further resistance, the enemy opened his cannon on the uncovered columns of Catholic pikemen.   Some parts of the ditch he levelled to the ground and drove the troops from it   Through these breaches the two first divisions of the royalists rushed, one against O'Neill and another against O'Donnell, who held the left wing, and some files crossed the ditch, to whose support Bagnal brought up the rear division.   At the same time the royalists, cavalry and musketeers pursued the cavalry and musketeers of the Catholics whom they drove from the ditch, and now both sides fought fiercely on the

level ground and the men on both sides commingling
dragged one another from horse back.   Hereupon the
Catholic pikemen, who had moved out of cannon range
from the ditch, seeing the enemy's cannon now paralysed,
charged the royalist division, though not yet formed into
ranks   At this instant, Bagnal who was protected by a
coat of mail and helmet which was proof against the shot
of a heavy gun, thinking that he had already conquered
and in order that he might more freely survey the whole
battle field and breathe easier, and fatigued with the weight
of his heavy armour, opened the visor of his helmet and
raised it but did not set it down and close it before he lay
lifeless on the ground struck by a bullet on the forehead.
By his death the 3rd division with which he had been was
panic-stricken.   The two divisions to whom the news of
their general's death was not yet announced stoutly stood
the brunt.   The Catholics in like manner were no way
backward in the battle.   O'Donnell protected himself by
the valour of the musketeers O'Neill's division seemed
in greater peril   In this doubtful state of things, O'Neill,
who kept on horseback beside his division with 40 horsemen
and as many musketeers ordered the musketeers to fire on
the royalists   On obeying this command the musketeers
seriously harassed and broke the ranks of the opposing
gunmen who had no assistance.   O'Neill added terror
to their confusion by charging with his 40 horsemen into
the midst of their corps.   His division of pikemen following,
O'Neill with a loud cry put the royalists to flight about an
hour after mid-day.   Those who were engaging O'Donnell
seeing this, also broke their ranks and turned tail and
Montague also retreated with the cavalry   The wings
of musketeers betook themselves to flight. O'Neill, O'Donnell
and Maguire, who commanded the cavalry, hung on the
rear of the fugitives   The dyke and ditch was then a
greater obstacle to the flying royalists than it had previously
been to them in making their attack, and falling over one
another they filled the dyke and were trodden down where
they fell by the hoofs of the horses and under the feet of
the infantry.   The rear division, in which Bagnal had been
was of no assistance to the others in their distress, being
itself depressed and panic-stricken by the death of its leader.
Maelmurray O'Reilly, surnamed the Fair, however, urged
the panic-stricken to pluck up spirit and resist the enemy
with him, crying out that it was more glorious to fall fighting
and avenged than to be slain with impunity in flight, and
that even now they might withstand the enemy's attack

and drive him back.   Some, reanimated by the Fair's appeal, especially young Irishmen allied to him in blood, renewed the fight   The Fair was to be seen everywhere amongst the combatants helping those most hardly pressed, and in greatest danger.   However, those few who stood by him were deserted by the royalists and fell covered with wounds inflicted by the Catholics who surrounded them, and the Fair himself, being left alone, was slain fighting most valiantly.   All the royalists scattered in flight took to their heels over the plain and underwood by which they had come, flying even to Armagh and slain as they straggled The horse and about 1,500 foot betook themselves to the Church of Armagh   More than 2,500 royalists perished in the battle among them Bagnal, the commander of the army, 23 captains, many officers, ensigns and sergeants, 34 colours were taken, all the military drums, the cannon, a great quantity of arms, and the entire commissariat.   Nor was this a bloodless victory for the conquerors, for although less than 200 were killed, yet more than 600 were wounded. Those who took refuge in the Churches of Armagh, which were held as royalist garrisons, were besieged by the victors. Montague escaped with the cavalry under cover of the darkness of night   Terence O'Hanlon, with some horse from O'Neill's camp, pursued him as he fled in disorder and confusion, and captured the baggage and two hundred horses, and slew three officers   Moreover, Romley, an English captain, was seized and slain the next day, as he was smoking a pipe of tobacco on the roadside   The foot capitulated and were dismissed without their arms, Armagh and Portmore being surrendered to O'Neill

CHAPTER VI.

SEVERAL SUCCESSES OF THE LEINSTERMEN AND OTHERS

OWING to this victory and the opportune arrival of Owny O'More many of the Leinstermen plucked up spirit and took up arms for Faith and Freedom, especially Donald Kavanagh, surnamed the Spaniard, because he had lived about four years in Spain   Owny reduced the whole of Leix to his sway except Maryborough and two other forts Daniel, the Spaniard, wasted with fire and sword a great part of Meath, because it had not joined the confederacy in defence of the Catholic faith against the English Raymond Burke wrested from the Earl of Ormond and held possession of Lower Ormond which is not far from Leix, and placed garrisons in the forts which had surrendered In Connaught many deserted from the English and some Ulstermen, who shortly before had gone over to the English, now returned.

TOME III. BOOK V.

OF

DON PHILIP O'SULLEVAN OF BEAR IN IRELAND

ON THE FIFTEEN YEARS' WAR.

WE will now relate some of the actions of the royalist armies under Ormond and Essex the Viceroy, and at the beginning of Blount's government. These actions were bloody and numerous, the war being now carried into Munster.

CHAPTER I

DESCRIBES THE STATE OF THINGS IN MUNSTER WHEN THE WAR BROKE OUT

WHILST the events we have so far recorded were taking place in Ulster, Leinster, and Connaught, MacCarthy More died leaving Helena, his daughter, betrothed to Florence, son of MacCarthy Reagh, and they disputed with the Queen of England the deceased's estates Moreover Daniel, an illegitimate son of More's, considered himself no ways unworthy of his father's estate and that his sister Helena should not be preferred to himself, but he did not trust his case to the English, whom he did not expect would be fair judges towards him However it is suspected that he would have promised them his support were it not that O'Neill was assisting him to obtain his father's chieftaincy. In addition there were James and John FitzGerald dissatisfied at seeing themselves deprived of the Earldom of Desmond since their father Thomas had adhered to the royalists against his brother Earl Gerald.

Therefore, it is said, they turned to O'Neill for assistance. Dermot and Donough MacCarthy were at law about the Chieftaincy of Duhallow, and not satisfied with the decision and rulings of the royalist judges Others also were ill-affected towards the English both on the general ground of religion and for personal grievances However, all enjoyed the most profound peace and were then, on account of present difficulties less worried by the English than at other times, and the Munstermen were very little inclined for rebellion with a few exceptions and these possessing little power or resources were not able to do anything worth mentioning. Thus Munster had a good supply of provisions and supplied such of .their own, and many of Connaught and some of Leinster, who came looking for victuals when their own countries had been laid waste. Their President, John Norris, had died, as we have seen, and his brother Thomas Norris, a trained soldier, succeeded him

---

CHAPTER II.

HOW THE WAR WAS CARRIED INTO MUNSTER AND WHO SECEDED IMMEDIATELY FROM THE ENGLISH.

IN this state of things Peter Lacy a Munster gentle-man of birth, full of courage and of some eloquence, fled from the English against whom he had committed some crime and came to Owny O'More in Leinster and persuaded him to make an incursion into Munster, repre-senting that most of the Munster men eagerly desired this and were anxious to rebel , that all the Geraldines would make James FitzGerald Earl of Desmond and follow his lead , that the MacCarthys would elect for themselves a Chief of Desmond Owny approving of this advice, and O'Neill consenting, he brought round to his views his friends who were carrying on the war in Leinster. These were Raymond Burke, Baron of Leitrim, and MacWilliam his brother ; Dermot O'Connor and his two brothers Carbery and Con, and Richard Tyrrell. Owny, at the head of 800 foot and about 30 horse, hastened into Munster sooner than anyone had expected, leaving his brother Edmond to look after Leix Earl Ormond, general of the royalist army, was expected to oppose his progress, but he did not turn up, either surprised by Owny's celerity or because he dreaded to venture a battle. Thomas Norris, an Englishman, President of Munster, perceiving the neces-sity of driving the enemy from his province, got together such forces as the shortness of time would permit, from the garrisons of his province, the muster of Munstermen, and chief persons of Munster, and summoned all to Mallow,

proposing to meet Owny there   As Owny came up he
sent bold letters challenging Norris to draw out his troops,
but the latter refused and leaving a garrison at Mallow,
retired to Cork   Owny followed and his light-armed
skirmished with Norris's rear guard with missiles. Instantly
more Munstermen than was at all expected seceded from
the English . Patrick FitzGerald, who was called Fitzmaurice
and Baron of Lixnaw ; William FitzGerald, Knight of Kerry
and Lord of Rathfinnan , Edmond FitzGerald, Knight of
Glin , Edmund FitzGerald, the White Knight and almost
all the Munster FitzGeralds, the majority of whom hailed
James FitzGerald as Earl of Desmond, by which title we
shall   henceforth   call   him   Dermot   and   Donough
MacCarthy, claimants to the Chieftaincy of Duhallow ,
Daniel son of MacCarthyMore, Patrick Condon, O'Donoghue
of Eoghanacht (or Onaght) , O'Donoghue of the Glen, also
joined the confederacy   Some other distinguished men
also seceded :—Roche, Viscount Fermoy, Richard Butler,
Viscount Mountgarret, who had married O'Neill's daughter,
Thomas Butler, Baron of Cahir , and others   Many,
however, remained friendly to the Queen, not only all the
cities and towns, but also chiefs and nobles   Hereupon
many flocked from Connaught who were suffering from
want in consequence of the devastation of their country
and were armed by the Munster-men and officered by
Dermot O'Connor, William Burke, Richard Tyrrell, Brian
O'Kelly and others   The Munstermen were also enrolled
and given captains   The war being thus kindled in
Munster, Owny returned to Leinster

CHAPTER III

STRUGGLES OF THE MUNSTERMEN WITH THE ENGLISH AND
WITH ONE ANOTHER

WHATEVER English were in the countries of those who took
up arms against the Queen, were plundered of their goods
and expelled   Some of their forts were stormed but were
of little importance, if we except Molahiff Castle which was
held by 30 royalists under Nicholas Brown, an English
knight.   William Burke, Thomas FitzGerald, surnamed
Oge, and some of the MacCarthys who lived on the river
Maine, attacked this castle with 300 foot, pouring in shot
on battlements and windows and compelling the besieged

to withdraw therefrom. The besieged defended the fort stoutly and bravely with missiles. One of them was such a wonderful marksman that he shot dead or wounded with leaden bullets sixteen of the assailants. A sow* was advanced to the castle under cover of which the soldiers undermined the wall. The garrison, manning the breach fought fiercely but were in the end beaten back and the assailants forced an entrance The besieged cast down on them paving stones and rafters which they tore up. While these were falling the assailants drew back a little but again charging captured the fort and slew the defenders. Dermot MacCarthy, claimant to Duhallow, deeming none more worthy than himself of the country and title of MacCarthy More, assembled a force of Connaughtmen and summoning his friends hastened to take possession of the Chieftaincy after the English had fled. Daniel, illegitimate son of MacCarthy, accompanied by a band of his friends and some Connaughtmen whom he had hired, marched against Dermot, asserting that the country and title of his father justly belonged to him Both sides gave pledges to abide by the decision of impartial arbitrators and refrained from war. Daniel, however, who remained in the country, was inaugurated MacCarthy, by Daniel O'Sullivan, brother of O'Sullivan More Forthwith Daniel, now in possession of the Chieftaincy of Clancarthy, and James Earl of Desmond sent troops to compel the Munstermen who had not yet seceded from the English to secede and to levy tribute or contributions from them. The land forces sent against MacCarthy Reagh and the men of Carbery were successful but the naval forces were worsted by the O'Driscolls Various other battles were fought between those Munster men who adhered to the Queen and those who had seceded from her, and there was slaughter on both sides Some shook off the English yoke of their own accord , some were compelled to do so, some were indifferent. Others, yielding to the victors for the time being paid tribute to both parties in turn.

CHAPTER IV

FIRST EXPEDITION OF THOMAS NORRIS AGAINST THE CATHOLICS

WHILE the Catholics of Munster were thus fighting and exhausting one another, Thomas Norris, President of

----

* See note on " Irish Arms ' in appendix

Munster, was enabled to collect his forces at Cork. He made a hosting of the Irish of his Province , consolidated the veterans and recent recruits from England ; and summoned some Munster Chiefs of his party , which in all gave him 2500 men. With these arranged in three divisions he set out to withdraw the veterans from the garrison of Kilmallock and leave the recruits there Hearing of this, William Burke, then in the Youghal district, unexpectedly came up with 300 foot and on Saturday, at the Pass of Ballaghawry, routed the rear division where were stationed the English recruits clad in red coats and driving them into the middle division killed many, seized the baggage, and amongst these the pet and hunting dogs which Norris prized However, Norris reached Kilmallock, and as he returned from thence on the following Monday to Ardskea, he was pursued by the Earl of Desmond, Viscount Mount-garret, Baron Cahir, Baron Loghmoe, William Burke, and Richard Tyrrell, with very nearly equal numbers, and fighting was kept up the entire day over eight miles of ground Some on both sides were killed and wounded but the royalists suffered most and of their noblemen Tamquin, an Englishman, perished. The contest ended only when Norris betook himself into Buttevant.

CHAPTER V.

SECOND EXPEDITION OF THOMAS NORRIS.

NORRIS prepared another expedition against the Catholics, and at the head of 2400 foot and 300 horse entered Viscount Roche's country, and occupied Bridgetown, a castle which, unfortified by nature or art, had been abandoned by the Viscount. Thence he proposed to make for Castletown Roche, half a mile off, but which was better protected by nature and by a garrison

The Viscount determined to defend this to the death and opportunely there came to his aid Daniel MacCarthy, who had obtained the Chieftaincy of Clancarthy, Earl Desmond, Dermot O'Connor, and William Burke, with about 2500 foot and less than 100 horse. Pitching their camp between Norris and Castletown Roche, they resolved to withstand his attempt. As soon as he marched his army they drove his wings back on the main body and compelled the entire army to return to camp. When the musketeers attacked the camp they were driven back by the artillery and the Catholics giving way were pursued by the royalist cavalry and gunmen and forced back on their own cannon, but these in turn drove back the royalists who were followed by the Catholics, and there was no more fighting for some days. Between both armies was a pretty ridge by no means impassable, the obtaining possession of which was accounted the victory and on the high ground of which the victors were wont to exhibit on poles the heads of slain enemies. Each strained every nerve to carry off from this ignominious position the heads of their own men, and hence arose fierce fights When twelve days had been spent fighting in this way more to the injury of the royalists than of the Catholics, and Norris had ceased to contest the ridge and seemed more disposed to retreat than advance, the Catholics leaving a strong garrison in Castletown Roche, sat down near Bridgetown, a place overlooking the road and near Norris's camp, in order to cut off his retreat.

Norris drew out before dawn his horse and 700 musketeers and suddenly poured in a heavy fire on this camp. Some of the assailed on that side suddenly panic-stricken fled William, coming to the rescue from the other wing reanimated his men and put Norris to flight and pursuing him to his camp killed and wounded some horse and foot. On the next day Norris, sending on his baggage before dawn, hastened to Cork, and the Catholics following him slew, at Monanimy 200 royalists. The rest being dispersed, the pursuit was abandoned

---

CHAPTER VI.

THOMAS NORRIS AND THE BARON OF CASTLECONNELL AND HIS BROTHER ARE SLAIN

SOME months later Thomas Burke, brother of Baron Castle-connell, and who had seceded from the English, got some soldiers from Baron Raymond and his brother William and attacked an ill-fortified fort in Muskerry. Norris and his army being in this district, hastened against Thomas with more than 200 horse and 1000 foot and came up with him and his cavalry and gunmen at Kilteely. Thomas, who had only 200 foot, meditated retreating. Norris not satisfied with this charged with his cavalry his rear ranks.

On this attack Thomas faced about and John Burke, a
Connaughtman of birth, struck Norris with a spear through
the helmet and left the iron point of his lance in Norris's
head Norris suffering from this wound, retired to Mallow
where he died within fifteen days. Dermot O'Connor,
accompanied by 100 men was marching through the
country of Richard Burke, Baron Castleconnell, when he
was surrounded by the Baron and his brother Thomas,
now reconciled to the English, at the head of 300 hired
troops and three companies of royalists sent from Limerick.
Compelled for his life to attack these in the desperate straits
in which he found himself, Dermot routed and put them
to flight and killed the Baron and his brother Thomas

CHAPTER VII.

THE BARON OF INCHIQUIN BEING DROWNED, THE GOVERNOR
OF CONNAUGHT BESIEGES THE FORT OF BALLYSHANNON ;
O'DONNELL RAISES THE SIEGE AND INVADES CLANRICKARDE.

WHILE these events were going on in Ireland, Dermot
O'Connor was litigating before an unjust tribunal in
England his claim against the Queen to the chieftaincy
of Sligo and neither obtaining his entire country nor getting
leave to return to Ireland lest in these troubled times when
many were in rebellion he should try to recover by arms
the property which was withheld from him
The Queen was conceding to him Ballymote castle but
not Sligo , but when Sligo was captured by O'Donnell,
then he was offered it instead of Ballymote When both
were lost by the Queen, she granted both to Dermot and
allowed him to return to Ireland and to recover and hold
for ever whatever of his chieftaincy he was able. O'Connor
reached Conyers Clifford, an English knight, at the time
he was preparing an expedition against O'Donnell with
4000 men amongst whom were Irish auxiliaries of no mean
rank :—the Earls of Thomond and Clanrickarde and
Murrough O'Brien, Baron Inchiquin. With this army he
marched to besiege Ballyshannon, a castle of O'Donnell's.
Proposing to cross Ballyshannon ford which was held by
O'Donnell, he attacked Ath-Culuain In the very ford,
as elsewhere, O'Connor and Baron Maurice disputed the
palm of valour and while each endeavoured to get before

the other Maurice's horse stumbled in the bed of the stream and threw him, and on account of the weight of his armour he sunk to the bottom of the river and rose no more. In spite of a few men placed there by O'Donnell, Clifford crossed the ford and assailed the castle with four cannons. The castle was held by Hugh Craphurt (*Crawford ?*) a Scotchman with 80 soldiers of whom six were Spaniards and the rest Irishmen On the first day of the assault a royalist foot soldier distinguished by his gilded coat of mail ventured too near the castle and was shot down and a comrade of his coveting his coat of mail was also shot with a leaden bullet when he incautiously came near the castle A third making the same venture was also shot and the besieged thereupon stripped the three of their arms and clothes. O'Donnell, few of whose men had yet come up, attempted to relieve the castle A cavalry fight ensued, in which O'Connor was wounded fighting valiantly When O'Donnell abandoned the attempt the royalists more freely battered the castle with cannon, fired into it, and destroyed its defences Moreover, advancing mantlets, they undermined the walls and closed with the defenders in the breach, but were repulsed. Changing their tactics they made a tunnel into the castle, through which some armed men entered but were destroyed by beams and stones rooted up and hurled on them by the besieged Meantime O'Donnell attacked the royalist camp night and day, hindering them from the assault and depriving them of sleep He was now joined by nearly all his mercenaries and followers, by O'Rourke and other allies and O'Neill coming to his aid was not far off. The royalists, fearing the increased Catholic forces, and every day more severely assailed by O'Donnell, and now tired out, raised the siege, leaving three cannon and shipping the fourth and at early dawn crossed the river over which they had come at a ford called Casan-na-gcuradh. They fled in such disorder that some perished. O'Donnell pursuing the fugitives slew some of them. On this day 300 royalists perished either in the river or by the sword After this O'Donnell invaded Clanrickarde's country where a few horse of Clanrickarde's meeting the wings of O'Donnell's cavalry, turned tail, dreading their numbers. Manus, brother of O'Donnell, who just for the first time donned the soldiers coat, followed one of the Clanrickardes too hotly. The latter dismounted and fled into a deep bog impassable to horse. Manus also dismounted and followed him and they joined in single combat with sword and shield, Manus eventually killing

his enemy.   A great part of this country was laid waste.
The town of Athenry was scaled and stormed and an
English company which garrisoned it was slain.   Not long
after this O'Donnell ravaged the countries of Baron
Inchiquin, of Turlough O'Brien, a knight, and of
O'Shaughnessy.

CHAPTER VIII

OWNY ENCOUNTERS ORMOND.   THE MEN OF OFFALY STORM CASTLE CROGHAN, AND ABOUT FATHER ARCHER.

MEANTIME in Leinster Owny O'More having cut Maryborough off from supplies had reduced it to great extremities.
Earl Ormond, general of the royalist army left Dublin with
more than 4000 cavalry and foot to relieve this fort, and
reached a small stream called the Blackford, where Owny
at the head of about 1500 men attacked him in the open
plain. They fought fiercely and stubbornly Owny
frequently drove the enemy's wings back on his main body,
but was in turn driven off by the numbers of the foe On
this day Ormond lost 600 men whose bodies he placed in
houses and burned, so that the full extent of his losses
might not be known, for it is the English custom to conceal
their own dead, and expose their slain enemies in public
places.   Sixty Catholics fell and about 80 were wounded.
Ormond forcing a passage by dint of numbers, victualled
the fort Cahir, Murrough and John O'Connor, gentlemen of Offaly, with 100 foot surprised and scaled with long
ladders, Castle Croghan in Offaly held by a garrison under
Thomas More, knight, and Sifford, both Englishmen, and
slew the defenders.
    Again Earl Ormond, commander of the royalist army
and Owny O'More, drew out their forces and faced one
another   There was at this time with Owny Father James
Archer of the Society of Jesus, an Irishman most zealous
to spread the Catholic religion and consequently very bitter
against the heretic enemy and therefore held in the greatest
hatred by the English.   And, indeed, he was most useful
first to O'Neill and afterwards to Owny and subsequently
to O'Sullivan and other Catholic opponents of base dogmas
by his zeal, advice, pains and industry   Even by his own
influence he often got Catholics to turn their arms against
the heretics   This religious, actuated by a hope of bringing
Ormond to reason, sought an interview with him. Ormond

agreed and so on one side Ormond, Donough O'Brien, Earl of Thomond and Chief of Limerick, and George Carew, President of Munster, mounted on horseback; and on the other side Archer on foot, accompanied by three Irish soldiers met at a conference in view of both armies without any safe conduct on either side. Here, as Carew did not understand Irish, Archer, who spoke English fluently, began to speak in English as was his wont piously and devoutly. Ormond interrupted, him advancing some silly argument against the holiness of the Pope. Irritated at this Archer changed his tone somewhat and at the same time chanced to lift in his right hand the staff or stick on which he was resting his aged limbs. The three Irish foot soldiers who accompanied him and did not understand English thought the priest wanted to strike Ormond with his stick. Hereupon, fearing some harm to the unarmed priest from the armed men and wishing to guard against it, two of them attacked and dragged Ormond from the horse and the third drew his sword. Several others from the Catholic army ran up to their assistance and dreading the numbers, Earl Thomond and Carew took to flight. The royalists rushed *en masse* against Archer and Con O'Reilly, sent by Owny, resisted these. On both sides the cavalry and musketeers attacked until night put an end to the fight. On the following day both parties quitted this place. Ormond was kept in custody by Owny and converted to the Catholic faith by Archer However, being safely released by O'Neill's orders in memory of ancient friendship, he returned again to his former heretical vomit. But I must not pass over Archer. He was held not merely in awe by the heretics but even in a kind of admiration or superstitious terror and they believed him able to walk dry-footed over the sea, to fly through the air, and to possess other superhuman power, arguing thence that he ought to be called Archdevil rather than Archer.

CHAPTER IX.

WHAT EARL ESSEX EFFECTED IN MUNSTER AND LEINSTER VARIOUS MATTERS RELATED

THINGS had now for so long gone against so many royalist generals and armies that the English determined to annihilate the Catholics with overwhelming forces. To this end

Robert, Earl of Essex, who at this time was credited with greater achievements than any Englishman of the period was made Viceroy of Ireland, second to no one* and Commander-in-chief ot the royalist army.   Setting out from London he landed in Dublin towards the end of March in the year 1599, according to Camden.   Here was mustered the greatest army that could be got together out of those who had recently come from England and those previously in Ireland, as if he were about marching against O'Neill, and so O'Neill prepared to meet him and O'Donnell was coming to O'Neill's aid.   But contrary to universal expectation, Essex set off for Munster at the head of 7000 foot and 900 horse   Owny O'More with 500 foot, met him in Leinster as he was leading his army through a narrow pass and routed his rear guard and killed some soldiers and officers and carried off some spoils amongst which were many helmet plumes, whence the place is to this day called the Pass of the Plumes (Bearna na gchleti).   When Essex reached Munster he immediately besieged Cahir, a castle of Thomas Baron Butler's, in which only seven or eight musketeers had been left as a garrison.   Earl Desmond, Baron Raymond and his brother William came to the castle's assistance, at the head of only 1000 foot and a few horse, forces very unequal to those of the royalists, for they were not prepared and had not expected Essex would have attacked them so soon.   There was access to the castle by a bridge which Winkle, an English captain, held with a strong guard.   On the second day of the siege William Burke with 500 foot and 200 horse marched to relieve the castle, dislodged Winkle from the bridge, cutting off some of the royalists, and placing James, brother of Baron Thomas with a garrison of 50 foot in the castle, returned safely. However the castle was beaten down by constant cannon adding notwithstanding the efforts of Desmond who by losing no chance of fighting endeavoured to raise the siege.   On the tenth night of the assault James and his soldiers abandoned the ruined castle and fled to their own people Essex, leaving a garrison in the fort, came to Limerick, the Catholics not venturing to oppose him.   Thence he made for Askeaton to strengthen the garrison   By this time Donal MacCarthy and Earl Desmond had got together 2500 men with whom

---

* The Lord Lieutenant of Ireland was usually an Englishman ; who never came over or discharged any function whatever, and the Government was carried on by a Lord Deputy.   O'Sullivan means that Essex was Lord Lieutenant.

they blocked the passes on the road. William was placed in the first post to oppose the enemy's march. In the second position was Dermot O'Connor in the difficult level ground, and in the last were stationed Walter Tyrrell and Thomas Plunkett, with 580 men in the narrowest passes of the road (Rower bog). If, as was hoped, the enemy could be caught between these three, he might have been destroyed with impunity. And such would have been the case had Peter Lacy, the chief of staff, commanded as many say he did, though Walter and Thomas deny it, that Walter and Thomas should first attack Essex and then Dermot and William fall on his rear. And so on Saturday Essex marched his forces in four divisions to the passes, and now the Earls of Thomond and Clanrickarde and Baron MacPiers with the first division of Irishmen passed William and Dermot without opposition as had been arranged. Then passing Walter and Thomas they deployed out of the passes into the open. When Dermot saw this, thinking that the enemy had escaped through the treachery of Walter and Thomas into the level ground where he was stationed, he began the battle and was forced by the numbers of the enemy to give ground and fall back on William. Both renewing the fight pursued the enemy for three hours fighting vigorously, but inflicting little damage because the enemy were free of the passes in which Walter and Thomas should have opposed them with all their strength However these latter allege they were ordered not to fight until the others had begun the battle but many assert the contrary and say that an arrangement was come to between them and Essex through one Tyrrell that they would not obstruct. Daniel MacCarthy thought they should be punished according to their crime, but the Earl disagreed fearing dissensions amongst the troops. Subsequently, a quarrel having sprung up, Thomas was killed by Peter Lacy. But to return to our subject. Essex reached Askeaton where the Catholics attacked his camp at night. Strengthening Askeaton with a stronger garrison, Essex not venturing further returned on the following Monday by another route. Here, at the village of Finniterstown, the Catholics sallying out from a wood attacked at once the first, rear and middle divisions. Henry Norris, an English knight, brother of John and Thomas, supported by a strong troop of musketeers charged the Catholics and was struck by a leaden bullet and fell from his horse Many other royalists and some Catholics were slain, for the fight raged from 9 in the forenoon to five in the afternoon, until Essex

halted at Croom.   Thence Desmond followed him for six
days as far as Decies, attacking night and day and thinning
his army.   After Essex's return to Dublin, Cahir castle was
speedily recovered by James Butler, brother of the Baron,
and the English garrison were slain.

Essex made another expedition against the O'Connors
of Offaly and the O'Moores against whom he had little
success and daily diminished his army, so that he asked
assistance from England to enable him to proceed against
O'Neill.

CHAPTER X.

THE GOVERNOR OF CONNAUGHT CUT OFF BY O'DONNELL IN
BATTLE.

At this time, Clifford, the Governor of Connaught, resolved
to fight O'Donnell, by land and sea, and in the first place
to attack Sligo and rebuild the castle O'Donnell had dismantled   To this end O'Connor Sligo went round amongst
the Connaughtmen on the Sligo side of the Curlew mountains, exhorting and beseeching them to desert O'Donnell.
A troop of O'Donnell's horse accidently met this O'Connor
accompanied by a few horse, and engaging him, forced him
with the loss of a few men to take refuge in Collooney fort,
where he was surrounded and attacked by O'Donnell.
O'Connor stoutly defended the fort for about forty days,
when it appeared he should surrender from want   Clifford
becoming aware of this, hastened his expedition in order
to recover Sligo, as he had already purposed, and on his way
to succour O'Connor, he ordered Theobald Burke, surnamed
Na-long (the naval) claimant to the MacWilliam's country
to sail from Galway with the fleet which was conveying the
provisions, cannon, lime and other materials for reconstruct-
ing the Castle, whilst himself with the rest of the forces took
the overland road   O'Donnell, well aware of this plan,
placed 400 foot under MacSweeny Fanad and MacWilliam
to garrison Sligo.   He ordered O'Boyle to continue the
siege of Collooney fort with 200 horse, while he himself with
the foot and O'Doherty held the Curlew mountains through
which Clifford's road lay   There were two roads through
this mountain, one very narrow and difficult, the other
wider.   He placed three companies in the more difficult
road with orders to prevent the enemy's advance until he
sent others to their aid   On the more open road himself

and O'Doherty with 2000 foot—an invincible column, pitched their tents.   O'Rourke was encamped not far off with 140 foot.   Meanwhile Na-long reached Sligo harbour with twenty ships and boats, but did not venture to land, awaiting Clifford's arrival.   Clifford got together 2500 picked youths and three troops of horse from the Irish and English regular forces and Irish auxiliaries.   Amongst the allies the most famous were—The O'Connor Don, chief of the plain of Connaught, Maelmurray MacSweeny, chief of Tuath, who, irritated against O'Donnell, had recently deserted to the English, and Richard Bourke, Baron of Dunkellin, son of Earl Ullick.   Clifford, advancing from. Athlone with 36 colours of infantry, and three of cavalry, reached Boyle.   O'Donnell directed trees to be cut down here and there and thrown across the path in that part of the mountain which is called Bellaghboy, to impede the enemy's advance and serve as a cover for his own defence, for he had decided to fight in this spot, and pitched his camp nearly two miles at the other side of it   The feast of the Assumption of the Virgin Mary being now at hand, all the Catholics obtained through Confession pardon of their sins on the vigil and on the feast itself received fasting the Body of the Lord Christ.   The day was dark with clouds and rain.   O'Donnell, therefore, thinking the enemy would not leave his camp, did not himself advance to Bellaghboy where he might fight with advantage.   However, MacSweeny thinking this a suitable opportunity, as he surmised O'Donnell would not leave his tents on account of the rain, persuaded Clifford to seize the Pass.   Clifford, leaving Griffin Markham, an English knight, and Master of the Horse, with the cavalry at Boyle, since a cavalry engagement could not be advantageously fought in the mountains, himself occupied the unguarded pass with his foot.   Scarcely had the Catholics received Communion when some mounted scouts returning brought the news that the enemy was at Bellaghboy and had passed the felled trees.   O'Donnell immediately ordered the soldiers to take their meal quickly so as to be all the stouter for the fight, and forthwith thus addressed them ·

" By the help of the Most Blessed Virgin Mary, Mother of God, we will this day utterly destroy the heretical enemy whom we have always heretofore worsted.   We fasted yesterday in honour of the Virgin, and to day we celebrate her feast.   Therefore in Her name let us fight stoutly and bravely the enemies of the Virgin and we shall gain the victory."

The soldiers being greatly inflamed to war by this speech, he sent on 600 musketeers under Eugene MacSweeny, Tuath, and Hugh and Tuathal O'Gallagher, with orders to attack and delay the enemy, while himself brought up the gallowglasses. The enemy had climbed out of the narrow passes to the middle and open part of the mountain, and about 11 a.m. the rain was ceasing when the gunners came up with O'Donnell's men. There on account of the favourable nature of the ground and the great spirit of the young men, a fierce encounter with leaden bullets at long range commenced, and many wounds were inflicted on both sides. The Irish gunners are giving way; their leaders remonstrate at this baseness, and at their fighting with such faint-heartedness for the Virgin. Stung with shame by these reproaches, and roused by zeal to fight earnestly for the Virgin they renew the contest. It is scarcely credible with what spirit and perseverance and skill the musketeers of both parties fought. The royalist gunners were driven back on the pikemen's division, and that division itself, overwhelmed with a shower of darts, and wounded, changed its front and from one side to another turned round three times in a circle, not knowing what it was doing. O'Rourke coming up with 140 foot to the support of the Catholics added terror to the already disorganised, and on seeing him the whole royalist army turned tail leaving behind a great heap of arms. The Catholics pursue. Although O'Donnell had hurried up with the gallowglasses, yet he did not find the fight going on. I do not believe the royalists would have been put to flight by the gunners, had it not been for the aid of the Virgin Mother. The Catholics hung on the rear of the terror-stricken fugitives for three miles. Clifford was carried for some time by two Irish soldiers to whom he promised a large reward, but was eventually overtaken and killed by a pike-thrust in his side. The felled trees and obstructed roads were great obstacles to the fugitives, and they left there not only their arms but even their garments. The Baron of Dunkellin had a narrow escape. Griffin with all the cavalry came out a mile from Boyle to the rescue of the fugitives, and put to flight the first of the Catholics, who were pursuing and slaughtering the enemy without any order ; but O'Rourke, supporting the Catholics, and rallying them, and withstanding the enemy, received two bullet wounds, one in the right hand and the other in the right thigh, and made the cavalry retire. The Catholics again pursued as far as Boyle, into which Griffin betook himself. Of the royalists there perished with their leader

Clifford, and Henry Ratcliffe, another English nobleman, 1,400, who were nearly all English or Anglo-Irish of Meath, for the Connaughtmen knowing the locality, escaped more easily Of the Catholics 140 were wounded and killed. Almost all the royalist arms, colours, military drums, baggage and clothes were captured. O'Neill, who was coming to O'Donnell's assistance, was two days' march away. When Clifford's death became known, Na-long brought back the fleet to Galway. O'Connor, submitting himself to O'Donnell's award, was restored by him to the whole Chieftaincy of Sligo and loaded with other presents, and he swore henceforth to aid against the Protestants.

CHAPTER XI.

WHAT DID ESSEX ACHIEVE IN ULSTER?

IN the following month of September, Earl Essex, receiving reinforcements from England, invaded Ulster. O'Neill, putting himself and his forces in evidence sought for a conference, through O'Hagan. Essex replied that he would be found in battle array on the morrow. On this day cavalry and musketeers advanced by both sides engaged in some slight skirmishing. O'Neill again asked for a parley which Essex did not think ought to be any longer denied. Both coming down alone to the banks of a river which lay between them, spoke from thence Here it was arranged that they should meet again on the 8th of September each accompanied by eight of the principal men of his army and they made a truce to the kalends of May of the following year on condition that either might renew the war on fourteen days previous notice to the other. In a short time Essex received very bitter letters from the Queen, upbraiding him for managing things so badly and sharply admonishing him, whereupon he crossed to England on the 28th of September and was cast into prison O'Neill sent a message to the English that there would be no truce if the management of affairs was changed and Essex cast into prison who had made and promised to observe the truce and that he would look to his own interests and let them beware of him when the fourteen days had expired Essex was put to death not long after this.

I

CHAPTER XII

AMBASSADORS FROM THE POPE AND KING OF SPAIN REACH
IRELAND   ACHIEVEMENTS OF O'NEILL IN MUNSTER, AND
OF BLOUNT THE VICEROY IN ULSTER   MAGUIRE AND THE
PRESIDENT OF MUNSTER SUCCUMB TO THEIR RESPECTIVE
WOUNDS

A FEW days after these events, Brother Matthew d'Oviedo,
a Spaniard, and Archbishop of Dublin, and Martin Cerdo,
a Spanish gentleman of birth, arrived in Ulster bringing
from the Pope indulgences and remission of sins to all who
would take arms against the English in defence of the Faith ;
and to O'Neill a plume of Phoenix feathers, and bringing
from His Catholic Majesty, Philip III (Philip II was now
dead) 22,000 pieces of gold to pay the army.

When the Spanish legates had returned home, O'Neill,
leaving strong garrisons in Tyrone, set off for Munster in
the middle of winter, accompanied by some of his allies in
war and at the head of by no means despicable forces.
His object was both to see the piece of the Holy Cross which
is said to have been in Holy Cross abbey, and to sound the
dispositions of the Irish and perhaps to defy the enemy.
He pitched his tent in County Cork.   Here Maguire, sallying
out from the camp accompanied by Edward MacCaffrey,
his standard bearer, Neill O'Dorney, and one priest, fell in
with Wareham St. Leger, an English knight, and President
of Munster, at the head of 60 horse.   Between these two
there was in addition to the general grounds of hostility a
personal jealousy because Maguire was universally recog-
nised as the bravest and best horseman amongst the Irish
and Wareham amongst the English.   Maguire seeing the
number of the enemy's cavalry did not think it consistent
with his honor to fly or surrender, but setting spurs to his
horse rushed into the midst of his foes.   As he was brandishing his spear Wareham shot him with a leaden bullet
from a pistol.   Nevertheless Maguire aimed his spear at
Wareham, and he wishing to avoid the blow by
bending his head, was pierced through the helmet,
and Maguire leaving the spear hanging from his
head escaped with drawn sword through the midst of the
enemy followed by his two comrades also wounded, and by
the priest.   Again wheeling his horse and charging he
routed and put the band to flight, but did not pursue them

far. Before reaching O'Neill's camp he dismounted and having got absolution from the priest, died of his wounds. Warcham also died within fifteen days raving from his wound. O'Neill taking with him Donough MacCarthy, claimant to Duhallow, lest he should return to the good graces of the English, returned to Ulster, notwithstanding Earl Ormond, who seemed disposed to fight. The year 1600 had closed when Charles Blount, Baron Mountjoy, was sent to Ireland as Viceroy, in February. He, setting out for Ulster did not advance as far as any of his predecessors but got only to Faughard   There he lay encamped more than three months and O'Neill having by daily battles and a ditch and dyke constructed across the road, prevented access to Armagh and Newry, Blount returned to Dublin without having effected anything   O'Neill suffered no loss worth mentioning except that he lost Peter Lacy, a stout cavalier of Munster, of whom we have above made mention, and who was wounded by a gunshot in the head.

TOME III. BOOK VI.

OF

DON PHILIP O'SULLEVAN OF BEAR IN IRELAND.

ON THE FIFTEEN YEARS' WAR.

So far the Catholics prospered. But now not only did their fortunes decline, but they came down with a crash, as will appear in the following books, and especially in this present book, in which the fiercest and most bloody struggles are recounted.

———

CHAPTER I

SUMMARY ACCOUNT OF HOW THE CATHOLIC FORCES DECLINED

THE English being in the greatest danger of losing Ireland and knowing that help would be sent to the Catholics from Spain, were distracted with various councils how to meet this disaster.

Finally, they resolved to reduce the whole of Ireland to the utmost poverty and want. They gained over to themselves the very Irish on certain terms and those who would not be conciliated they destroyed by artifices and practices inciting them one against another In this, fortune favoured the English First of all brass money was sent to Ireland by which all Irish gold and silver was withdrawn to England while the brass money itself soon became worthless. In this way the Irish were defrauded of their own money and reduced to the utmost poverty. Moreover the corn was cut down and other devastations were committed.

———

CHAPTER II.

BY THE DEATH OF OWNY O'MORE, LEINSTER IS AT PEACE.

OWNY O'MORE with an inferior number of men came up with the Viceroy Blount on his way to victual Maryborough, a fort of the Chieftaincy of Leix, and Owny having incautiously advanced with one comrade beyond his own troops was struck by a leaden bullet and killed. On his death almost all the Leinstermen lost heart and very soon afterwards the Viceroy Blount received into favour Daniel, the Spaniard, Felim O'Byrne, the O'Tooles and others, and almost the whole of Leinster wasted and weary of war was pacified. Raymond brother of Owny O'More alone held out.

———

CHAPTER III.

CONCLUSION OF THE WAR IN MUNSTER

THE Munstermen were, so far, too well equipped for war to be easily defeated by English arms, but were overcome by this device:—Florence, son of MacCarthy More, was as we have seen, disputing the Chieftaincy of Clancarthy with the Queen. The Queen gave him leave to wrest the chieftaincy, if he could, from Daniel MacCarthy and hold it for ever. Florence was hailed by his followers, mercenaries and friends, and Daniel was deserted, not even the Earl of Desmond coming to his assistance However in a short time Florence himself was seized and sent by the English into England, where he was thrown into prison in the Tower of London, and Daniel having no forces surrendered to the English on getting a pardon Thus half the force of those who were carrying on the war in Munster was broken down.

Another young James Fitzgerald, son of Earl Gerald, was released from the confinement in which he had been kept in England, and being instituted Earl of Desmond by the Queen, was sent into Ireland in opposition to James then Earl of Desmond, and was received by many of the Irish However the Catholic Earl made so stout a resistance, the English promised a large reward to Dermot O'Connor, his lieutenant, to betray the Earl to them. Dermot was gained over both by the bribes and for the sake of the young Earl whose sister he had married, and imprisoned the Catholic Earl in Castle Lisin in order to deliver him thence to the English. A report of this having got abroad, Fitzmaurice, Baron of Lixnaw, Dermot MacCarthy Reagh, The Knight of Kerry, William Burke, Brian O'Kelly, and Peter Lacy at the head of 1,800 men stormed the Castle. Dermot was not far off, but being inferior in numbers dare not try to raise the siege. He expected George Carew, an English knight and President of Munster, and who had left Kilmallock, would relieve the fort, but Fitzmaurice prevented this by sending troops to block the road. The Earl was released on the seventh day of the siege, the garrison stipulating that with O'Sullivan More and other hostages they should be sent to Dermot Dermot, thinking he would not be safe either with the Irish against whom he had committed so great a crime, or with the English, since he did not fulfil his compact, returned with his followers to Connaught. Richard Tyrrell attacked and wounded him on his march, slew many of his men, and liberated O'Sullivan More and other Munstermen Dermot was scarcely cured of his wounds when he was cut off in battle by Na-long. Na-long informed the Irish that he had done this on account of Dermot's base crime against Desmond, while to the English he gave his reason that Dermot had always been an enemy to the Queen.

William Burke disagreeing with the Earl as to his hire betook himself to his brother the Baron in Eliogarty. While the Catholics were unsettled and weakened by these domestic feuds, Carew bombarded with cannon and reduced Glin Castle, the fortress of the Knight of Glin. Desmond having only 600 men set off for Eliogarty and joined Raymond the Baron, and William, who had possessed themselves of a great part of that country. This expedition cost him little more than the loss of Maurice his illegitimate son, who fell fighting bravely. Afterwards, while suffering from fever and being nursed in hiding, he was betrayed by the White Knight to the English, by whom he was committed to the Tower of London, where he died Before his death, his rival the young Earl was recalled to England, having served the purpose. Fitzmaurice, Peter Lacy, and others fled to O'Neill. The rest submitted to the English and so the war in Munster was at an end.

— — —

CHAPTER IV.

O'NEILL'S RESOURCES ON THE WANE.

THE Ulstermen of O'Neill's party, whose countries had been the seat of war were now exhausted of their means and resources, and therefore quite unable to carry on the fight any longer. They begged and pressed O'Neill to allow them to make peace with the Queen through him. He praised them all for their constancy and fidelity to himself and their fight for the Catholic religion and country, but admitted that their complete destitution forced them to submit to the English. Magennis, O'Hanlon, and Ever MacMahon son of Julius, were received into favour by Blount, and he himself advancing as far as Armagh and Portmore placed garrisons in them He was prevented from advancing further by O'Neill, although his forces were weak enough, yet after Blount's return, O'Neill suddenly entered Armagh and carried off all the horses of its defenders.

CHAPTER V.

O'DONNELL'S RESOURCES GREATLY BROKEN DOWN.

O'DONNELL alone kept his forces intact until they were in great part destroyed on him in this way :—As he had preserved his country by successful battles on land, making Connaught the seat of war, a fleet was organised in England which, sailing between Scotland and Ireland, put into Lough Foyle in O'Donnell's country. In this fleet was no Irishman of standing except Maelmurray MacSweeny Tuath who had quarrelled with and deserted O'Donnell. He had fought against him at Ballaghboy on the day Clifford was slain and having distinguished himself by his valour in Leinster, had been knighted by Essex and had subsequently crossed to England.

However, on the night in which the English reached this port, he jumped overboard, swam ashore, and coming to O'Donnell begged his forgiveness on bended knees and got restored to all his possessions. The English, who were 4,000 under Henry Dowcra, a knight, landed and occupied the unfortified town of Derry, the famous episcopal seat of Saint Columba, overhanging the lough and fortified it with works and batteries. On the second day after their landing O'Donnell came up and carried off 168 of their horses and again the Catholics seized some horses grazing near the town, which the English pursued. A cavalry fight ensued. Hugh O'Donnell, surnamed Oge, wounded Dowcra, piercing his helmet with a spear and breaking his head. An English gentleman fired a pistol placed close up to Daniel O'Gallagher, an Irish gentleman, and though the bullet grazing the eye passed out through the nose, yet the powder burned out O'Gallagher's eye. Daniel wresting the pistol from the Englishman struck him with it on the head and knocked out his brains. The English were driven back into the town from whence they seldom afterwards ventured out. Therefore, O'Donnell leaving John O'Doherty, Chief of Innishowen, and Niall O'Donnell, surnamed Garve, his kinsman son of Con nephew of Calvagh, formerly chief, to manage the campaign against them, himself invaded Thomond and laid waste a great part of it and returned home safely. Meanwhile Dowcra's lieutenant having advanced out of Derry was killed in battle by O'Doherty. And now the English regretted having entered the Foyle, and not getting aid from any of the Irish, would soon undoubtedly have withdrawn, were it not that Art O'Neill, son of the chieftain Turlough, addressed himself to them, and by his offices Garve was also won over, because of a difference with O'Donnell as to the town of Lifford which O'Donnell had appropriated to himself although it had been given to Garve by his father, O'Donnell giving Garve, Castlefinn. The latter was also in hopes that if the English conquered he would be made O'Donnell and chief of his nation, as the English already began to style him and offered him other great inducements. And so when O'Donnell again set off into Thomond, Garve thinking it a good opportunity, went over to the English (on which he was deserted by his wife Nuala, sister of O'Donnell) and gave them up Lifford which had been entrusted to his charge The English placed a garrison of ten companies here. When O'Donnell heard this he abandoned his incursion into Thomond and pitched his tents not far from Lifford. Garve was a man of great spirit and daring, skilled in military matters and had many of the men of Tyrconnell on his side, fortified by whose aid and valour he did not decline a fight with the Catholics in the open. However he always retained the Catholic faith and kept aloof from heretical rites as did Art who soon died. There was frequent and sharp fighting between the royalists and the Catholics round Derry and Lifford We may mention a cavalry fight in which the royalists being routed, Manus, a brother of O'Donnell's, would have run through with his spear Garve as he retired, had not the blow been parried by Owen O'Gallagher, surnamed Oge, a comrade of Manus, but actuated by his devotion and affection for Niall's family who were their lords. Cornelius O'Gallagher was differently disposed to this family, and is said to have persuaded Garve to go over to the English, and who wounded Manus at Monin, near Lifford, where a cavalry fight was suddenly sprung on both parties and Manus charging into five Irish royalists was struck in the right side by a spear thrust from Garve and being surrounded was struck by Cornelius under the shoulder. However the points of the spears did not penetrate the cuirass but nevertheless reached the body of Manus. Roderic coming to his brother's rescue aimed his spear at Garve's breast. Garve tightening the reins raised his horse's head which received Roderic's blow by which the horse fell dead under Garve ; but he lifted up by his men, returned to Lifford when O'Donnell was coming up with the foot Manus died of his wounds within fifteen days and shortly after Cornelius was captured by O'Donnell and hanged.

On another day Roderick accompanied by two horsemen fell in with eight English foot soldiers who came out of Derry to gather wood, and attacking them, slew six, releasing one whom he captured but who said he was a Briton The eighth who was sergeant of a company, held out with great valour, being often struck by Roderick's spear and thrown down but again quickly getting up unwounded, as he was protected by a jerkin of oxhide, he attacked Roderick with drawn sword and got in sixteen thrusts on Roderick's right arm, which was, however, protected by the sleeves of the cuirass. When Roderic was unable to hurt his enemy with his spear, and he seemed likely to escape, the former attacked with his sword but this also was unable to penetrate the hide, whether owing to the toughness of the leather or to some spell, I do not know. Finally the sergeant tried to cross the nearest stream but as he was crossing Roderick struck him with his spear in the back and kept him down under the water until he was drowned.

Ships carrying provisions from Derry to Lifford were pursuing the even tenor of their way over the lough, when, near Lifford, where the lough narrows, they were attacked by the Catholics showering missiles on the boats from the banks. The garrison of Lifford coming out to the fight were driven back to the town and the boats, provisions and clothes were captured. Many of the royalists perished on this day Roderic was slightly wounded in the thigh by a bullet

About this time O'Connor, Chief of Sligo, being suspected by some persons of plotting mischief against O'Donnell, was imprisoned by the latter. O'Doherty ended his days (a great blow to O'Donnell) leaving his son, Cahir, a child, unable to manage affairs, so that O'Donnell inaugurated Felim O'Doherty chief of Innishowen Hugh, foster-father of Cahir, took offence at this, and he and his party deserted O'Donnell and gave up Castle Birt, the capital of Innishowen, to the English.

O'Donnell was now in great straits, having lost Derry, Lifford and Innishowen, and deprived of the aid of O'Connor, whom he kept in prison. Moreover the Connaughtmen whom he had hired became disaffected and mutinous. However he invaded Innishowen where Cahir's party had a great quantity of arms stored in Birt which was strongly defended by its natural position and by ancient fortifications. O'Donnell determined to assail this and the Cahirites decided to defend it. The Connaughtmen would not form the first line as ordered by O'Donnell. A company of Tyrconnellians placed in the van broke into the fortress but were not supported by the Connacians, and therefore this company, which was very inferior in number to the Cahirites, was overwhelmed with showers of bullets and being partly destroyed, escaped with difficulty from another portion of the fort Meantime Garve, burning with a great desire for the Chieftaincy of Tyrconnell, was by no means idle A man of bold spirit, and particularly well acquainted with the roads, he secretly conducted Irishmen of his faction and Englishmen over land and water from Lifford and surprised the monastery of Friars Minors called Donegal, and occupied it, and fortified and placed a garrison in the dismantled castle which stood an arrow-flight off, and in another monastery of Franciscans of the Third Order which is called Maherabeg, half a mile away, from which the monks fled and which up to that day had ever been regarded as sacred and inviolable sanctuaries By this move O'Donnell was forced to send his moveables and baggage into Sligo while himself and his army surrounding Donegal disputed with Garve during nearly three months the monastery and castle, now advancing mantlets to the walls, now setting up against them sows* and breastworks. But the royalists suffered for their violation of the monastery, for one night the powder, either by means of some one detailed by O'Donnell, or by accident, or providentially fired, suddenly burned up the monastery and partly blew it into the air. The defenders were partly consumed by the fire, and partly crushed by the falling roof and walls. O'Donnell

---

* See Appendix "Irish Arms."

thinking this a good opportunity, made an attack on the monastery. Garve, encouraging his men, forced some of them to take arms, others he could not get to overcome their terror, and they fled to Lifford in boats. The Catholics were slow to enter the monastery on account of the darkness of a very dark night, and fearing the fire which was not yet quenched might harm them if they were in the monastery, and being resisted by a few got together and encouraged by Garve. Meanwhile, Garve knowing that he had not enough of men to defend the walls of the burnt monastery by day and not losing his presence of mind, getting out alone by a secret passage, brought half a company from Maherabeg monastery into the burnt monastery now almost ungarrisoned. On this night about 1,000 royalists perished by sword, fire, water and falling debris, amongst whom was found Con O'Donnell, brother of Garve, buried under fallen stones. Of the Catholics only five or six were lost. O'Donnell continued the siege in the former fashion.

On the other side, Earl Clanrickarde by command of the Queen, made an incursion against O'Donnell and led the royalist forces against Elphin, an episcopal town. O'Donnell advanced to meet him. For some days there were cavalry and musketeer skirmishes and the Earl then returned without having effected anything

---

CHAPTER VI.

THE EMISSARIES SENT BY O'NEILL AND O'DONNELL INTO MUNSTER RETURN. ON EARL CLANRICKARDE AND DERMOT THE BISHOP.

WHILE O'Neill and O'Donnell were in these straits, they nevertheless sent over 1,000 men under Donough MacCarthy, claimant to the chieftaincy of Duhallow, Thady O'Rourke, and Raymond, Baron of Leitrim, to renew the war in Munster and assist Earl Desmond, whose forces were now shattered. However, while on the march, Donough was unfortunately killed by a leaden bullet fired by one of two musketeers who fired from ambush two shots, at the army as it passed, and it was rumoured that Desmond had been captured. Hereupon Thady and the Baron abandoned the journey to Munster. Earl Clanrickarde, to prevent their return, followed them closely with his forces, but they wheeled about and defeated him in the open plain and he died within fifteen days after.   As to his death two reports went out, some saying that he had died of a wound received in this battle, others asserting that he succumbed to disease. His son succeeded him.   The Catholics lost in these days, Thady O'Brien, son of Turlough, a youth of the highest nobility who fell fighting bravely for the Catholic faith.

Amongst the Catholics' misfortunes at this time must be accounted the death of a most upright and illustrious man, Dermot MacCarthy, Bishop of Cork and Cloyne, who had for more than 20 years laboured with great pains to preserve the faith in this Island and had displayed much zeal and energy during this war in animating the Catholics to take up arms for Christian piety   By his death the resources of Irishmen were not a little weakened.   For his services to the Church of God and realm of Ireland, his head was long vainly sought for by the English, who offered a large sum of money to whoever would slay or arrest him. With such insatiable hatred did they pursue him that they did not hesitate to destroy his kinsmen.   Amongst these they seized Thomas MacCarthy, the Bishop's nephew by his brother, Thomas, and endeavoured by threats and bribes to make him desert the Catholic faith.   Disappointed in this attempt they beheaded this man of noble and Catholic spirit.   But since we have alluded to the bishop, we must not omit mentioning this great and peculiar trait of his, that although he wrote with the greatest difficulty, and no one ever saw him write even one letter otherwise, nevertheless he turned out so accomplished and learned that he was advanced to Doctor *in utroque jure*, and publicly taught Sacred Theology at Louvain for some years, for such was his intellectual keenness and so strong his memory that even as a pupil he had no occasion to take notes.   He left to posterity a work on Christian doctrine written in Irish, whose precepts the youth still study in that Island.

CHAPTER VII.

ARRIVAL OF DON JUAN DE AQUILA IN IRELAND.

WHILST these events were taking place in Ireland, his Catholic Majesty, Philip III., solicitous to assist the Irish, raised such an efficient army as O'Neill and O'Donnell had asked for At the time when it was expected this army would have been transported to Ireland, the King's fleet was sent to the Azores to meet the English fleet said to be there, and to protect the ships bringing gold and silver from India By this delay the army destined for Ireland was in greater part broken up, the soldiers dying or deserting. The remainder set out under command of Juan Aquila, a Spanish gentleman, of military skill, who, in Armoric Gaul had displayed great valour against the French and English.

Having returned from the Azores, Diego Brochero, a noble Spanish gentleman, of the Order of St. John, and distinguished in the art of war on land and sea, took Aquila on board the King's fleet, which he commanded, and sailed for Ireland.

When he got out to sea a storm arose, and divided his fleet into two portions One portion, consisting of seven ships, followed the vessel of Peter Zubiaur, the second in command, and after drifting about some time on the ocean, was driven by the winds into Corunna, a town of Gallicia The other division, which was larger, followed the Admiral's flag, and in the month of September, 1601, reached Kinsale, a town of Munster, which overhangs a large and excellent harbour facing to the south Also overhanging the harbour are two forts, one on either side, and if these were fortified with cannon, access to the harbour could not easily be gained in opposition to them On one side rises a hill, artillery planted on which might easily either assail or defend the town. The river washing it on the west afforded a landing-place for the auxiliary force.

The townsmen, expelling the English garrison, conducted the Spanish general and his army (2,500 foot) into the town with great enthusiasm and open arms (as they say). Aquila, thinking he would not be long here, placed a single company as a garrison in Ringcurran, one of the two forts which commanded the harbour He took from the ships only one piece of artillery, as he had embarked the artillery assigned him in the ships under Zubiaur's command. Jealousies and disputes arose between him and his captains, and Matthew Oviedo, Archbishop of Dublin Daniel O'Sullivan, chieftain of Bear and Bantry, sent a messenger to Aquila to say he and his friends had 1,000 armed men and as many unarmed men enlisted, and that if Aquila would only supply arms for them they would block the Viceroy's road and prevent a siege until O'Neill and O'Donnell came to his assistance. Aquila replied (as O'Sullivan told me) that he had no supply of arms which were being brought by Zubiaur, and, moreover, he had no notion of enlisting more Munster men, pending advice from O'Neill and O'Donnell.

Blount, Viceroy of Ireland, was at this time in Athlone, where he had mobilised his forces, not ignorant that the Spaniards would make a descent on Ireland, as English spies had advised. Now making for Kinsale, with the Earl of Clanrickarde, the Anglo-Irish, the Irish Privy Council, and all the Queen's forces —amounting to 7,000 men—he surrounded and beseiged Aquila, and stormed Ringcurran without much difficulty. Placing cannon on the hill, he vigorously attacked Kinsale. The Earl of Thomond, who was at this time in England, was sent to Blount's assistance with 8,000 English recruits. The Queen's fleet occupying the harbour, battered the town on the other side with their cannon. The Spaniards, no way discouraged, bestirred themselves to defend the town with the cannon they had taken from their fleet and two others which were in the town. On one side they drove off the English ships from the attack, and on the other side attacked the enemy's camp and destroyed their tents. By day they fought stoutly and bravely on the walls, and by night made frequent sallies, slew the watches and sentinels and spiked the cannon. In this way more English than Spanish were killed, because the Spaniards are famous for the steadiness with which their infantry maintain their ranks. Charles MacCarthy, captain of an Irish company which had come from Spain, fell fighting bravely against the English, having first slain two English captains and spiked a cannon. At the commencement of the siege O'Sullivan, chieftain of Bear, had refused to answer the Viceroy's summons, alleging that he had to look after himself at home, to defend his country from neighbouring enemies, and he began a mock war which he got up with some of his followers.

CHAPTER VIII.

ZUBIAUR LANDS IN IRELAND AND SUCCESSFULLY ENCOUNTERS
THE QUEEN'S FLEET.

ZUBIAUR, with the seven ships laden with ammunition and supplies, soon followed Aquila, and was in some danger, drifting near the rocks of Castlehaven (Cuan an Caishlean, for fort and port have the same name in Ireland) At that time this place was in the possession of the brothers Donagh, Dermot, Cornelius, and Darius (*Dairine ?*) O'Driscoll, who pointed out the entrance to Zubiaur, and delivered to him the port, and Dermot, a shrewd man, not unskilled in Latin, gave him an account of the state of the kingdom. In a short time, the Queen's fleet, excellently equipped and superior in number of men, entered the harbour, and with impunity battered with their cannon the fort, which had no artillery, and also Zubiaur's ships, which were not adequately equipped for fight, but, were transports, somewhat tried by the voyage and now drawn up on shore The English seemed actually about to land themselves, but Zubiaur, being uncommonly well-informed of existing circumstances, and foreseeing the danger that threatened him, acted differently to Aquila, and sending letters to O'Sullivan, Chieftain of Bear, besought his assistance in the name of his Catholic Majesty. Within 24 hours after receipt of Zubiaur's letters, O'Sullivan and Dermot, my father, who were then at Bantry, five leagues distant from Castlehaven, arrived on the spot with 500 foot and a few horse of picked young men, at the very moment when the English were taking to the small boats in order to overwhelm the few Spaniards in a land battle. Thither also came O'Driscoll More, with his son, Cornelius and others, O'Donovan and gentlemen of the MacCarthy's. At their arrival the English were daunted and remained in their ships, and Zubiaur, elated and emboldened, took his cannon from the vessels and for two days right vigorously bombarded the English fleet. Finally, the balls rendered red hot by the rapid firing, pierced the English ships which they struck from stem to stern, hurling men and planks into the sea The admiral's ship especially, riddled with numerous cannon shots, was destroyed. Zubiaur's first shot into this ship killed 60 men, who, were seated at table, and under the succeeding shots, soldiers and sailors fell right and left. Upon this, soldiers flocked to its assistance from the other ships. At last this ship being nearly destroyed, the others, in confusion, cut their cables, abandoned their anchors, and took to flight when a favourable and light breeze arose, having, indeed, waited so long only because they had been forced to do so by contrary winds.

In this battle 575 English fell. Of the Catholics, one Spaniard, a kinsman of Zubiaur's, was killed, and two were wounded—one a Spaniard, the other an Irishman.

After this Dermot O'Sullivan, my father, conducted Vasco Sahavedra, a Spanish captain and his company to Dunboy, supplying them with provisions and beasts of burthen, and by O'Sullivan's order delivered to them the principal castle and the harbour of the Chieftaincy of Bear, and provided him with about two month's victuals. Thither also he caused to be transported in boats, which he sent therefor to Castlehaven, artillery, brazen balls, powder, lead, tow-match, and other ammunition, so that he might keep open for the Spanish fleet access to that harbour, which is a safe and much frequented one, and keep out the enemy therefrom. O'Driscoll also admitted a Spanish garrison into his harbour and fort for the good of the cause.

CHAPTER IX

THE CATHOLICS UNFORTUNATE AT KINSALE

O'DONNELL and his allies, O'Rourke, M'Dermot, MacSweeny Tuath, O'Kelly, Baron Raymond (*Burke*), his brothers Roderick and Caffrey (*O'Donnell*) Daniel, brother of O'Connor Sligo, and William Burke, brother of Baron Raymond. marched 3,000 men, of whom 400 were horse, to Aquila's assistance. Carew, the English President of the Munsters, hastened to meet them, leading 4,500 foot and 500 horse from the Viceroy's camp into Ormond's country, where he blocked up the passes and narrow roads. O'Donnell having lit large fires to present the appearance of a camp, led his army safely past Carew by night, and in different places for forty days awaited O'Neill's arrival. Carew, completely foiled in his object, marched his forces back to the Viceroy's camp before Kinsale.

O'Neill, finding an opportunity, invaded Meath, where he ravaged the English and Anglo-Irish far and wide, and returned home laden with booty, having slain Darcy of Platten, who had followed provoking a battle Thence he made for Kinsale in mid-winter. Accompanying him were M'Mahon, Cuconnacht, brother of Maguire, who had been killed in Cork, Ranald M'Donnell, chief of The Glens, Fitzmaurice, Baron of Lixnaw, Richard Tyrrell, and others of his retainers, amounting in all to 2,600 foot and 400 light armed horse. With these O'Neill joined O'Donnell in Orriria Barria (*Barry Oge's country?*), and both then pitched their camp in that part of Carbery which

is called Kinalmeaky. Thither came O'Sullivan Bear
bringing the forces of his own he had at Castlehaven, and
300 Spaniards he had got from Zubiaur, and which were
commanded by Alphonso Ocampo. Accompanying
O'Sullivan were O'Connor Kerry, Daniel, son of O'Sullivan
More ; Magnus (Manus ?) and Daniel MacSweeny, and other
gentlemen. Thence all advanced to Coolcarron Wood, and
pitching their camp a mile from the enemy, they fenced it
round with a ditch. Here, they kept the English in great
straits, hemmed in between themselves and the Spaniards
(*in Kinsale*) preventing corn and provisions from being
supplied to them from the towns and villages, or any
quarter, and cutting off such as came out of the
camp to forage. The English therefore, became more
cautious and timid in foraging, and did not venture to go
far, so that they might, when pressed, have a cover close at
hand, and when they met a slight rebuff or saw an enemy
in the distance they threw down their burthens and fled.
After this they lay still by day and foraged by night, but
eventually they did not venture to leave the camp for
foraging at all, and whatever provisions they had previously
got were now nearly all consumed. And so first want,
then hunger, and at last pestilence broke out amongst
them The Irish army had plenty of provisions The
Spaniards also had many days' supply of victuals which
they had themselves brought from Spain or the town
supplied, and they were safe from the enemy's attacks
in their own valour and the fortifications they had made.
The Munster magnates, who had so far favoured neither
side, now promised adherence to the Catholic cause and
defence of their country, and that they would come to the
rescue as quickly as possible The Irish regular soldiers
and auxiliaries, backed by whose valour the English were
holding their ground, promised O'Donnell through in-
termediaries, that they would go over to him within three
days, and they had commenced to fulfil their promise,
deserting the English in two's, three's and ten's. Now,
if the desertion of all had been waited for, it would have
been all up with the English, for out of 15,000 men, whom
they had at the beginning of the siege, 8,000 had perished by
the sword, hunger, cold, and disease, and of those remaining
the greatest part were raw recruits lately sent from England,
and unequal to trials and difficulties. Of the remainder,
scarcely 2,000 were English, the others being Irish and
Anglo-Irish. The Viceroy, alarmed at this danger, determined to raise the siege, and retreat to Cork, and at

K

least defend the walls. In this manner the Catholics might
have obtained a victory without a struggle or any loss
but our sins stood in the way of this consummation

In the first place, Aquila sent many letters again and
again, urgently pressing O'Neill to form a junction with
him.   O'Neill, O'Sullivan, and others thought this risk
ought not to be run, but that they should rather await the
coming over of the Irish and the flight of the enemy.
O'Donnell and several others were of a different opinion,
and so the majority in numbers overruled the more prudent.
A day was appointed, on dawn of which O'Neill was to draw
up near the enemy's camp, so that Aquila, making a sortie
from the other side, should unite with him.   Aquila's
letters to O'Neill on this arrangement were intercepted by
the Vceroy.   O'Neill, with his forces arranged in three
columns, set out for the place agreed on.   The English,
who were well aware of the Catholics' plan, went by night
to the spot whither O'Neill was to proceed, and feigned a
battle with beat of drum and sound of trumpet and report of
musketry.   Aquila's scouts are said to have informed him
that this was a mock fight.   O'Donnell with his column
wandered about all night owing to his guides' ignorance
of the route, and was far off   The columns of O'Neill and
O'Sullivan, hearing the sound of fighting, and thinking
Aquila had advanced to the appointed spot, quickened their
pace, and arrived there at night.   Thereupon the enemy
retired behind their fortifications, and when the camp was
seen perfectly quiet and silent, the Irish perceived the
stratagem, and after waiting a little under arms, and it
being now daybreak, they advanced a little beyond the
appointed place, and the front of O'Sullivan's column,
which was in the van, halted not far from the trenches,
although not seen by the enemy, as a low hill cut off their
range of vision.

When it was quite lightsome, O'Neill, wondering why
Aquila did not come out, nor give the signal for battle,
went up to the top of the hill with O'Sullivan, the Spanish
captains and a few others, and closely examined the enemy's
came   It was very strongly fortified with a trench, ditch,
towers and cannon ; the soldiers were under arms, and the
horses were bridled.   Moreover, they were   superior in
numbers to the Irish, many of whom, especially Munstermen, were absent, having on the previous day left the
colours to forage and get corn.   O'Donnell with the third
column had not arrived.   In this state of things O'Neill,
according to the captains' advice, putting off the enterprise

to another time, ordered the divisions to retreat These, having retreated half a mile, met O'Donnell, and at the same instant the Viceroy's cavalry turned up. O'Donnell with his cavalry attacked these after they had crossed the ford of the adjacent stream, and drove them back over the same ford The Viceroy's cavalry returning, again tried to cross the ford O'Donnell, thinking he could easily destroy them between himself and the ford, gave ground a little, in doing which some of his own horse, turning about either by accident or somebody's contriving and treachery, bore down on O'Donnell's own division, and forced the foot to open their ranks The disordered foot took to flight. O'Neill's division did the same, and likewise O'Sullivan's, although the enemy were not pressing, and the chiefs vainly recalling them.

Thus all were panic-stricken, or, rather, scattered by Divine vengeance. The royalist cavalry did not venture to pursue the fugitives, fearing they might be drawn into a snare. Many Irish gentlemen who had adhered to the English, vainly reassured the Catholics, coaxing them to return to the fight, and promising themselves to help them. O'Neill and O'Donnell could not recall their men to the fight O'Sullivan, Tyrrell, the Spanish captains, and a few who returned in part, withstood the enemy's attack. On this day, of O'Neill's army, 200 foot perished. Of the English, three noblemen fell. The Earl of Clanrickarde was for his valour dubbed a knight by the Viceroy.

CHAPTER X.

O'NEILL RETURNS TO ULSTER · O'DONNELL SAILS FOR SPAIN : AQUILA FOLLOWS.

O'NEILL, who, after the loss he had sustained, was no weaker, wished to continue the war against the enemy in the old way, but he was wholly unable to get his followers to agree to this For O'Rorke returned to defend his country against his brother, Thady O'Rorke, whom he had left in Breiffny, and whom he had heard was now disposed to possess himself of the chieftaincy Ranald followed suit, and others were influenced by their example, and forced O'Neill also to retire, much against his will. O'Donnell, delegating his authority to his brother Roderick, set out for Spain with Raymond the Baron, and a few others, to seek assistance.

O'Sullivan, collecting his own Munstermen and the Spaniards received from Zubiaur, and taking into his pay Richard Tyrrell and William Burke, resolved to cut off the English supplies, and force them to raise the siege, and abandon their camp. He wrote to Aquila not to lose courage or be dispirited, and not to surrender the town, but Aquila struck a bargain with the enemy, whereby he and his army and all their effects were at liberty to return to Spain, and the town was not to be surrendered until the Viceroy had provided ships and sailors, and Aquila had sailed, giving pledges for return of the ships. And so Aquila returned, having lost in this expedition 500 foot, and the English in the whole siege of Kinsale having lost more than 8,000, who perished by the sword, hunger, cold and pestilence. O'Neill and Roderick, brother of O'Donnell, having left the Munsters, parted from each other on the road, and O'Neill arrived in Tyrone.

CHAPTER XI.

RODERICK (O'DONNELL) RECONCILED TO THE QUEEN.

As Roderic was passing by Lough Sewdy, a town in Meath, the town artisans and English mechanics, and Anglo-Irish garrison, thought they would do a brave feat and prove their loyalty by pursuing him and so they rashly engaged in battle armed, some with staves, some with swords, some with spears, but at the first onset of Roderic's cavalry they quickly turned tail. The garrison endeavoured to rally the fugitives, but being surrounded by the cavalry, about 200 of them were cut off, scarcely enough to tell the tale escaping the slaughter. Roderick, having returned home, suffered for some months from dysentery. Meanwhile the royalists made expeditions by land and water from Donegal, and without opposition besieged and battered with cannon Ballyshannon fort. Tuathal O'Gallagher, who held the fort with 56 Irish and 4 Spaniards, made a brave and protracted defence to maintain the walls and when these were broken down fled with his men by night, leaving only one sick man, Owen O'Dwyer, who on the following day, as the royalists entered, killed one of them with a gunshot and brandished his spear until promised quarter, but the enemy treated him with the faith of the English religion, and having taken his arms from him put him to death with the women and boys, in number 300 Oliver Lambert, an English knight and Governor of Connaught, set out to establish a garrison in Sligo. Roderick, who was now well again, routed him in a battle in the Curlew mountains, and slew many in the pursuit to Boyle, whither they retired, and as they proceeded thence to Roscommon with the cavalry and musketeers, one behind each horseman, Roderick overtook and cut off many of them Oliver was again prevented marching to Sligo by Roderick and O'Connor Sligo whom Roderick had set at liberty, and who successfully fought Lambert not far from Boyle However although unable to reach Sligo by land, the English occupied it by sea. Seven companies of Englishmen under Leonard Guest, a knight, unexpectedly landed there, and quickly fortified the place Roderick ordered the adjoining crops to be cut down The English sallied out to prevent this and Roderick came to support the reapers A battle ensued in which 300 English were laid low and the rest fled to their fortifications.

Although the English abhorred the titles and names of Irish chiefs and had often issued proclamations to abolish them, nevertheless they were sometimes content to create chiefs in order that they might ruin one another. Thus Richard Burke, the son of Deamhan-an-chorrain, was made The MacWilliam by the royalists, and cut off in battle by Roderick. Meantime an army was being assembled in Spain to be sent into Ireland with O'Donnell, but he most unfortunately died, and on hearing of his death Roderic's comrades were filled with grief and despair of any aid from Spain. MacSweeny Banagh joined Garve. Tuath took his own course. Roderic, exhausted of powder and other ammunition, made peace with the Queen, and so did O'Connor Sligo and others Garve had himself inaugurated O'Donnell by O'Ferrall, and for so doing was imprisoned in Derry by the English, who hate the Irish titles and wished to abolish such inaugurations. Garve escaped to a thick wood where he assembled his forces and party. Roderic and Dowcra, joining their forces, stripped him of his goods and shattered his resources. Hence it came to pass that of his party 4,000 men women and children died of famine, and himself reduced to poverty fled into England less valued now by the English than Roderic

CHAPTER XII.

O'NEILL ACCEPTS TERMS OF PEACE.

AFTER the return of the Spaniards, Blount recruited the remains of his army during the winter and sent Samuel Bagnal to provision the garrison of Armagh. O'Neill with 1,000 men attacked him and his 15 companies and 3 troop of horse at Mullaghcros. First the cavalry, then the musketeers, and finally the pike-men of both sides rushed into the fight Samuel came to the rescue, but he lost 700 men and O'Neill about 70.

In the following spring Blount moved his forces, increased by Anglo-Irish auxiliaries, into Tyrone He began to rebuild the fort of Portmore, calling it Charlemount after his own name O'Neill, by some successful skirmishes, prevented him advancing further. However, O'Neill learning of O'Donnell's death, and now deserted by his own clansmen, was reduced to want and despair. Accompanied, therefore, by only 400 men, he concealed himself in the thickly wooded valley of Glenconkeine, and there endeavoured to defend himself The enemy burned his towns and cut down his crops. Con and Henry O'Neill, sons of the Chieftain Shane, assisted the English and acted as guides for them and many of the Tyrone men followed suit. The powder and ammunition placed in a strong fort and entrusted for safe keeping to Patrick O'Donnelly, was put upon pack-horses and carried off to the English At this time—it being now the year 1603—Elizabeth, Queen of England, died

On her death bed the English Council had obtained authority to make a treaty with O'Neill, and he, although he had by two successful skirmishes, prevented the English entering the valley, nevertheless being exhausted of his resources , his ammunition gone , and himself surrounded on all sides, without any hope of aid ; and ignorant of the Queen's death, accepted terms of peace

O'Rourke still preserved his country and stood out against the English and was joined by MacWilliam. Con Maguire was set up as The Maguire against his kinsman Maguire, by the royalists, and was called by the Irish the English Maguire. He seduced Maguire's followers and mercenaries, so that the royalists got possession of Fermanagh and Maguire was driven to O'Rourke. Mac-Geoghegan also held out.

TOME III. BOOK VII.

OF

DON PHILIP O'SULLEVAN OF BEAR IN IRELAND.

THE FIFTEEN YEARS' WAR.

WE have seen nearly the last of the affairs of Ulster, Leinster, and Connaught. Now the extremely bitter and vigorous struggle in the Munsters under O'Sullivan, Chief of Bear, challenge our attention as strange and astonishing, both in the vicissitudes and hardships of the toils of war.

CHAPTER I.

O'SULLIVAN'S ASSOCIATES AND RESOURCES, AND WHAT HE DID IN THE BEGINNING OF WINTER.

AFTER Aquila's treaty, O'Sullivan sent into Spain, to beg speedy assistance, Dermot O'Driscoll, a man of tried fidelity and prudence, and his eldest son, Daniel as a pledge of and hostage for, his father's fidelity. With these went other noble youths and myself, then a boy, and we were most graciously received by Count Carazena, Governor of Gallicia, a distinguished man of ancient and noble lineage, and very much attached to the Irish people. There I learned grammar and humanities and skill in Latin from Patrick Synott (Patric oig Sinot), one of my own countrymen ; Philosophy from Roderic Vendanna, a Spaniard of keenest intellect ; and other subjects from other masters.

Meantime, O'Sullivan thought by every plan and device to defend himself against the enemy's attack until assistance would come to him from Spain. To his aid came Daniel MacCarthy, son of the Chief of Clancarthy ; Daniel, son of O'Sullivan More, Cornelius and Dermot, sons of O'Driscoll More, Dermot O'Sullivan, my father; Dermot, the two Donoghs, and Florence, of the MacCarthy Reaghs; gentlemen of the MacSweenys; and Donogh O'Driscoll, with his brothers.

To him fled O'Connor Kerry; Fitzmaurice, Baron of Lixnaw; the Knight of Kerry; the Knight of Glin; and John Fitzgerald, brother of the Earl (*of Desmond*), and James Butler, brother of the Baron Cahir, both of whom in the previous war had been dispossessed of their belongings O'Sullivan having also enlisted William Burke, Richard Tyrrell, and other mercenaries for pay, had, with his allies, about 2,000 picked young men With these in this winter he possessed himself of Carriganass Castle (Carraig an neasaig), which was the only castle in Bantry held by Owen O'Sullivan, who had always adhered to the Queen's side, reducing it partly by raising a rampart, partly by towers, mantlets, sows and gabions, and partly battering it with brass cannon. He ravaged the countries of O'Donovan who had gone over to the English, and other helpers of the English. He drove the Queen's Munster forces, terror-stricken, into fortified towns and castles.

CHAPTER II.

PREPARATIONS AND STRENGTH OF THE ROYALISTS—CAREW'S FIRST EXPEDITION—DEATH OF MACCARTHY

THE English were much distressed and uneasy at these achievements and determined to direct against O'Sullivan the greatest force they could command

George Carew, president of the Munsters, summoned the Royalist forces to Cork and called up the Irish auxiliaries. He had with him some Anglo-Irish, the levies of Ormond's county, auxiliaries sent by divers persons, and the following Munster magnates without whom he could have done little to hurt O'Sullivan—namely, Donogh O'Brien, formerly chief of Limerick and Earl of Thomond; MacCarthy Reagh, chief of Carbery, Charles MacCarthy, chief of Muskerry, Barry More, Viscount Buttevant, O'Donovan, the White Knight, Owen O'Sullivan, who, although a kinsman of O'Sullivan's, was his bitterest enemy, Dermot, brother of O'Sullivan More; Donogh and Florence, brothers of MacCarthy, and who had deserted O'Sullivan. The whole army contained more than 4,000 men, of whom scarcely 500 were English.

The rest were Irish and Anglo-Irish who in the existing desperate circumstances, thought it would be very unsafe and dangerous for them to disown the Queen.

With these forces, Carew, setting out from Cork in the month of March, 1602, unexpectedly arrived in Bantry ; threw a garrison of eight companies into Whiddy Island, by means of ships and boats which he had sent round before-hand , and quickly returned again to Cork. In Whiddy the Royalists fortified themselves behind a ditch and trench. O'Sullivan getting together shipping, resolved to attack this garrison Meantime, the Royalists having remained two months in the island, cut off from assistance by O'Sullivan, and filled with alarm, abandoned the island, and under the guidance of Owen O'Sullivan, took the road to Cork.

O'Sullivan pursued and captured the baggage, but killed only a few, because the fugitives were met near Bantry by Carew and his whole army coming to their rescue. Dermot MacCarthy was ravaging the lands of the English abettors in Carbery, when, as he was driving off the prey, he met his kinsman, MacCarthy Reagh, accompanied by a few men, and having embraced one another in all friendliness they parted. Reagh having assembled a larger band of soldiers again sought out Dermot, and fired on him at a distance. Dermot, a man unsullied by crime, restraining both parties from fighting, and calling on Reagh by name, was shot by a dastardly trooper, leaving to O'Sullivan a sad loss.

CHAPTER III.

CAREW'S SECOND EXPEDITION—DESTRUCTION OF DUNBOY AND DURSEY ISLAND—MARTYRDOM OF DOMINICK O'CALLAN

(*Collins.*)

CAREW, having increased his forces to over 5,000 men, again resolved to crush all O'Sullivan's resources, and, entering Bantry, encamped in the open plain at Gurteenroe, purposing to penetrate from thence to Bear and attack Dunboy fort and other castles of O'Sullivan's O'Sullivan, occupying the road, pitched his tents half-a-mile from the enemy. He was very inferior in point of numbers, but, backed by valour and the favourable nature of the ground, he warded off the enemy's advances, and cut off supplies. Carew, fortifying himself with a ditch and trench, kept his men for two months within the bounds of their camp, until there arrived off the adjoining coast eighteen ships of war and transports, and other small vessels sent from Waterford, Cork, and England, in which he embarked his army and landed it near Dunboy to besiege the castle. This was now held by 120 foot, placed there by O'Sullivan, under command of Richard MacGeoghegan, an illustrious hero. This garrison, sallying out, fought valiantly against the enemy before the walls, and, for a long time, prevented an assault on the castle, and when they were driven behind the fortifications, they stoutly defended themselves from the battlements, windows, and towers. Carew attempted to carry the castle by main force with his cannon, but was worsted in this by the besieged making sorties and hurling missiles from the fortifications. Thereupon, he drew a ditch two cubits higher than a man round the castle, and ran a transverse rampart in the teeth of sharp opposition from the besieged, who kept interrupting the work   Into the trenches, when not exposed to the towers of the fort, he brought five cannon, which he placed on the transverse ditch, and therewith incontinently battered the castle. Meantime, the besieged made frequent sallies, endeavouring to drive off the enemy from the assault, engaging in hand to hand skirmishes, and at longer range, firing from the fortifications red-hot balls from muskets and cannons. But, now, from the continuous cannonading, the walls were shaken, and the fabric of the castle was collapsing. A large part fell in and another portion following, tumbled down   The royalist army made an assault on the castle through the breach, and, after great slaughter on both sides, the besieged withstood the attack. The royalists again set themselves to destroy the castle at long range with their cannon and with their muskets to drive the defenders from the walls and towers   An immense piece of the works tumbled in ruins, carrying with it the men, and burying the soldiers under the falling stones.   The royalists rushed in through the breach; the besieged overwhelmed them with shot and stones, ran them through with pikes, slew them with swords, advanced barriers, rolled up stones, and drove them headlong out again through the breach and repelled all attack. Hitherto, the royalists had cannonaded the fortifications from a distance, but now they safely advanced their artillery, the works being sufficiently ruined, and the besieged, falling on all sides, could not defend the breach.   The assailants rushed through it and into the great hall, up to which the fort was destroyed, and occupied half of it with three companies. There the besieged rallying, a bloody conflict ensued.   Many wounds having been inflicted on both sides, and many lives having been lost, the royalists were forced to turn tail and quit the hall and every part of the ruin.   The enemy, carrying off their wounded, again made an attack, in which fresh and active men engaged the wearied and wounded, and large numbers attacked few.   The breach was first contested.   The defenders being beaten from this, seven companies carried their colours into the hall, which was not large enough for them, as they could not deploy in it.   The fight was long protracted there , many fell under wounds on both sides.   There lay a great heap of bodies and arms, the whole hall ran streams of blood. Far the greatest part of the defenders fell, especially the Captain,   Richard,   whose   high   spirit   was defending the chieftaincy with the valour of his race. Fighting with the utmost vigour, he fell amongst the corpses, covered with many deadly wounds and half dead   Of the rest none were unwounded   The survivors, abandoning the hall,   were forced to betake themselves to the basements. There they fought strenuously, as well in valour as in despair, which is oftentimes a great incitement to die bravely. They prevailed so far as to deprive the enemy first of the hall and then of the whole castle.   Thereupon night put an end to the struggle.   On the next day the Royalists sought to finish the business by treaty   The defenders, seeing the greater part of the castle tumbled and destroyed, their leader lost, themselves exhausted with wounds, and wearied with various trials, stipulating that they be dismissed in safety, surrendered the fort in the month of September on the fifteenth day of the siege.

After the Royalists had entered the fort, Richard, who was still alive, when he heard the voice of the English, recalled his fading spirit, and tried to set fire to the gunpowder, of which there was no mean store in the fort, and undoubtedly he would have blown up the enemy were it not that before he accomplished his object life failed him. The treaty and compact was kept with English scrupulosity, for men and women were hanged.   All are not agreed as to the numbers of the assailants who perished , some say 600 , some say less, others more.

During the days on which the castle of Dunboy was being attacked, Owen O'Sullivan and John Bostock, an Englishman, sailed over to the Island of Dursey, in which was a monastery, built by Bonaventura, a Spanish Bishop, but dismantled by pirates, a church dedicated to Saint Michael the Archangel, and a fort built by my father, Dermot, which was garrisoned by a few of Cornelius O'Driscoll's men. The inhabitants were terrified by the sudden arrival of the enemy, some sought the protection of the altars, some ran to hide, some betook themselves to the fort, which the few armed men surrendered on the enemy's promise of safety, as it had no cannon or fortifications. The English, after their wonted manner, committed a crime far more notable for its cruelty than their honour. Having dismantled the fort and fired the church and houses, they shot down, hacked with swords, or ran through with spears the now disarmed garrison and others, old men, women, and children, whom they had driven into one heap. Some ran their swords up to the hilt through the babe and mother, who was carrying it on her breast, others paraded before their comrades little children, writhing and convulsed, on their spears, and, finally, binding all the survivors, they threw them into the sea over jagged and sharp rocks, showering on them shots and stones. In this way perished about 300 Catholics, the greater part of whom were mercenaries of my father, Dermot.

Having acomplished these feats, the Royalists sailed from Bear and returned to Cork, carrying off Dominick O'Colan (*Collins*), a lay brother of the holy Society of Jesus, who had been sent by the garrison of Dunboy as a messenger to those in the island. He was in vain tempted by the Protestant clergy with cunning arguments, and offers of great rewards, especially ecclesiastical dignities, to desert Christ's religion and profess the Anglican doctrines. Spurning these, he was dragged at the tails of horses, hanged with a halter, and, his breast being cut open with sharp knives, he rendered his soul to God in the year 1602, on the last day of October.

In his youth he had served as a cavalier in campaigns in France under King Henry IV. Converted to a better use of life, he dedicated himself in religion. He was born of citizens of the town of Youghal in Ireland.

CHAPTER IV.

DERMOT O'DRISCOLL RETURNS FROM SPAIN—CORNELIUS IS SENT THITHER.—O'SULLIVAN CAPTURES SOME OF THE ROYALISTS' CASTLES.

DURING the days in which these disasters befell O'Sullivan, Dermot O'Driscoll returned from Spain and brought O'Sullivan from his Catholic Majesty 20,000 gold pieces to pay his soldiers, and letters promising assistance and ammunition. But after the loss of the castle, O'Sullivan sent Cornelius O'Driscoll, son of O'Driscoll More, to Spain to press for speedier succour. Meantime, he himself, no way dispirited, led into Muskerry, towards Cork City, 1,000 men, and reduced into his power two forts, Carrigna-curra and Dundareirke, setting up against them gabions and sows. He forced the inhabitants who surrendered to join him in rebellion, and compelled O'Donoghue of the Glens, whom he had captured, to surrender the castle of Macroom and join the confederacy. Whilst he tarried at Macroom, south of the river Lee, Charles Wilmot and Samuel Bagnal, with 2,000 men, crossing this river from the north to the same side as O'Sullivan, halted at Carrigadrohid, not further than one league from the fort. On these days a great storm suddenly arose, and so unusually swollen were the waters that they carried away the bridges, so that it seemed improbable the royalists would venture to recross the river. O'Sullivan seized this opportunity, and, leaving a garrison at Macroom, swam across the river with his forces and wading the River Laney (?), whose waters came over the men's shoulders, he ravaged Cork country far and wide, and drove off a great booty to Bear. After his return the royalists advanced from Carrigadrohid to Macroom, and besieged the castle. The garrison fired the buildings round the fort lest they should afford a vantage point to the besiegers. The fire spread from these buildings to the fort, so that it could not be in any way saved. From the fort itself, thirty soldiers who garrisoned it, fled (as usually happens in misfortune) from fire to sword, and, bursting through the midst of the serried ranks of the enemy, happily escaped wholly unhurt through the clouds of smoke, their agility, the nearness of the wood, and their own valour.

CHAPTER V.

PERILOUS FLIGHT OF THE CHIEF OF MUSKERRY, O'SULLIVAN
STORMS A FORTIFIED CASTLE, AND OTHER MATTERS.

AT this time Donogh and Florence, brother of MacCarthy, shifted their dislike from O'Sullivan to the English. The sons of Thady MacCarthy likewise went over to him, but these having got some of the Spanish money, again went over to the English, denouncing Charles MacCarthy, Chief of Muskerry, as secretly friendly to and treating with O'Sullivan. Whereupon Charles was imprisoned in Cork and in danger of his life.

Owen MacSweeny, a youth in years, but in courage more than manly, and six other followers, resolved to rescue him, and for their master's sake to peril themselves. Owen, getting into Charles's cell by night, as if on some other business, cut with a file the leg fetters and freed the feet from one another, and enabled him to escape through the window.

Holding out before the gates a lighted lamp, Owen gave his six comrades the signal to approach and catch Charles as he jumped down. But as Charles was long hesitating and afraid to throw himself from so high a window, Owen threw him out and himself escaped safely another way. The six confederates caught Charles unhurt in the air, and before he touched ground in a cloak spread out for the purpose, and stealthily made for the town walls. The fugitive's fetters, striking some stones roused the guards, who pursued with a mob of the neighbours, and now there was uproar throughout the whole city and calls to arms. Lamps and torches flared up in the streets and windows of the houses. Meantime, two of Charles's six men halted, and, with drawn swords, for a short time withstood the attack of the pursuers. Of the other four, two jumping down from the wall, caught Charles, let down by the other two, and the remaining four, leaping from the high walls, and all six carrying Charles over the fords of the river Lee, surrounding the town, escaped partly by swimming and partly by wading. Charles mounting a horse which had been in readiness on the bank of the river, fled to O'Sullivan.

O'Sullivan, learning of this event from general flying rumours, hastened with half of his army to meet the fugitive in Muskerry. There Charles, striking a bargain with O'Sullivan, promised that his affection and assistance would henceforth be given him. On his way, O'Sullivan thought to try whether Carrigaphooca, which was held by Thady MacCarthy's sons, could be reduced and injuries inflicted by them avenged The fort was strong in its natural situation and difficult to storm In the first place, there was no passage for cannon, situated as it was, amongst the mountains and woods, nor could it be undermined, as it was built on a rather cut-away and steep rock, and surrounded by a double stone wall, one near the base, two cubits higher than a man, the other higher still, near the top, and from the lower to the higher wall, the ascent was by a narrow and steep path. However, 500 marksmen, posted by O'Sullivan showering bullets on the windows, towers and battlements of the castle drove back the defenders and rendered them powerless Things went hard against the terrified besieged, and a great panic seized all hearts Some burst their muskets when firing, others accidentally burnt themselves with the powder. Meantime, pikemen sent by O'Sullivan having burnt the gates of the first wall, unexpectedly climbed the rock to the second wall, and partly burnt and partly burst in the doors And now the fort began to totter when the besieged terror-stricken surrendered, and, being disarmed, were sent away as agreed, the castle being dismantled. Herein were found the Spanish gold which Thady's sons had got from O'Sullivan, and various other treasures, deposited for safe-keeping by the neighbours.

This and the other two forts of Carrignacurra and Dundareirke, which were in the chieftaincy of Muskerry. O'Sullivan handed over to Charles to be garrisoned by him. O'Sullivan himself ravaged the Cork Country to the town's suburbs and, distributing his soldiers in winter quarters amongst the villages and killing the Protestant officers of justice, he returned to Bear laden with booty. At this time, Charles Wilmot held Dunkerron Castle with a garrison of 1,000 men, and three captains, and other English and Anglo-Irish of birth and considerable military rank coming to him from Askeaton were intercepted and annihilated by Daniel, son of O'Sullivan More.

CHAPTER VI.

O'SULLIVAN DESERTED BY HIS OWN IS DRIVEN FROM BEAR

IN the heat of this war word of O'Donnell's death was brought to Ireland, whereupon those who were following O'Sullivan lost hope of Spanish aid and became dispirited. First of all Charles (*MacCarthy*) deserted, with the three castles which he had received from O'Sullivan and the rest of the chieftaincy of Muskerry. Daniel MacCarthy the Knight of Kerry, Daniel O'Sullivan, and others sought favour from the English. Tyrrell with his troops, of which he was commander, betook himself to Connaught. By these defections the English were emboldened, and, assembling the Munster magnates, the Anglo-Irish, and all the royalist forces, they got together about 5,000 men of whom scarcely 500 were English. Charles Wilmot an Englishman, was made governor of Bear, and marched this army to Glengariff, where O'Sullivan then was, and pitched his camp at Gortnakilly, and issued a proclamation in which pardon was promised in the Queen's name to all deserting O'Sullivan. O'Sullivan reduced to a few armed men, fought with the enemy continuously for four days, in which time he was being daily more and more deserted by his followers, so that he had left few more than 300, of whom by far the greatest number were Connaught men. And now the Connaught-men with one accord quitted the camp and watches at night, and took themselves off to Connaught. O'Sullivan, O'Connor, Dermot O'Sullivan (my father), William Burke, and other nobles followed them, accompanied by a few men, and with them fled more than 200, whom they could not prevent as they preferred flight to falling unprotected into the hands of the enemy. Thus O'Sullivan was driven out of Glengariff with the loss of scarcely fifteen men, whilst in these four days 300 of the enemy perished by the sword, cold, or sickness. The royalists laid waste all Bear, replete as it was with divers riches, and received the surrender of the castles of Ardee and Carriganass. O'Sullivan's wife, Johanna Sweeny, my mother, and other gentlewomen concealed themselves in the gorges and the tops of the mountains.

CHAPTER VII.

THE MEN OF CARBERY AND THE ROYALISTS ENCOUNTER WITH
LOSS ON BOTH SIDES ; TWO PRIESTS KILLED ; FITZMAURICE
RECOVERS HIS COUNTRY.

AT this time the two Donoghs and Florence MacCarthy;
Dermot, son of O'Driscol; Thady, son of O'Mahony, Carbery;
Maur, and other gentlemen of the MacSweenys were in
Carbery, and against them came towards Cork, Maurice
Fitzgerald, the White Knight, Taaffe, an Anglo-Irish Captain
of a troop of horse, the infantry of Muskerry and Fermoy,
and some English, in all about 400. The former were
inferior in point of numbers. They encountered at Clodagh
wood, with little success on either side. On the first day,
Thady, charging the Muskerry infantry, killed 14, and
put the rest to flight. On the next day also, MacCarthy's
foot, Dermot and the MacSweenys, attacking a crowd of
the enemy's infantry, slew about forty of them. At the
same time the others of MacCarthy's foot, scattered about,
were surrounded by the royalist cavalry, and twenty of
them cut off, and the rest routed. The White Knight
pressed eagerly on the rear of the fugitives, and, having
followed Thady O'Crowley, surnamed Furiosus (?), into
ground unsuitable for horse, he dismounted, and, attacking
with his sword, was deprived by Furiosus (?) of two fingers
of his left hand, his signet ring, ear, and horse. During
this confusion, Owen MacEgan, a priest of most spotless
and innocent life, who had lately returned from Rome,
honoured with the degree of Doctor in Sacred Theology,
and appointed by the Pope, Bishop of Ross, was struck
down with a sword blow, and mortally wounded by the
Royalists, even clad as he was, in his holy vestments, and
carrying in his hands his spiritual weapons—the Breviary
in one hand, the Rosary in the other. To those friends
who murmured and mourned him as slain by the royalists,
he said : "To me these unhappy people have brought
life ; for themselves they have earned death." When
he breathed forth his soul, a bright halo is said to have appeared over his mouth and face. Dermot MacCarthy,
surnamed Roe, a priest and son of Conald, was captured
and carried off to Cork by the royalists, as, prompted by
piety, he went around absolving from their sins in their

L

last moment the soldiers of both parties lying wounded on the battle field. There, after he had spurned the Protestant bribes, he was dragged through the streets at horses' tails, hung with a halter, cut down half alive and his intestines torn out, which were exposed by the English in public places, a sad spectacle to the Catholics.

After this encounter the MacCarthys and their comrades, as soon as they heard that O'Sullivan was driven off, owned allegiance to the Queen, except Thady O'Mahony, who, being captured by treachery, was put to death. Fitzmaurice, accompanied by a few comrades, fled from the pursuing royalists through Slieve Lougher, and, inflicting loss on the English, with some difficulty obtained pardon and restoration of his barony. And thus the war in Munster was ended

---

CHAPTER VIII.

O'SULLIVAN'S VARIOUS ACTIONS AND ALMOST DAILY BATTLES DURING THE FIRST SEVEN DAYS OF HIS FLIGHT.

Now let us see the fortunes and perils and trials which O'Sullivan suffered in his flight from the hands of the enemy. He had to accomplish a long journey of about 100 leagues ; the winter weather was most unsuitable therefor. His soldiers little exceeded 400 in number, of whom thirteen were cavalry, the others infantry, pikemen, musketeers, and a few targets. He had a large crowd of women and sutlers. All the roads were beset with enemies, and a large sum of money was promised to whoever would slay him. Hence it came to pass that he endured almost incredible toils and faced tremendous risks. I will briefly relate these circumstances in their order.

On the 31st December, in the year of our Redeemer's birth, 1602, O'Sullivan set out from Glengariff, and at night pitched his tents twenty-six miles away in Muskerry country, at a place which the natives call Augeris.

On the next day, the 1st of January, 1603, starting off in the early morning, he reached, before midday, the populous village of Ballyvourney, dedicated to Saint Gobnata.

There the soldiers paid such vows as each one list, gave vent to unaccustomed prayers, and made offerings, beseeching the saint for a happy journey. Advancing thence they were pursued by the sons of Thady MacCarthy with a band of natives, harassing their rear ranks with missiles, and again and again returning to the skirmish after being driven off by O'Sullivan's wings of marksmen. Four hours were spent in continual fighting of this kind, and some on both sides were wounded. At last O'Sullivan, by making an attack with his whole column and killing some, put the enemy to flight. Covering twenty-four miles in that day, he pitched his tents at nightfall in O'Keeffe's country. Sentinels being posted, the soldiers abandoned their way-worn limbs to rest, but the natives annoyed them throughout the whole night rather by yelling than hurting Hunger also greatly weakened them, because they had had no food the whole day, the provisions which they had taken with them for only one day having been all consumed. On the following dawn O'Sullivan marched his men by the base of Slieve Lougher towards Limerick City. Not far from this road was an English garrison under Cuffe, who, with Viscount Barry's nephew, and a band of his dependents, occupied the ford of a river O'Sullivan had to cross The ford was contested with red hot balls from both sides for about an hour, until Cuffe was forced to abandon the place. In this fight four of the Catholics fell , the royalists lost more, many were wounded, and perhaps more would have perished, although they were superior in numbers, were it not that the Catholics, through want and weariness, were unable to pursue them, The Catholics having buried their dead and in turns carrying the wounded in military litters, accomplished a march of thirty miles that day, and on a stormy night pitched their camp in a desert place and vast solitude, near the woods of Aherlow, the guards being scarce able to keep awake through hunger, weariness, and fatigue. On the following day they refreshed themselves with cresses and water and hastened along in a direct route before sunrise.

The inhabitants in the usual way pursued. The Gibbons, mercenaries of the White Knight, natives of Limerick City, and a few English superior in numbers, but very undisciplined, attacked, not in column, but in a mob. However, they charged boldly and fiercely in front, rear, and baggage, which was carried in the middle, attacking all at once Both sides fought with guns. Such heavy showers of bullets rained on all sides that O'Sullivan could not, as usual, bury his dead or carry off his wounded. Such a cloud of smoke from gunpowder darkened the air

that one party was often unable to see the other. After
the contest had continued in this way for eight hours,
O'Sullivan, reached at night Kilnamanagh, where fires
were lit, for as soon as the fighting was over the cold of
a very severe winter pinched. The soldiers, in whom
want had produced starvation, fed on plants and roots
and leaves of trees. As they proceeded on the following
day, their rear ranks were engaged with the enemy's
musketeers until they had reached Donohill fort, which
the soldiers stormed for the sake of getting food. Whatever
prepared food was there, the first who entered devoured
right off. The rest set themselves to feed on meal, beans,
and barley grains, like cattle. Carrying their packs, they
covered about twenty miles, and halted in the village of
Solloghod.

At this time Dermot, second son of O'Sullivan, aged
two, was left in charge in unhappy Bear, where he was
secretly nursed for two years by some gentleman of rank,
and afterwards sent into Spain. From thence, at break
of day, they took the route to Slievefelim, where far larger
forces sent by Ormond blocked the way. On learning
this the Catholics were filled with terror, but as things
were come to such a pass that the enemy could force them to
fight against their wills, they resolved to attack the enemy
first. When the enemy saw this they were stricken with
greater fear and quitted the ground

Hunger pinching them bitterly, Thomas Burke and
Daniel O'Malley, by O'Sullivan's order, made a slight
detour, with sixty men to look for booty and food.
These were suddenly attacked by the enemy, Daniel
and twenty men killed, Thomas captured, and the rest
routed, but saved by O'Sullivan coming to the rescue,
and immediately he rescued Thomas flying from the enemy
after having broken his bonds, his helmet on, but stripped
of his sword, pike, and dagger. He halted in the village
of Latteragh, and threw his men into a rather small church
and its enclosure. There was in this village a fort from
which he was annoyed the whole night with firing and by
sallies of the garrison   He withstood the attack from the
fort and momentarily awaited with drawn sword, prepared
muskets and couched pikes a larger crowd of the enemy
assembled not far from the camp ; the men going on sentry
and to sleep in turns.

It was now the 6th of January, when at dawn, a storm
of red-hot balls blazed on O'Sullivan as he advanced. This
was, indeed, a daily salutation with which the enemy

honoured him ; a farewell as they drew off at night , a greeting as they turned up in the morning.

Throughout the whole day his rear column was con- tinually engaged in fight and some' fell on both sides, nor was O'Sullivan's only disadvantage that with a few he had to meet many, but, in addition, he had to oppose, with wearied and wounded, fresh and staid enemies The fighting was usually with missiles. Whenever O'Sullivan halted the enemy fled, when he advanced they quickly pursued. Night putting an end to the contest, O'Sullivan reached the village of Brosna.

CHAPTER IX.

O'SULLIVAN LANDED IN A TIGHT CORNER, FROM WHICH HE WAS DELIVERED BY AN ADMIRABLE DEVICE OF DERMOT'S.

O'SULLIVAN seemed to be landed here in a very tight corner, as he could not cross the broad and navigable river Shannon since the enemy had removed all boats and ships, and warned every ferryman under the severest penalties not to carry him over. Moreover, the soldiers were nerveless from want. Every heart was hereupon filled with giant despair. In this critical state of things, my father, Dermot O'Sullivan, announced that he would in a short time make a ship and put an end to the soldiers' hunger.

On the following day, which was the 7th of January, they, by Dermot's advice, concealed themselves in the thick and secure wood of Brosna, and having cut down trees, arranged them like a ditch and surrounded themselves with a small trench In two days they built two ships of osiers and trees, covered with the skins of twelve horses, which they killed, and on whose flesh they all fed except O'Sullivan, Dermot, and Dermot O'Houlaghan. The ship planned by Dermot was made in this way .—

Two rows of osiers were planted opposite each other, the thickest end being stuck in the ground, and the other ends bent in to meet each other's *vis-a-vis*, to which they were fastened with cords, and so formed the frame of the ship turned upside down. To this frame the solid planks were fixed, and seats and cross beams were fitted inside. Outside it was covered with the skins of eleven horses, and oars and dowels were fitted on. The keel was flat, both on account of the material used and in order to avoid rocks and stones. It was twenty-six feet long, six feet broad, and five feet deep, but the prow was a little higher in order to stem the tide.   The other ship, which was built under direction of the O'Malleys, was made of osiers without joinings, having a circular bottom like a shield, and sides much higher than the bottom suited.   It was covered with the skin of one horse drawn over the bottom. These ships were carried by night on the men's shoulders to the bank of the Shannon called Portland, and O'Sullivan began stealthily to ferry his men across in them.   Ten of the O'Malleys got into his ship, but it perished in the midst of the river with its men, being too small and imperfectly built to bear the weight.   Dermot's ship, which carried thirty armed men at a time, brought the others across safely, drawing after them the horses swimming and tied to the poop.

At daybreak, after the soldiers had been got over, Donogh MacEgan, who held the adjoining port of Kiltaroe, surrounded the baggage with an armed band and began to destroy the packs, to sprinkle the earth with the blood of the sutlers and drive the terror-stricken women into the river.   Thomas Burke, with about twenty pikes and as many marksmen, had been placed on guard and in ambush by O'Sullivan to protect the others until they were brought over the river, and now rousing his men, he unexpectedly attacked Donogh, whom, with fifteen of his comrades, he slew, and routed the rest, nearly all wounded.   The natives, attracted by the report of the guns, flocked down to both banks of the river   Hereupon Thomas, with his guards, women, and sutlers in a great panic, tumultously pouring into, sank the ship, but so near the shore that no one perished, and the ship being again floated carried over the guards.   Some of the sutlers swam across the river , others, not being able to get over on account of the natives coming up, dispersed in different directions and hid themselves.   O'Sullivan ordered the ship to be broken up lest it should prove useful to the enemy.

CHAPTER X.

O'SULLIVAN, IN A WONDERFUL MANNER, ROUTS ROYALIST FORCES FAR SUPERIOR IN NUMBERS.

As O'Sullivan advanced from the banks of the river he was not given one single moment's rest from the attacks of the enemy. O'Madden assembling a crowd of natives, fired on him, but O'Sullivan, no whit daunted, divided his famished troops into two parts when he had reached Magheranearla, before mid-day, and each part in turn withstood the enemies' assaults.

Entering the houses, they gathered up sacks of wheat, beans, and barley, and refreshed themselves on the grains, and by drinking malt or beer. This kind of food and drink seemed, to their parched palates and hungry stomachs, regular nectar and delicacies. Whatever other kind of food had been in the village the natives had removed Advancing thence, O'Sullivan sent eighty armed men in front, the baggage followed immediately after, and he himself, with 200 men (for he now had no more), brought up the rear. Here he was obliged by the pursuers' fire to leave behind some worn out beasts of burthen, and to abandon some men exhausted by the march, or weakened by wounds. When he had reached a place called Aughrim, Henry Malby, an Englishman, Thomas Burke, brother of the Earl of Clanrickarde, and Richard Burke, with five companies of foot and two troops of horse, and a band of natives, came against him. The neighing of their horses, the sheen of their brilliant armour, the braying of their trumpets, the sound of their pipes, the beat of their drums, all joyously and proudly anticipating victory, unnerved the small band of Catholics and struck terror into their souls. The eighty men who were in advance to protect the baggage, abandoned it and fled at first sight of the enemy. O'Sullivan thus addressed the others.—

"Since on this day our desperate circumstances and unhappy fate have left us neither wealth, nor country, nor children, nor wives to fight for, but, as on this instant the struggle with our enemies is for the life that alone remains to us, which of you, I ask in God's eternal name, will not rather fall fighting gloriously in battle and avenging your blood, than like cattle, which have no sense of honour, perish unavenged in cowardly flight? Surely our ancestors, heroes famed for their high spirits, would never seek by a shameful flight to shun an honourable death even when they could fly. For us it will be proper to follow in their footsteps, especially as flight offers no salvation. See the plain stretching far and wide without hindrance of bog, without thick woods, without any hiding-places to which we could fly for concealment. The neighbouring people are no protection for us. There is none to come to our aid. The enemy block the roads and passes, and we, wearied with our long journey, are unable to run. Whatever chance we have is only in our own courage and strength of our own arms. Up, then, and on them, whom you excel in spirit, courage, achievements past, and holy faith. Let us remember this day that enemies who have everywhere attacked us have heretofore been routed by the Divine mercy. Above all let us believe that the victory is the gift of God. Let us think that Christ our Lord will be with His servants in their utmost need, and that for His name and holy faith we join issue with heretics and their abettors. Fear not the worthless mob of enemies who are not as used to fight as we are, much less as famous. Wherefore, I do hope they will turn tail when they shall see us heartily resist, even as I expect you will show forth your faith and courage."

O'Sullivan had scarcely concluded this speech when the royalist cavalry were down full tilt upon him, endeavouring to run the foot through with their spears, to trample them under the horses' hoofs, and throw their ranks into confusion. O'Sullivan, avoiding the shock of the enemy's cavalry, marched his column through an adjacent swampy and boggy ground to a thin low copsewood not far off. The royalist cavalry dismounted and joined their pikemen, and both, running through the bog, tried to get before O'Sullivan, and seize the copse, whilst his column was not fully arranged and his ranks were open. The royalist musketeers sharply pressed O'Sullivan's rear. O'Sullivan sent William Burke with forty gunmen against these musketeers, but he was driven back to O'Sullivan by the enemy's numbers with the loss of fourteen marksmen. At this instant O'Sullivan suddenly turned round his division on the enemy's column, which was within a dart's throw, and was followed by the chieftains and the brave though abandoned by cowards and dastards. This sudden and unexpected *volte face* struck terror into the royalists, and when ordered to fall into line some fled to the rear ranks and, one following another, they wheeled round in a circle. Some fled.

The chief and bravest, however, held their ground against O'Sullivan. Shortly before he came within a spear's length of them, twenty marksmen, whom O'Sullivan had posted flanking his front ranks, shot down eleven royalists. Forthwith, the advance lines of both parties fell to with drawn swords and couched spears First of all, Captain Maurice O'Sullivan closed with Richard Burke, but before he had got firm ground he was struck on the chest and knocked down by Richard, who was standing on firm ground. He was, however, not wounded, being protected by his coat of mail. Donogh O'Hinguerdel (?) with a blow of a sword cut off Richard's right hand as he was making a second thrust with his pike, and Maurice quickly getting up again ran him through with his spear, and Hugh O'Flynn finished him off with his sword as he fell half dead. Dermot O'Houlaghan and Cornelius O'Morogh killed Malby. Then the fight became general, each attacking his foe as he met him. The fight going against the royalists, Thomas Burke, who was heavily armoured, was got on his horse by his sevrants and rode off. And now a heap was formed of bodies and arms and the rest not slowly, but pell-mell, made for the adjoining fort of Aughrim

O'Connor, a peer of the bravest in the fight, shouted victory ! The conquerors hung on the rear of the enemy. And now those who had not dared to charge with O'Sullivan against the opposing foe, were quick enough to fall on the routed enemy, arrogating to themselves with great blusterings the glory of the victory obtained by others, and anxious by a show of spirit to wipe out the abject disgrace of their ill-timed cowardice.

However, the routed were not pursued far. O'Sullivan ordered a recall to be sounded, having seen John Bostock with some companies coming to the rescue of the fugitives, and who, with the others, betook himself to Aughrim fort. Whilst this was taking place, Malby's musketeers and a crowd of those who, following the Catholics' division, had been annoying them all day with throwing javelins, were engaged in plundering O'Sullivan's baggage, and when the royalist column was routed they also sought safety in flight

In the battle about 100 royalists fell, the flower of their forces, their general. Malby, Richard Burke, three standard-bearers, as many adjutants, more sergeants, and the rest were Irish, Anglo-Irish, and English gentlemen. The conquerors lost the fourteen whom I have mentioned. O'Sullivan, collecting the enemy's arms and colours, fled that evening and following night through a host of surrounding enemies through O'Kelly's country with such haste that he left some soldiers worn out on the road, and overcome with sleep.

.

CHAPTER XI.

STRUGGLES OF THE FOLLOWING COUPLE OF DAYS RECOUNTED.

AT dawn of the following day O'Sullivan crossed Slieve
Murry, and, as he came near the villages, beat the drums
and displayed the standards captured from the English at
Aughrim, pretending that his men were Royalists and
English, so that the food might not be hidden by the inhabitants However, this device did not avail him, for the flocks
and herds were removed, food and drink hidden, or carried
into the fort, and MacDavid, the lord of the village, assembling a large, though for the most part unarmed, crowd of
men, attacked him from a distance with missiles, and followed
annoying, throughout the whole day, and cutting him off
from food At nightfall O'Sullivan concealed himself in
the thick woods of Slieve O'Flynn.   There, having lit fires,
the soldiers, exhausted by the continuous watchings of the
previous night and their great toils, had scarcely begun to
yield their wearied limbs to rest when a man came to them
to announce that the natives had decided and arranged to
surround and destroy them at daybreak   Thereupon they
kindled larger fires, as if all were encamped there, and
quickly moved off, enduring with patience tremendous
sufferings of an unseasonable march and time.   The rain
so poured on them that they were scarcely able to bear the
weight of their soaked clothes.   Quite tired out, they sank
into deep snow as if into pits, and, when lifting one another
out, were rather dragged down by their comrades than
the latter pulled out.   Nor was darkness the least of their
trials, for, if any stars did shine, the boughs of the trees, inter-
woven with one another, formed an unbroken screen and
shut out their light, so that they wandered about as if blind,
following only the sound of familiar voices.   And, moreover, the winds rustling the branches made a louder noise
than mere whistling, and made hearing difficult   However,
through the skill of their guides, they got through the wood,
having covered four miles   When at daybreak the natives,
under MacDavid, surrounded the quarters deserted by
O'Sullivan, and found nothing but fires, they followed the
track of the fugitive, and having come up with him about
nine o'clock, attacked with missiles until he reached the
top of a high hill   There some of O'Sullivan's men, whose

strength was failing from weariness and hunger, swore they would rather hazard the worst in fighting the enemy than quit this spot before they had taken food and sleep, and the rest chimed in with the same vow O'Sullivan was not unequal to the emergency, exhorting them to put all their trust in valour.   And, indeed, martial ardour and courage are not to be despised in soldiers, however few (there were in sooth not more than 60 capable of fighting) or worn with toils.   Quickly drawing up, they offered fight to the enemy, thinking that those who show fight with great confidence of success, or, hating a burdensome life, seek an honourable death, are more likely to perish well avenged or return safe to their wives, than peril their safety. O'Sullivan's men killed two horses, and, after all but the three who had previously declined horseflesh had eaten their fill, they took at night about six hours' long and peaceful sleep.   They made brogues of the horses' hides, for they had worn out their boots, and made tracks for the wood which is called Diamhbhrach (Bracklieve ?), that is, " Solitude."   When they had entered this wood sleep again overcame them, and, scattered about without any order, bodies were stretched here and there, heedless of danger, each one resting until daylight wherever he chanced to settle down.   O'Sullivan perceiving this, and having with himself but 12 companions, ordered a fire to be kindled, thinking, as in fact happened, that the stragglers when they awoke would gather round the blaze.

CHAPTER XII

TOILS OF THREE DAYS RELATED

WHEN day broke, the natives, coming to investigate the strange fire in such a wilderness, spent a long time talking with O'Sullivan, and then brought him a present of food, reporting to Oliver Lambert, President of Connaught, that the fire had been lit by labourers.   Here some of the Catholics grew foot-sore from the hard weather and long march.   O'Connor suffered intensely.   On account of this, O'Sullivan tarried in the wood the following day till night. A night march was necessary for all, but O'Connor was so bad that he could not mount his horse.   The highways and horsepaths were here and there blocked by enemies,

and therefore the route was through narrow passes and
obstructed valleys, so that they could not have struggled
through were it not for one often helping the other.   And
so, O'Connor, lying stretched on the ground, thus addressed
his feet ·—" Have you not gone through the most difficult
trials these last three nights?   Why do you now shrink
from the toils of one night?   Are not my head and the
safety of my whole body more precious to you, my most
delicate feet?   What doth it avail to have fled so far if
through your sloth we now fall into the hands of the enemy?
I will assuredly make you shake off this sluggishness."
Forthwith, with the utmost effort and weight of his armour
he struck his feet against the ground, and squeezing out
the matter, pus, and blood, he got up and began to march
with the rest.   Now, however, a guide was wanted, and
him God supplied   For a man clad in a linen garment,
his feet bare, his temples bound with a white wreath,
carrying in his hand a long wand tipped with an iron point,
and presenting an appearance well calculated to inspire awe,
appeared and greeted O'Sullivan and the rest, and being
saluted by them in turn, thus spoke :—

" I know that you are Catholics tried by divers misfortunes, fleeing from the tyranny of heretics, that at
Aughrim hill you routed the royalist forces, and are going
to O'Rourke, who is 15 miles off, but you want a guide.
Therefore a desire has seized me to conduct you thither."

O'Sullivan long pondered whether he could confide in
this man, and ordered 200 gold pieces to be given to him.
These he took. " This gift," said he, " I accept not as a
reward, but in token of my good will towards you, as I
have resolved of my own good will to do you this service."
The darkness of night, the unknown country, the suspected
guide, multiplied the fears of those groping along.   The
feet slipping over loose stones, the snow heaped up by the
wind, exhaustion, swollen feet, all tried the unhappy
fugitives.   O'Connor suffered more than anyone, the causes
of his pain increasing.   The greater part of his feet and
legs was inflamed   Lividness supervened, and in turn
gave place to blisters, and these were succeeded by ulcers.
He was terribly afflicted and only able to bear up because
he suffered for Christ Jesus   In the dead of night they
reached the little village called Knockvicar, where they
refreshed themselves with fire and purchased food.   When
they decided to move on, O'Connor, whose ulcers had been
crustated by the fire, was not able to stand, much less walk.
Four of his comrades carried him on their shoulders until

in the twilight they found a stray beast, lank and worn with age, on which they placed him without bridle or saddle, the sharp bone of the lean back pricking the rider. Some led the blind beast, others whacked him along Having got over the Curlew hills, they reached a plain, when O'Connor began to walk. After daybreak, the guide showed O'Sullivan O'Rourke's castle in the distance, and bid the rest farewell, assuring them all danger was now past. They reached Leitrim fort about eleven o'clock, being then reduced to 35, of whom 18 were armed, 16 were sutlers, and one was a woman. The others, who were over 1,000 leaving Bear, had either perished or had deserted their leader, or lingered on the road through weariness or wounds Some followed in twos and threes. I am astonished that Dermot O'Sullivan, my father, an old man near 70, and the woman of delicate sex, were able to go through these toils, which youths in the flower of age and height of their strength were unable to endure. O'Rourke received O'Sullivan with most honourable hospitality, giving directions to have his sick cured, and all necessaries to be supplied just as he had afforded comfort to MacWilliam and Maguire, who had been driven to him. And he would have succoured O'Sullivan had he delayed longer here.

TOME III.   BOOK VIII.

OF

DON PHILIP O'SULLEVAN OF BEAR IN IRELAND.

WE have shown how the resources of the chief leaders in this war were shattered.   We shall in this volume relate some memorable struggles : How on the death of the Queen of England, the King of Scotland obtained Ireland , and shall discuss the justness of the Irish war.

CHAPTER I.

O'SULLIVAN AND MAGUIRE SUCCESSFULLY ENCOUNTER THE ROYALISTS, AND THE LATTER RECOVERS HIS COUNTRY.

AFTER O'Sullivan had stayed some days with O'Rourke and refreshed the few soldiers, survivors of his flight, he and Maguire, accompanied by Richard Tyrrell and 300 armed men and several sutlers and unarmed people, undertaking a difficult journey, set off to treat with O'Neill as to renewing the war.   Now O'Neill was more than 100 miles off, three rivers, flowing into the famous Lough Erne, and which, it now being winter, could not be forded, had to be crossed.   Besides, other places of the intervening country, the whole lough and its islands and Maguire's country round it, was held by a royalist garrison under Cornelius Maguire, surnamed Roe, Maguire's kinsman, who adhered to the English and had been by his own faction elected The Maguire, but by others was called the English Maguire.   He had brought over to the Queen's side many Irish, especially mercenaries and followers of Maguire's people, although at the same time he shrank as much as the others from the false religion of the English.   O'Sullivan and Maguire crossed the rivers in pontoons brought down for the purpose. Not knowing this fact, the English Maguire, O'Malachy, and Lawrence Esmond, with 500 armed men from their encampments, sailed over the lough in boats and ships and uselessly blocked the ford at the end of the river called Belturbet, with intent to meet O'Sullivan and Maguire.

O'Sullivan and Maguire encamped that night six miles beyond the ford. When on the next day they learned that the enemy were away in ambush at the ford, they attacked and captured their camp, which was six miles further away. They stayed there that day and night, hung fifty of the defenders, and got together a great prey of flocks and herds. On the next day Maguire, thinking it a good opportunity whilst the enemy were at the ford 12 miles off, went out of the camp with 200 light armed soldiers to raid the friends and abettors of the English. O'Sullivan, who was left only 100 armed men, fearing lest in Maguire's absence he should be overborne by the rush of a numerous enemy, whose arrival he dreaded, dismantled the camp, burnt the tents, and betook himself with the spoils to the dense wood of Alfarcan. In a very short time the enemy having heard of the storming of the camp and capture of the prey, returned in their ships and disembarked not far off. When they came in sight of O'Sullivan they arranged their column with intent to take vengeance. O'Sullivan placed his armed men in front, the sutlers at the rear, the boys and women, holding long staves for spears, he placed as if in reserve, so as to frighten the enemy by a show of numbers.

The royalists, wondering how confident of success O'Sullivan appeared, and considering his numbers, which rumour magnified, and being ignorant that Maguire with 200 men was absent, spent a great time in doubt as to whether they ought to give battle. Meantime, towards evening, Maguire returned safe with an immense booty. The royalists, cursing their lot that, deceived by O'Sullivan's device, they had let victory escape their hands, retreated to their ships, seeing the camp destroyed and booty lost, and resolved merely to preserve the garrisons which they had in the islands on the lough, until larger forces were sent to their assistance. There was on the route to the ships a deserted old fortress built of small stones, and surrounded by a trench and lofty trees planted on the sides. It was called O'Neill's Fort by the natives because he used to inaugurate Maguire there. The royalists were seen by the Catholic scouts to enter this fort at night, as they could not reach the ships before dark. Thence on the following dawn they started for their ships, which they reached about four hours after sunrise, and, after Esmond with a few men had been ferried over, the rest were, at a sudden signal for battle, surrounded by a division of the Catholics, who had silently followed.

Panic-stricken by this sudden and unexpected attack, some jumped into the boats in such haste and confusion that some were sunk ; others loaded the nearest ships with such a crowd that they went down with them ; others, throwing themselves into the lough, were drawn down by the weight of their armour ; others were killed by the Irish. There was one ship a little larger than the rest, which, when filled inside with fugitives, was also surrounded outside with frightened people hanging from the thowels and trying to climb into the ship, and this, being kept where it was by the rope tied to the bank, was deluged with a shower of bullets.   However, the rope being cut, it got off, and most of those hanging on were either pierced with javelins or drowned in the lough.   The English Maguire, with his two sons and three men, fled for safety in a small boat. O'Melachlin and 40 men perished by sword and water. The Catholics thence sailed to the islands in the lough, took seven garrisons, hanged the defenders, and having put to flight the English Maguire and Esmond, Maguire was restored almost completely

---

CHAPTER II.

MAGUIRE AND OTHERS RECEIVED INTO ENGLISH FAVOUR.
O'CONNOR GOES FOR SCOTLAND.   O'SULLIVAN RETURNS
TO O'ROURKE.   OTHERS MAKE PEACE.

O'SULLIVAN and Maguire forthwith passed the English garrison, and after a three days' march reached Glenconkeine.   There they found that O'Neill was gone for Dublin, having accepted terms of peace as already shown. Maguire accordingly returned home and was received into English favour, like other Ulstermen, on the terms granted to O'Neill. O'Sullivan returned to O'Rourke.   O'Connor Kerry, going for Scotland with a single comrade, was most honourably received by King James, and being invited into England, was reinstated in his country   Tyrrell, William Burke, and others went over to the English, stipulating for pardon and reward.   In Leinster, Raymond O'Moore, reduced to poverty. and deserted by his own, sought safety in making his peace.

CHAPTER III.

O'ROURKE IS STRIPPED OF HIS POSSESSIONS AND DIES
MACWILLIAM DIES IN SPAIN

MEANTIME, the Munster rising being quelled after O'Sullivan's expulsion, the English assembled an army against O'Rourke out of those troops which had been enlisted against O'Sullivan and of the survivors of the Aughrim slaughter, and got together 3000 Irish and Anglo-Irish under command of Oliver Lambert, Governor of Connaught. In the month of March, 1603, Lambert marched his forces to the south side of the Shannon, not far from Leitrim Castle. Here he was for twelve days foiled in his attempts to cross a ford by O'Rourke, who had assembled a small band of soldiers On the thirteenth night John Bostock secretly brought over in boats and pontoons seven companies to Gleann-na-mochart, and quickly fortified himself in its chapel with a ditch and rampart. From this post Bostock could easily raid and waste O'Rourke's country, and when he had perceived this on the sixth day after his arrival, he sallied out with 300 men and drove off a prey O'Rourke came up with him and endeavoured to rescue the booty A battle ensued and the English were defeated. Some, including Bostock, their captain, were slain , some returned terror-stricken to their entrenchments, bearing tidings of the loss of their captain and spoils. The victors lost only two. Hereupon the English began to regret having crossed so large a river and undoubtedly would have been more sorry had not Fortune, never weary of injuring the Irish, at this time absolutely raged against them. For Thady, brother of O'Rourke by a different mother, and who now adhered to the English party because he was disputing with O'Rourke about his inheritance and patrimony, attacked him on the other side and detaching many followers and mercenaries from his brother, occupied the greater part of the country of Breifny. O'Rourke himself caught a bad fever and died, deserted by those to whom he had entrusted his government, and who made peace. O'Sullivan, with some difficulty, procured a safe conduct for a few days In this state of things Philip III., King of Spain, sent Martin Cerdo with two ship-loads of powder and other ammunition and 30,000 pieces of gold

M

to O'Neill and Roderic, and no doubt had they received this aid sooner they would not have laid down their arms, but having done so, they would not accept the King's money or ammunition MacWilliam accompanied Cedro to Spain and there died shortly after. At this time Cornelius O'Driscoll, whom we have seen had been sent to Spain by O'Sullivan, got from his Catholic Majesty 2000 pieces of gold and put into Munster. Not finding O'Sullivan here, he returned to Spain, taking his wife and other women with him

———

CHAPTER IV

RISING OF THE MUNSTER CITIES.

AFTER the pacification of Ireland, the death of Elizabeth, Queen of England, who a few days previously had passed away in delirium and great pain, became known. Immediately on receipt of this news, Waterford, Cork and Limerick, cities of Munster, and also intervening towns, not knowing what Prince to obey, took counsel together and hastened to publicly celebrate Mass and carry out the ancient ecclesiastical rites. If they had done this before, when the Irish chiefs and entire Catholic party were flourishing, the English would have been driven out of the whole realm Now, however, there were none to help or defend them and by themselves they did not seem capable of withstanding the power of the heretics, and this, indeed, turned out to be the case The English Privy Council with the utmost despatch called James Stuart, King of Scotland, to be their king also. This assuredly, on account of the ancient enmity between the English and Scotch they would never have done, had they not known that England, the home of error, would be maintained in its madness, and had they not been aware that if the Irish, who could never he detached from the Catholic faith nor be brought over to English views, and the Scots, who seemed to claim the sceptre of England as their King's hereditary right, were joined in attacking England, it would go hard with the English between two such warlike races, which in ancient times had conquered and made England subject to them. James having got the sceptre, Charles Blount with the royalist army arrived at Waterford from Dublin John White, a priest and Doctor of Theology came into his camp

with a deputation from Waterford, carrying and displaying
the Crucifix, and assured the Viceroy that the people of
Waterford would never willingly yield allegiance to any
prince who would attack and persecute the Catholic religion.
To the same effect spoke brother Edmond O'Callaghan of
the Order of St. Dominic, a man renowned for his holiness
and learning, and Brother Candidus of the Order of St.
Bernard, assuredly candid not only in name but also in
learning, piety, and manners   Blount, on account of the
difficulties of the times, and the anxieties which perplexed
him, dissembled, treated the monks and doctor with civility,
and speaking them fair, received the surrender of Waterford
and other lesser towns   The Corkonians suffered more
severely in this *inter-regnum*, for having expelled the
English garrison they fought daily battles for two months,
with Charles Wilmot, Vice-President of Munster, at long
range and close quarters ; from the fortifications and before
the walls ; in the harbour and docks , on land and sea.
In these skirmishes Charles lost more than the Corkmen,
but a few fell on each side.   When Blount arrived the
Corkmen submitted to him, being now advised of the new
king   As soon as Blount entered the city he ordered three
persons to be publicly hanged :—Christopher Muriach
(*Murray ?*), a man well skilled in military matters and who
had inflicted no small damage on Wilmot's troops ; Eugene,
a teacher of Latin, because when our Lord Christ in the
Blessed Sacrament of the Eucharist was being carried
through the streets of the city, with great pomp and incredible joy of the whole town, he, looking up to heaven
with outstretched arms, had prayed God never to permit
Cork to want power to preserve so happy, holy, and divine
a custom : and William Buler, because he had stayed the
cruelty of Dominic Sarsfield, a judge of notoriously truculent
and wicked disposition, who used to condemn to death
priests and other holy and innocent men   Then he sought
out the movers of these disturbances, and would have treated
most honorable citizens with the greatest harshness and
cruelty, were it not for the magnanimity of one William
Meach (*Meade ?*). This man preferring that he alone should
die for all the citizens, than that all should perish with him,
avowed himself the sole instigator and leader of the rebellion
and prime mover therein.   He was imprisoned and put
in chains on this confession and now it appeared that if he
were acquitted the others must also go scathless, but if he
were condemned then all who had taken part in his schemes
must suffer the like punishment.   This matter, according

to the English law, was to be submitted to the verdict of
twelve men, who were to pronounce whether he were guilty
or not of the crime, and if found guilty the punishment
was meted out by the judge in manner heretofore described
by us at length.   William, distrusting the virtue of his
own fellow-citizens, chose, to try him on the capital charge,
twelve Irish gentlemen, some of whom had served under
O'Sullivan in the Catholic Party.   It must, however, be
remembered that if the twelve men acquitted against the
direction of the English judge, they were at least fined and
often put to death.   Lest the twelve men should, through
dread of this penalty, be afraid to acquit William, the
Corkmen, who knew that their own safety depended upon
William's acquittal, promised the twelve to pay the fine for
them.   These gentlemen, at the peril not only of a fine,
but even at the risk of their lives, boldly and bravely
acquitted   They were heavily fined, and the Corkmen
failing to pay up, some of the jury were reduced to poverty
by the enormousness of the fine, and some who could not pay,
had to quit the country.   William, being released from
prison, also went for Spain, where he was granted 40 gold
pieces a month by his Catholic Majesty, and where he died.

CHAPTER V.

O'NEILL AND OTHER BELLIGERENTS GO TO ENGLAND TO THE KING

AT this time O'Neill, Roderick, O'Sullivan, Garve, and other
Irish chiefs betook themselves into England to congratulate
the new king and treat of their own affairs.   O'Sullivan
could not by any means get pardon or restitution of his
country.   By the Catholic King, however, to whom he fled,
he was granted 300 gold pieces a month and made a Count,
and decorated with the Cross of the Equestrian Order of
St James, which was also bestowed on his sons Daniel,
who shortly after died from an accidental wound in the head,
and Dermot   My father, Dermot, was allowed fifty gold
pieces a month, and many others received other grants.
    O'Neill was allowed by King James to retain his pos-
sessions and directed to be satisfied with the title of Earl
of Tyrone   Roderick was left O'Donnell's country, and
given the title of Earl of Tirconnell   Garve was awarded

only those possessions which he had had before he joined
the English and was offered the title of Baron. Filled with
vexation, he refused to accept this title, and after his return
to Ireland, appeared before the Council in Dublin and railed
bitterly against the Councillors and English people, asserting
that the Catholics had been defeated and conquered and
Ireland preserved to the English crown, not by the English,
but by him, and that the Council and the English had
treated him unjustly and faithlessly, and had not kept their
promises. Then he heaped terrible curses on himself for
having ever kept faith with the English or helped them.
And so as Garve was garve,* so he wound up his speech
with great asperity.

CHAPTER VI.

WHAT WAS THE CONDITION OF IRELAND AFTER THE WAR ?

THUS the war was finished Ireland was almost entirely
laid waste and destroyed, and terrible want and famine
oppressed all, so that many were forced to eat dogs and
whelps : many not having even these, died. And not only
men but even beasts were hungry. The wolves, coming
out of the woods and mountains, attacked and tore to pieces,
men weak from want. The dogs rooted from the graves
rotten carcases partly decomposed And so there was
nought but abundance of misery and a faithful picture of
ruined Troy as given by *Virgil*, Book II., Æneid —

> That night of slaughter and of gloom
> What pen can paint or tears atone ?
> An ancient city meets it's doom
> It's rule of ages is undone
> The streets are strewn with silent dead,
> E'en homes, aye God's abodes, are graves
> Not only Trojan's blood is shed ,
> The foeman's gore the streets belaves,
> And Trojan valour smites the Greeks.
> Around the cruel anguish spreads,
> And all with death and terror reeks

As a result of this almost total destruction of Ireland,
many Irishmen scattered themselves amongst foreign
nations. A great number passed into France, and a far
larger number into Spain. The Exiles were kindly and generously received by Catholics on account of their faith. So great

---

* Garve signifies " rough "—hence O'Sullivan's joke

was the affection of the King of Spain for them, and such his kindness and generosity, that one could scarcely find words to express, or mind to conceive, all they owed him.. Receiving all, to begin with, most honourably, he heaped presents on them. To the Chiefs he allowed monthly sums of money according to their rank, and to others he gave appointments in the army He had a legion embodied out of them in Belgium, which, under the command of Henry, and after his death, of John, sons of The O'Neill, fought faithfully and bravely against the Batavians In the royal fleet in the ocean, he had also employed some companies who exhibited great valour After his Catholic Majesty the most illlustrious of the Patrons of the Irish were the Duke of Brigantia, a Lusitanian, Cardinal Surdi, Archbishop of Burdigal, a Frenchman ; The Marquess of Caracena, a Spaniard, and Fabius O'Neill, a rich citizen of the city of Valladolid.

END OF BOOK.

APPENDIX I

IN his lectures on the manners and customs of the Ancient Irish, Professor O'Curry deals exhaustively with our ancient military organisation and weapons. Mr. Joseph C Walker, M.R I A , etc , in "An Historical Essay on the dress of the Ancient and Modern Irish, to which is subjoined a Memoir on the Armour and weapons of the Irish. Dublin, 1788," has developed the same subject as appearing in later times

Scattered through many of the old English writers' works on Ireland will be found descriptions of the national mode of warfare, but I transcribe the following as being at once the most complete and succinct of the descriptions of the period of our narrative

Dymmok's treatise was written in 1600, and applies to the campaign of 1599 It is printed in "Tracts relating to Ireland," published by the Ir Arch Socy , vol ii., Dub., 1843 He says (pp 7-8).—

"Theire forces consist of thre sortes, Horsemen, Gallow-glass and Kerne.

"The horsemen are armed with headpeeces, shirtes of mayle or jackes, a sworde, a skayne, and a speare They ryde vpon paddes or pillowes without styrvps, and in this differ from ours · that in joyninge with the enemy, they beare not their staves or launces vnder arme, and so put it to the reste, but taking yt by the midle, beare yt aboue arme, and soe encounter

"Every Horseman hath two or thre horses, and to euery horse a knave his horse of service is allwaies led spare, and his knave, which caryeth his harness and speare, rydeth upon the other, or els upon a hackeney

"The Gallowglass ar pycked and scelected men of great and mightie bodies, crewell without compassion. The greatest force of the battell consisteth in them, chosing rather to dye than to yeelde, so that when yt cometh to handy blowes they are quickly slayne or win the fielde. They are armed with a shert of maile, a skull, and a skeine : the weapon they most vse is a batle axe. or halbert, six foote longe, the blade whereof is somewhat like a shomaker's knyfe, and without pyke; the stroake whereof is deadly where yt lighteth And beinge thus armed, reckoninge to him a man for his harnesse bearer, and a boye to carry his provision, he is named a spare of his weapon so called, 80 of which spares make a battell of Gallowglass

"The kerne is a kinde of footeman, sleightly armed with a sworde, a targett of woode, or a bow and a sheafe of arrows with barbed heades, or els 3 dartes, which they cast with a wonderfull facility and nearnes, a weapon more noysom to the enemy, especially horsemen, then yt is deadly, within theise few years they have practized the muskett and callyver, and are growne good and ready shott Some will have the Dalonyes or horseboys to be a fourth sorte for that they take them into the fight; they are the very skumme and outcaste of the countrye, and not less serviceable in the campe for meatinge and dressinge of horses, then hurtfull to the enemy with their dartes."

Appended to Dymmok's "Treatice," is an interesting old State paper of 17th November, 1568, on "what the wages and entreteynment of every sparre of her Majesties Gallowglasses oughte to be." Here every sparre or speare (Hastatus in O'Sullivan) is reckoned two men The number of men in a battalion or "battell" varied. This old paper gives the numbers and pay of the Gallowglasses cessed on the different "countries."

The skeine was, according to Walker, a dagger (p 119), sgian is now a common word for a knife.

The poet Spenser gives a short description of Irish arms, in his "View of the State of Ireland" (Thom's Tracts, I., 479-80), and O'Clery, one of the Four Masters, in his life of Hugh Roe O'Donnell, incidentally gives us an insight into the weapons, etc, then in use (See Father Murphy's translation, pp. 65, 73, 99, 101, 143, 153, 211-7). See also *Paccata Hibernia*, pp 150, 237, 345.

The Irish often flung their skeines (*Pac. Hib.*, 45), and had thongs attached to their javelins, whereby they might recover them after casting (Miscel Celtic Soc 303) Don Juan remarked that the Irish horses were small (*Pac Hib.*, 345), but Derrick, writing in 1578, praises the "gallant stouryng steede" (p 30).

The following passage relating to an Irish army in 1598, taken from the *Life of O Donnell* (pp 167-9), may, I think, be added to Dymmok's account.—

"The weapons and dress of these were different, for the Irish did not wear armour like them (i e, the English),

except a few, and they were unarmed in comparison with
the English, but yet they had plenty of broad-shouldered
darts, and broad, green spears, with strong handles of good
ash. They had straight keen swords and light shining axes
for defeating the champions, but their were neither rings
nor chains on them as there were on the axes of the English
The implements for shooting which they had were darts,
made of wood, and elastic bows, with sharp-pointed arrows,
and lock-guns, as was usual with the English."

And here is a description of a battle in 1599. "When
they came near each other the Irish discharged against them
terrible showers of beautiful ash-handled javelins and
swarms of sharp-pointed, whizzing arrows from their long,
elastic bows, and volleys of blood-red spherical balls and
leaden bullets from their straight-shooting, sharp-sighted
guns. They were responded to by the English soldiers in
the same way exactly with sharp-wounding leaden balls
from their iron-lock guns, and their far-sounding muskets,"
etc, etc. (*Life of O'Donnell*, p 217).

The Kernes have not been without their Fenimore
Cooper, and Mr Small has, in recent years (1883), republished "A Discouerie of Woodkarne by John Derricke,
1581," with all the original plates and quaint versified
legends.

The first plate shows a horseman, his knave, boy and
steed.

"Wherein is bravely paynted forth, a nat'rall Irish
grace,
Whose like in cu'ry poynt to vewe hath seldome stept in
place."

Amongst the military engines used in attacking fortified
places, one of the most usual at this period was that known
as the sow.

The following quaint description of a "sow" is taken
from Maurice Cuffe's account of his gallant defence of
Ballyally Castle in 1641, published by Crofton Croker in
"*Narratives Illustrative of the Contests in Ireland in* 1641
and 1690," amongst Camden Society's publications (Lon.
1841, p. 17). It reads refreshingly like Cæsar's description
of Testudo :—

"The great sow was 35 foote long and 9 foote broade ;
it was made upon 4 wheeles mad of whole timbar, bound
aboutt with hoopes of iron, there axell trees where one
she was run was great round bars of iron, the beames she
was bult upon being of timbar   Thare had cros beames

within to worck with there levars, to forse har along as
thaie pleased to gide har The hindar part of the sow
was left open for there men to goe in and outt at. The fore
part of the sow had 4 dowres, 2 in the ruffe and 2 one
the lower parte, which did hang upon great iron huckes,
but were not to open tell thaye came close to the wale of
the castell, where thaie intended to worck through the
castell with there tooles thaie had provided The ruffe
of the sow was built lick the ruffe of a howse, with a very
sharp ridge ; the lower part as the wales of a howse,
She was dubell plancked with manie thik oken planckes,
and driven very thik with 5 stroke nailes, which nailes cost
5 li, being intended for a howse of correction which should
have bin bult at Inish. This sow was lickwaies covard
ovar with two rowes of hides and 2 rowes of sheepe skinnes,
soe that noe musket bullet or steele arow could pearse it,
of which triell was often made "

Mr Croker thought it necessary to gild this gem with
a note (p 114) The engine called a sow was at this time
well known in Munster and in constant use. (*Pacata
Hib , Dub.*, 1820, p. 124)

For illustrations and descriptions of Gabions, see Lieut.
General Sir Charles W. Pasley's "*Rules for Operations
of a Siege*" 3 Ed. Lon., 1857 See also *Pacata Hibernia*,
pp 116, 563, etc., and plan of Glin Castle, where several
gabions (wicker-work pillars) are representing flanking
cannon

Fynes Moryson, the secretary of Lord Mountjoy, and who
has written an exhaustive account of his master's Irish
campaigne, says of the Irish soldiers —" The Irish kerne
were at the first rude soldiers, so as two or three of them
were imployed to discharge one Pieece, and hitherto they
have subsisted especially by trecherous tenders of sub-
mission, but now they were growne ready in managing
their Peeces, and bold to skirmish in bogges and wooddy
passages, yea, this yeere and the nevt following, became so
disasterous to the English, and successful in action to the
Irish, as they shaked the English Government in this
Kingdome, till it tottered, and wanted little of fatall ruine."
(I i., 24)

Writing to the Queen on the 25th June, 1599, Mountjoy
himself says —" These Rebels are more in number than
your Majesties Army, and have (though I doe unwillingly
confess it) better bodies, and perfecter use of their
Armes, then those men which your Majestie sends
over " (I. i., 36.)

On the 5th June, 1602, Lord Mountjoy wrote to the English privy Council ·—At my first arrival, I found the rebels more in number than at any time they had bin since the conquest, and those so farre from being naked people, as before times, that they were generally better armed then we, knew better the use of their weapons then our men, and even exceeded us in that discipline, which was fittest for the advantage of the naturall strength of the country, for that they being very many, and expert shot, and excelling in footmanship all other nations   *   * In regard whereof I presumed that man's wit could hardly find out any othet course to overcome them, but by famine " (*Id* III , i., 211) Mountjoy also speaks of their " good art and admirable industry," in raising fortifications. (*Id* III., i., 213.)

Spencer had advised that famine was the only way to reduce the Irish, and Mountjoy adopted this as his policy. He cut down all the corn and burnt and devastated the country, a terribly graphic account of which and of its awful results is given by Fynes Moryson from what he himself saw, and the reports of the captaines.

On the 11th September, 1602, Mountjoy reported to the English Privy Council, " wee found everie where men dead of famine, in so much that O'Hagan protested unto us, that betweene Tullogh Oge and Toome there lay un-buried a thousand dead, and that since our first drawinge this yeere to Blackwater, there were above three thousand starved in Tyrone." III., i., 237-8. See also Fynes Moryson's account, III., i , 271. 258 *et alibi*

APPENDIX II.

PLACE NAMES

O'Sullivan often translates names of places into the Latin equivalent of their signification; and for the benefit of the topographical etymologist I append a list of such names and of O'Sullivan's Latin versions of them. Where O'Sullivan has given the Irish names also, I transcribe them as spelled by him.

PLACE NAMES	O'SULLIVAN'S RENDERING
Abhain-mhor	Fluvius magnus
Antha-dubh	Vadum nigrum
Ardfert	Tumulus miraculorum (Ardfearta)
Ardskea	Tumulus Scutorum (Ard Scieth)
Ath-culuain	Vadum prati (Beal antha Cuoin)
Baile an-Caislean	Oppidocastellum
Baile an drohid	Oppidopons
Ballylahan	Vadum Corn (Beal antha an leathair)
Bealach Finnuse	Via Finnuis
Beal antha an Bhorin	Vadum semitae
Beal atha bui	Vadum pallidum
Beal antha Killoter	Vadum Otirensis Ecclesiae
Beal antha nam-brisgi	Vadum biscoctorum panum
Bearna na gchleti	Transitus plumarum
Belacooloon	Vadum prati
Bellaghboy	Pallidus (Bealach bui)
Benburb	Pinna superba (Benburb)
Carrickfergus	Rupes Fargusiae
Carricklea	Rupes Cana
Carrick-on-Suir	Rupesiurius
Carrigadrohid	Pontirupes (Carraig an Drohaid)
Carriganass	Torrentirupes (Carraig an neasaig)
Carrigaphooca	Rupes Lemurum (Carraig an phuca)
Carrignacurra	Chorirupes (Carraig na Chori)
Casan na gcuradh	Semita heroum
Castlehaven	Portucastellum (Cuan an caishlean)

PLACE NAMES.	O'SULLIVAN'S RENDERING.
Castletown Roche	Oppidocastellum
Clontibret	Pratum fontis (Cluoin Tiburuid)
Cloonacastle	Angulus murorum (Kul na gchasil)
Crickstown	Balarriecha
Diambrach	Solitudo
Donegal	Munimentum externorum
Drogheda	Oppidum pontanum
Drumflugh	Collis madidus
Dundareirke	Munimentum jucundi prospectus (Duin Dearairc)
Eanach-beg	Parvae Nundinae (Eanach beg)
Glenagenty	Sylva Cunei
Glengariff	Vallis aspera (Gleaunn Garaibh)
Glenmalure	Maluria Sylva
Goart-na-pisi	Ager lentis (Goart-na-pisi)
Gortnakilly	Ager anus (Goart na Kailli)
Gurteenroe	Angellus ruber (Gurtin Rua)
Kilcloney	Ecclesia prati (Kill cluona)
Kilnamanagh	Sylva Monachorum (Cuill na Monach)
Kiltaroe	Sylva rubra (Cuillthe Rua)
Knockgraffan	Mons Graffunnus (Cnoic Grafuin)
Knockvicar	Mons Vicarii
Lathach-na-ndaibh	Lutum boum (Lathach na ndaibh)
Magheranearla	Planicies comitis (Machaire an Earla)
Magherabeg	Planicies parva
Monanimy	Monasterium Montis (Mainister na Mona)
Mullaghbane	Tumulus albus (Mollach ban)
Mullaghbrack	Collis Maculatus (Molach breac)
Mullaghcros	Tumulus crucis
Mullaghmast	Maisum Castrum (Mollach Maius)
Portmore	Munimentum Magnum (Portmor)
Tobermesson	Fons Masanus (Tober masan)

SOBRIQUETS.

————❖————

The following translations of usual sobriquets are added as being perhaps of interest.

Boy or Bui=Pallidus, see Rossa bui McMahon.
Duff or Duv=Niger, see Thomas Butler, etc
Gorm=Caeruleus, see MacSweeny-Fanad
More=Magnus, see MacCarthy-More
Na gceann=Calvaria, see Theobald Burke
Oge=Junior, see MacSweeny Tuath, etc
Reagh=Fuscus, see MacCarthy Reagh, etc
Roe=Ruber, see Hugh Roe O'Donnell, etc

INDEX.

N

O

PRINTED BY SEALY, BRYERS AND WALKER, MID. ABBEY ST , DUBLIN.

Copy Map of Ireland made by JOHN NORDEN, bet

Preserved in State Paper Office, Londo

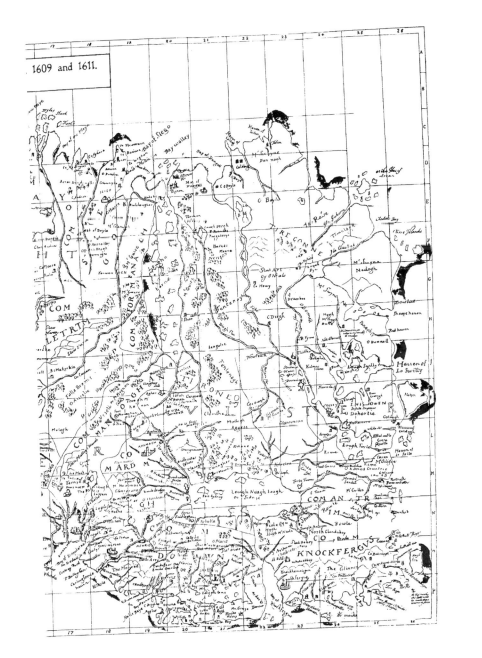

1609 and 1611.

------ ❖ ------

NAMES OF SUBSCRIBERS.

NAME	ADDRESS	COPIES
R B Armstrong, Esq ..	6 Randolph Cliff, Edinburgh N B .	1
Rt. Rev J C Beardwood	Mt St Joseph's Abbey, Roscrea	6
Rev J Begley, C C. ..	St Munchin's, Limerick ..	1
J P Boland, Esq , M.P.	12 King's Bench Walk, Temple, London, E C	2
M. S Brews, Esq , J.P .	Ballyerra House, Kilrush .	1
Rev. J. Bric, C C.	Castlegregory, Co. Kerry .	1
N A Brophy, Esq	Glenlevan, Limerick	1
Rev. M Browne, S.J	St. Stanislaus College, Tullamore, King's County ..	2
Jas Buckley, Esq , Sol. ..	154 Portsdown Road, London, W ..	1
Miss Annie Byrne ..	24 Frankfort Avenue, Rathgar	2
Rev T B Carroll ..	Presentation Monastery, Douglas Street, Cork	1
Rev. A. Clancy, P P. ..	Killiner, Co. Clare ..	2
Rev J Clancy, C C	Kilkee	1
James Coleman, Esq	11 Manchester Street, Southampton	2
Messrs Combridge & Co ..	18 Grafton Street, Dublin	3
Very Rev J. Conmee, S J	Presbytery, Upper Gardiner St.	1
J. T. Counihan, Esq , M D.	Kilrush	1
Sir Francis Cruise, M.D.	93 Merrion Square, Dublin ..	1
J B Cullen, Esq ..	40 Kenilworth Square, Rathgar	1
M F Cox, Esq , M.D.	45 St Stephen's Green	1
Rev. E. A D'Alton, C.C.	Belcarra, Castlebar ..	1
Very Rev W Delaney, S J	University College, Dublin .	4
John Dillon, Esq , M P	2 North Great George's Street ..	1
E. R. Dix, Esq., Sol.	2 Pembroke Road, Dublin ...	2
E. Dowden, Esq LL.D. ..	Highfield House, Rathgar, Dublin ..	1
Sir T. H Esmonde, Bart , M.P.	Ballynaslough, Gorey ..	1
C. L Falkner, Esq , M.A.	9 Upper Merrion St., Dublin .	1

NAME	ADDRESS	COPIES
Miss Gibson	"Kildare" Downes Park Road, W., Hackney	1
Rev P Glynn, P P	Carrigaholt, Clones	2
Geo Hanks, Esq	Sally Mills, Rathangan, Kildare	1
Rev J Hannon, C C.	Kilrush	2
H R Harris, Esq., J.P.	Millview, Dublin	1
Very Rev. L Healy, C.S.Sp.	Clareville, Blackrock	1
Maurice Healy, Esq, Sol	Ashton Lawn, Cork	1
T.M. Healy, Esq, K C, M P	1 Mountjoy Square, Dublin	2
Rev W. Healy, P P	Johnstown, Kilkenny	1
Very Rev L Hickey, O P	St Saviour's, Dominick Street	2
P H. Hore, Esq.	41 Batts Road, Bedford Park, London	1
Rev P. Hurley, P.P	Inchigeela, Cork	1
P W Joyce, Esq, LL D	Lyre-na-Grena, Leinster Road, Rathmines	1
E. F. Kelly, Esq.	Northernwood Park, Lyndhurst	2
T Kelly, Esq, Sol.	Kilrush	1
Rev W T. Latimer	Eglish, Dungannon, Tyrone	1
Rev T Lawlor, P P	Killorglin, County Kerry	1
John Loton, Esq.	Librarian, Public Library, Rathmines	1
J P Lynch, Esq., Sol.	34 Kildare Street	1
P J. Lynch, Esq.	Limerick	2
J McCarte, Esq.	51 South George's Hill, Everton, Liverpool	1
Mrs B Elligott	The Square, Listowel	3
J A MacFarlane, Esq	Kilrush	1
J McInerney, Esq.	Killaloe, Co Clare	1
Rev J McKenna	Enniskillen	1
Very Rev S Malone, P.P., V.G.	Kilrush	2
Rev. P. Meegan, P P	Lisnaskea	1
M Molloy, Esq.	493 King's Road, Chelsea	1
R T Molloy, Esq.	78 Kenilworth Square	1
Dr. Monaghan	King's Road, Chelsea	1
Rev H Moore	Kildare Place, Dublin	1
D P Moran, Esq	*The Leader*, 200 Gt Brunswick St	2
The Librarian	Mount Mellary, Cappoquin	1
Hodges, Figgis & Co.	Grafton Street	1
O. Neary, Esq.	Cookstown House, Ardee	1

NAMES OF SUBSCRIBERS

NAME	ADDRESS	COPIES
R. B. O'Brien, Esq ..	100 Sinclair Road, W , Kensington W.	1
R. V. O'Brien, Esq , J P.	Ballyalla, Ennis ..	1
Major G B O'Connor ..	Illane Roe, Rochestown, Cork .	2
Dr O'Doherty	84 Rushholm Road, Manchester	1
F H O'Donnell, Esq ..	Irish Club, 205 High Holburn	1
Rev P O'Donnell, C.C	Presbytery, Rathmines	1
Most Rev Dr O'Dwyer	Bishop of Limerick .	2
Rev J S O'Keeffe, P P .	Ballinasig, Cork	1
Rev. E O'Leary, P P	Balyna, Moyvalley, R S O	1
A O'Malley, Esq	The Quay, Westport	2
Mrs. O'Meara .	Drumbane, Birr, King's County	2
O'Neill De Tyrone	59 Qua das Flores, Lisbon .	2
Rev. P. O'Neill, P P. .	Fracton, Cork .	1
Very Rev. H Canon O'Riordan, P.P.	Cahirciveen ..	1
R O'Shaughnessy, Esq .	3 Wilton Place, Dublin	1
P. O'Sullivan, Esq , Sol.	42 Cecil Street, Limerick ..	4
H. Rowntree, Esq .	Kilrush	1
Dr. M Ryan	15A Gower St , Bedford Sq , London	1
Rev. J. J. Ryan .	St Patrick's College, Thurles	2
Sister M Shanahan .	Presentation Convent, Lixnaw, Kerry ..	4
F C Silles, Esq.	131 Wandsworth Bridge Rd., London	3
R. O'C Silles, Esq J P , .	Newtown House, Kilkee ..	5
D B Sullivan Esq , K C	56 Mountjoy Square .	1
N J Synott, Esq. ..	Furness, Naas, Kildare .	1
W F. Trench, Esq , M.A...	Queen's College, Galway .	1
Right Hon. Geo. Wyndham, M P.	Dublin Castle ..	3

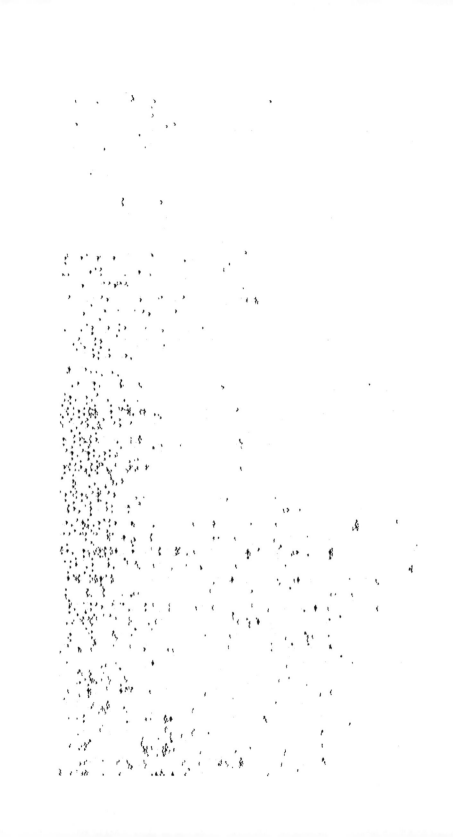